AMC'S **BEST DAY HIKES** ALONG
THE MAINE COAST

T0108862

FOUR-SEASON GUIDE TO **50** OF THE BEST TRAILS
FROM THE MAINE BEACHES TO DOWNEAST

CAREY MICHAEL KISH

Appalachian Mountain Club Books
Boston, Massachusetts

AMC is a nonprofit organization, and sales of AMC Books fund our mission of protecting the Northeast outdoors. If you appreciate our efforts and would like to become a member or make a donation to AMC, visit outdoors.org, call 800-372-1758, or contact us at Appalachian Mountain Club, 10 City Square, Boston, MA 02129.

outdoors.org/books-maps

Distributed by National Book Network.

Front cover photograph © Talanis / Dreamstime.com—Man Jumping on Rocks Photo
Back cover photographs © Carey Michael Kish; Couple hiking with sticks, © auremar/Bigstockphoto.com
Interior photographs by © Carey Michael Kish, unless otherwise noted.
Maps by Ken Dumas © Appalachian Mountain Club
Cover design by Gia Giasullo/Studio eg
Interior design by Eric Edstam

Library of Congress Cataloging on file.

The paper used in this publication meets the minimum requirements of the American National Standard for Information Sciences-Permanence of Paper for Printed Library Materials, ANSI Z39.48-1984. ∞

Interior pages and cover are printed on responsibly harvested paper stock certified by The Forest Stewardship Council®, an independent auditor of responsible forestry practices.
Printed in the United States of America, using vegetable-based inks.

For Mom, my biggest fan.
Thanks for a lifetime of love and support.

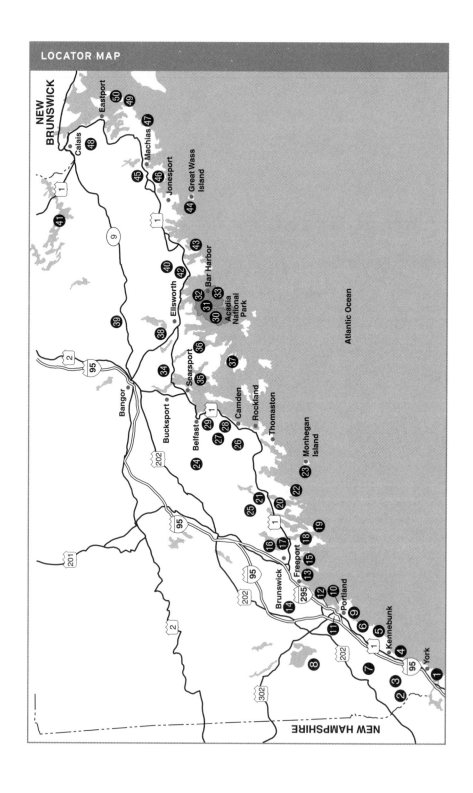

CONTENTS

SECTION 3: MIDCOAST

SECTION 4: ACADIA NATIONAL PARK

SECTION 5: DOWNEAST

NATURE AND HISTORY ESSAYS

AT-A-GLANCE
TRIP PLANNER

#	Trip	Page	Location	Difficulty	Distance & Elevation Gain
	YORK COUNTY				
1	Rachel Carson National Wildlife Refuge	3	Kittery	Easy	1.8 mi, 40 ft
2	Vaughan Woods Memorial State Park	7	South Berwick	Easy	2.2 mi, 131 ft
3	Mount Agamenticus Conservation Region	12	York	Moderate	3.9 mi, 620 ft
4	Wells Reserve at Laudholm	18	Wells	Moderate	4.2 mi, 50 ft
5	Edwin L. Smith Preserve	23	Kennebunkport	Moderate	8.7 mi, 280 ft
6	Saco Beach Loop	29	Saco	Easy	4.1 mi, minimal
7	Bauneg Beg Mountain Conservation Area	34	North Berwick	Easy	1.5 mi, 340 ft
8	Sawyer Mountain Highlands	38	Limerick/Limington	Easy	3.0 mi, 680 ft
	CASCO BAY				
9	Eastern Trail/ Scarborough Marsh	45	Scarborough	Easy	4.2 mi, minimal
10	Spring Point Shoreway	50	South Portland	Easy	2.4 mi, minimal
11	Forest City Trail	56	Portland	Strenuous	10.0 mi, 260 ft
12	Mackworth Island	64	Falmouth	Easy	1.5 mi, 60 ft
13	Wolfe's Neck Woods State Park	69	Freeport	Easy	2.2 mi, 160 ft

Estimated Time	Fee	Good for Kids	Dogs Allowed	Public Transit	X-C Skiing	Snow-Shoeing	Trip Highlights
1.5 hours		✓			✓	✓	Tidal estuaries, salt marshes, mixed forests
1.25 hours	$	✓	✓		✓	✓	Loop amid century-old trees on Salmon Falls River
3.0 hours		✓	✓		✓	✓	Cleared mountaintop, coastal woods and hills
3.0 hours	$	✓			✓	✓	Saltwater farm, estuarine habitats, sandy beach
4.5 hours		✓	✓		✓	✓	Large block of undeveloped forestland
2.5 hours	$	✓	✓		✓	✓	Mixed woods, salt marshes
1.0 hour		✓	✓			✓	Scenic loop over two undisturbed forested peaks
3.0 hours		✓	✓			✓	Mountain amid large block of undeveloped land
2.5 hours		✓	✓	✓	✓	✓	Wildlife walk through expansive salt marsh
1.5 hours			✓	✓		✓	Beach, forts, two lighthouses
5.5 hours		✓	✓	✓	✓	✓	Urban green spaces, rivers, waterfalls
45 minutes		✓	✓	✓	✓	✓	Easy, scenic island trail
1.5 hours	$	✓	✓		✓	✓	Views of Casco Bay islands and Harraseeket River

Estimated Time	Fee	Good for Kids	Dogs Allowed	Public Transit	X-C Skiing	Snow-Shoeing	Trip Highlights
3.0 hours		✓	✓		✓	✓	Old feldspar mines, woods walking, open ledges
1.75 hours		✓	✓		✓	✓	Cliff-top views of tidal estuary
2.5 hours					✓	✓	Spectacular stretch of winding river, waterfalls
3.5 hours		✓	✓		✓	✓	Tidal creek, suburban wilds
3.0 hours		✓	✓		✓	✓	Pondside walk, granite ridges
2.5 hours	$	✓	✓		✓	✓	Long sand beach, wildlife-rich wetlands
2.5 hours		✓	✓			✓	Salt marshes, tidal river, secretive basin
2.0 hours		✓	✓		✓	✓	Tidal estuary, oyster midden
2.0 hours		✓	✓		✓	✓	Mature forests, mile of spectacular oceanfront
3.5 hours		✓		✓		✓	Remote island, rugged cliffs
2.5 hours		✓	✓		✓	✓	Forests and fields along river headwaters
3.0 hours	$	✓	✓		✓	✓	Ecologically diverse forestland, pond and huts
3.0 hours		✓	✓			✓	Ridge walking, extensive open ledges, scenic views
2.5 hours		✓			✓	✓	Mature forests, miles of scenic lakefront
4.0 hours	$	✓	✓			✓	Ridge walking, cliff-top vistas
2.5 hours		✓	✓		✓	✓	Two undeveloped reservoirs, scenic stretch of river
2.5 hours	$		✓			✓	Cliff-top walking, fire tower, lake and ocean views
5.0 hours	$		✓	✓		✓	Eight trails, six open summits, ocean views

Estimated Time	Fee	Good for Kids	Dogs Allowed	Public Transit	X-C Skiing	Snow-Shoeing	Trip Highlights
4.5 hours	$		✓	✓		✓	Long ridgeline traverse of high alpine-like peak
2.0 hours	$	✓	✓	✓	✓	✓	Shoreline walk with sandy beach, coves, cliffs
2.0 hours		✓	✓				Bedrock trail, mountaintop cliffs, far-reaching views
2.0 hours			✓		✓	✓	History, hilltop forests overlooking two rivers
3.5 hours			✓			✓	Island and bay views
2.0 hours		✓	✓			✓	Human history, island views, lobster boats
1.5 hours		✓	✓		✓	✓	Mature spruce and pines, pristine lakefront
2.0 hours		✓	✓		✓	✓	Forested loop past two remote ponds
3.0 hours		✓	✓		✓	✓	Extensive ledges, series of pristine ponds
3.5 hours		✓	✓		✓	✓	Shoreline walk along expansive and pristine lake
3.0 hours		✓	✓		✓	✓	Upland forests, granite ledges and hilltops
1.25 hours		✓	✓		✓	✓	Pine forests, cobble beaches, bay views, lighthouse
4.0 hours						✓	Rugged walk on remote beaches, oceanfront rocks
2.5 hours		✓	✓		✓	✓	Wild and free-flowing river, converted rail trail
1.5 hours	$	✓	✓		✓	✓	Maritime forests, cliffs, cobbles
6.0 hours						✓	Oceanfront headlands, coves, cobble beaches, bogs
3.0 hours		✓	✓		✓	✓	Old roads, wilderness footpaths, downed fire tower
3.0 hours	$	✓	✓		✓	✓	Oceanfront cliffs, maritime forests, interesting peat bog
2.0 hours	$				✓	✓	Oceanfront headlands, island and bay vistas

ACKNOWLEDGMENTS

A journey of a thousand miles begins with a single step.
—Lao-tzu, *The Way of Lao-tzu*

THROUGH THE WRITING OF THIS BOOK, this adventurer has enjoyed the unique opportunity of exploring the Maine coast from Kittery to Eastport and experiencing the wealth of natural beauty that defines its parks and lands and preserves, as well as its people, food and accommodations. What an incredible journey it has been!

So many individuals across the state of Maine provided support, assistance, enthusiasm, advice, review, and comment, as well as companionship along the meandering two-year path that was this book project from start to finish. Thank you from the soles of my hiking boots to the depths of my heart to the smile on my sunburned face; I am truly indebted to all of you.

First and foremost, thanks to my lovely wife and favorite trail companion, Fran Leyman, who accompanied me on each and every one of the 50 hikes and the two dozen or so other hikes that didn't make the cut. Fran endured with a smile the often slow pace necessitated by copious note taking, fiddling with the GPS and posing as a subject for photos; the enormous mess I made of the house with files and papers and books; and the countless hours and days of actual writing when I could not accompany you for many of the everyday fun things in life. All my love; you're the best.

Sincere thanks to my friends at the Appalachian Mountain Club for the chance to make this new book a reality, especially Peter Tyson, AMC's Editor-in-Chief and Publisher, and Victoria Sandbrook Flynn, AMC's Books Editor, both of whom guided me through the long and sometimes arduous process, and Heather Stephenson, AMC's former Editor-in-Chief and Publisher, and Kimberly Duncan-Mooney, AMC's former Books Editor, who got me started on this endeavor what seems so long ago.

Thanks to the dedicated folks at the land trusts and conservation organizations who do the most amazing work: Robin Kerr, John Branigan, Mount

Agamenticus Conservation Region; Tom Bradbury, Bud Danis, Dave Jourdan, Kennebunkport Conservation Trust; John Gold, Saco Bay Trails; Ann Gamble, Tom Gilmore, Bob Summa, Deb Dubay, Patti Gilmore, Great Works Regional Land Trust; Dick Jarrett, Hilary Wallis, Alison Truesdale, Francis Small Heritage Trust; Carole Brush, John Andrews, Eastern Trail Alliance; Linda Woodard, Scarborough Marsh Audubon Center; Steve Jocher, Jeff Ryan, Tom Blake, South Portland Land Trust; Kara Woldrik, Jaime Parker, Portland Trails; Alan Stearns, Kyle Warren, Royal River Conservation Trust; Don Miskill, Harpswell Heritage Land Trust; Cheryl Sleeper, Matt Dubel, Cathance River Education Alliance; Angela Twitchell, Brunswick Topsham Land Trust; Carrie Kinne, Becky Kolak, Kennebec Estuary Land Trust; Brenda Cummings, Dan Dowd, Bob Cummings, Phippsburg Land Trust; Diane Gilman, Michael Warren, Nick Ullo, Boothbay Region Land Trust; Steve Spencer, Steven Hufnagel, Damariscotta River Association; Donna Minnis, Pemaquid Watershed Association; Clare Durst, Lillian Harris, Monhegan Associates; Anna Fiedler, Buck O'Herin, Sheepscot Wellspring Land Alliance; Jay Astle, Annette Naegel, Georges River Land Trust; Ellen Skoczenski, Kristen Lindquist, Coastal Mountains Land Trust; Cloe Chunn, Skip Pendleton, Belfast Bay Watershed Coalition; Cherie Domina, Great Pond Mountain Conservation Trust; Tim Glidden, Warren Whitney, Jane Arbuckle, Jeff Romano, Kris Campbell, Maine Coast Heritage Trust; George Fields, Eileen Mielenhausen, Blue Hill Heritage Trust; Mike Little, Anne Beerits, Marissa Hutchinson, Island Heritage Trust; Alan Hutchinson, Kristen Hoffman, Forest Society of Maine; Laura Hunt, Tanya Rucosky, David Montague, Downeast Lakes Land Trust; Tom Sidar, Frenchman Bay Conservancy; Tom Rumpf, Nancy Sferra, Misty Edgecomb, Dan Grenier, The Nature Conservancy; Rich Bard, Becky Lee, Downeast Coastal Conservancy.

From the state and federal agencies, thank you to: Rex Turner, Gary Best, Maine Department of Agriculture, Conservation, and Forestry, Bureau of Parks and Lands; Samantha Wilkinson, Reid State Park; John Christie, Bill Elliott, Camden Hills State Park; Rich Donaher, Roque Bluffs State Park; Julie McPherson, Quoddy Head State Park; Doug Denico, Maine Forest Service; Ward Feurt, Connor Casey, Rachel Carson National Wildlife Refuge; Paul Dest, Wells National Estuarine Research Reserve at Laudholm Farm; Charlie Jacobi, Gary Stellpflug, Stuart West, Acadia National Park; Beth Goettel, Brian Benedict, Maine Coastal Islands National Wildlife Refuge; Bill Kolodnicki, Moosehorn National Wildlife Refuge.

And thanks to so many others from various and sundry corners of Maine: Harold Borns, professor emeritus, Climate Change Institute and the School of

Earth and Climate Sciences, University of Maine; Mary Braley, Davis Memorial Library, Limington; Adele Floyd, Limerick Historical Society; Gina Perrow, Reed Coles, town of Harpswell; Will Honan, Highland Green; Michele Gagnon, John Wedin, Elena Piekot, city of Ellsworth; Deirdre Fleming, *Portland Press Herald*; Melissa Waterman, April Gilmore McNutt, Maine Lobstermen's Association; Caroline Paras, Greater Portland Council of Governments; Tony Barrett, East Coast Greenway Alliance.

Finally, one of the best things about hiking along the Maine coast is the near total absence of crowds on the trails. Thanks to Dana Thurston, Tim Nagle and John Wilson for joining me on a few hikes, providing a good measure of levity and for making the trails seem at least a little bit busy.

INTRODUCTION

THIS NEW GUIDE IS DESIGNED TO TAKE YOU ON A JOURNEY of discovery along the coast of Maine, a geographic expanse of 230 miles from Kittery to Eastport as the crow flies, but an incredible 3,500 miles when every nook and cranny and some 3,000 islands are accounted for on the undulating margin along the Gulf of Maine between New Hampshire and Canada.

The topography of the Maine coast is as varied as could be, a natural museum of sandy beaches and rocky headlands, bold ocean cliffs and blueberry barrens, quiet salt marshes and wildlife-rich estuaries, long finger-like peninsulas and deep-water coves, spruce-studded islands and wide bays, pristine lakes and ponds, free-flowing rivers and streams, woods of pine and oak, maple and birch, gentle forested hills and mountains peaks of pink granite.

Hundreds of miles of foot trails will lead you on many hours and days of exploration through the wealth of conservation lands that protect these special places, from state parks and public lands to federal wildlife refuges, from a national park and an estuarine research reserve to private land trusts and conservation organization properties of every shape and size and character. In fact, in just the last four decades the total amount of land in conservation in Maine has increased from just 1 percent of the state's area to an estimated 20 percent, or 3.97 million acres. Of that, more than 1.73 million acres are owned by conservation organizations, the state of Maine, or the federal government; 2.24 million acres are held in conservation easements.

The many hundreds of miles of trails on Maine's public and private lands, whether along the coast or inland, exist because of the generosity of landowners and the stewardship of many organizations and individuals.

The Maine coast can be segmented into two distinct physical regions, the coastal lowlands and the hilly belt of the interior. The coastal lowlands include the long stretches of sandy beaches; coves and bays formed by peninsulas, all exposed to the ocean and its moods by varying degrees; plentiful islands of every size, whether connected to the mainland by tidal bridges or separated by many miles of water; and a stretch of interior hills and mountains. This geology is the result of a series of complex natural forces. Much of the natural landscape we observe today in Maine was shaped by the glaciation events that started about 35,000 years ago. The 10,000-foot-thick Laurentide Ice Sheet spread across southern Quebec and New England, covering the highest mountains in the state, including Katahdin. The sheer mass of the ice sheet depressed the land many hundreds of feet, and its movement scoured the mountains and valleys, eroding the rock and carving enormous basins out of the mountainsides, while moving great quantities of sand and gravel southward. When the glaciers began to retreat about 21,000 years ago, the melting waters flooded as far as 75 miles inland, creating the long peninsulas and islands that exist today and leaving behind more than 6,000 lakes and ponds in the interior.

The hikes are geographically dispersed along the coast so as to provide the best glimpse into the many and varied possibilities along Maine's lengthy coastline and coastal interior. Each specific hike was selected for its unique natural and scenic character and the availability of foot trails to ensure a pleasant and satisfying outing.

Given Maine's geographic location on the eastern edge of the North American continent, its climate is influenced primarily by continental air masses flowing across the land on the westerly winds. This can be the cold, dry air from Canada or the warm, moist air from the Gulf of Mexico. The climate is influenced to a lesser degree by cool, moist air from the Atlantic Ocean, which serves to moderate the temperatures along the coast. Maine's northern location makes for generally mild, but not hot, summers and cold winters. The mean January temperature along the coast averages 20 degrees Fahrenheit, while the mean July temperature is 65 degrees Fahrenheit. Coastal areas receive around 50 inches of rainfall and up to 80 inches of snow annually.

Maine occupies a transition zone between the predominantly deciduous forests to the south and the predominantly coniferous forests to the north. Within this zone the broad mix of forest-cover types is influenced to some degree by latitude, although soil variation and local climate also play a role. Along the coast from Casco Bay east to Passamaquoddy Bay, the dominant tree species are spruce, fir, cedar, and larch. In southwestern Maine, and in parts of the hilly interior belt, the dominant species are oak, white pine, and hemlock. The northern hardwood mix of beech, maple, and birch dominates in the hilly interior of Washington County.

Maine's diverse landscape and flora offers a wide variety of habitats and an abundance of animal, bird, and marine life. Maine has more moose, lynx, black bears and marten than any other state east of the Mississippi River. The woods are also home to white-tailed deer, red squirrels, porcupines and beavers, among the more common mammals. More elusive are the coyotes, red foxes, and fishers. Loons populate thousands of lakes and ponds, and their distinctive black-and-white bodies and mournful calls make them a Maine woods classic. Bald eagles, hawks, ospreys, falcons, and owls are common predatory bird species. Eider ducks, buffleheads, mergansers, guillemots, and cormorants are common along the coast. The colorful Atlantic puffin with its clown-like beak can be viewed at a handful of protected offshore island sites. Wading birds such as herons and egrets are found among the waters and wetlands, while black-capped chickadees, warblers, and woodpeckers inhabit the wooded environs. In all, 292 species of birds are found in Maine. Finback, humpback, and minke whales summer in the ocean waters, which also hold harbor seals and porpoises. Inland, waters teem with trout, salmon, bass, and other game fish.

After the retreat of the glaciers, indigenous peoples inhabited the territory that is now Maine for more than 10,000 years, from the mysterious "Red Paint" people through the Wabanaki, or "People of the Dawn," members of a large Algonquin confederation that ranged from New England to the Great Lakes. The Wabanaki were the people first encountered when Europeans began to arrive in the region during the late fourteenth and early fifteenth centuries. Four Wabanaki tribes continue to inhabit the state, including the Passamaquoddy, Penobscot, Maliseet and Micmac.

The first European settlement in North America was established by French explorer Pierre Dugua, Sieur de Mons, in 1604 on an island in the St. Croix River not far from present day Calais. The first English settlement in Maine was the short-lived Popham Colony, founded in 1607 near the mouth of the Kennebec River. English settlement continued in the 1620s along the coast of Maine, but most endeavors failed due to the harsh climate and difficulty of securing enough food in the wilderness.

Despite the fact that the Massachusetts Bay Colony had purchased most of the land claims in Maine, the territory remained in dispute between the French and the English until the French surrendered all land claims in the New World after the French and Indian Wars in 1763. English settlement resumed after the wars and thriving fishing, lumbering, and shipbuilding industries were developed here. During the Revolutionary War, several important naval battles were fought along the Maine coast, at Portland (then called

Falmouth), Machias Bay, and Castine; Benedict Arnold traveled through Maine on his ill-fated attempt to seize Quebec. Maine joined the Union as its 23rd state under the Missouri Compromise in 1820. After statehood, manufacturing enterprises harnessed Maine's abundant water resources to power textile, paper, and saw mills. Ice harvesting and granite and lime quarrying also became important industries. This robust industrial growth lasted through the Civil War and into the first half of the twentieth century.

Today, Maine's bountiful natural resources and scenic beauty continue to play key roles in the state's economy, with forest products, fishing, agriculture, tourism, and outdoor recreation being major contributors to the state's gross domestic product. Maine's population is just over 1.32 million people.

HOW TO USE THIS BOOK

WITH 50 GREAT HIKES TO CHOOSE FROM, you may wonder how to decide where to go for a hike. Start with the locator map at the front of this book to help you narrow down the trips by geographic location along the coast of Maine from Kittery to Eastport. The At-a-Glance Trip Planner that follows the table of contents provides a summary of key information about each hike to further guide you toward a decision.

Once you decide on a destination and turn to a trip in this guide, you will find a series of icons at the top of the page that indicate if a fee is charged, if the hike is a good one for kids, if dogs are permitted, if the trailhead is accessible via public transportation, and if the hike is suitable for cross-country skiing or snowshoeing in winter.

Information on the basics of the hike follows: town or township location, difficulty rating, distance, elevation gain, estimated time, and maps. The difficulty ratings of easy, moderate, and strenuous are based on the author's personal experience and are estimates of what the average hiker will experience. You may find them to be easier or more difficult than stated.

Distances are presented in miles and calculated for round-trip hikes returning to the same trailhead and for point-to-point hikes ending at a different trailhead, depending on the particular trip.

The elevation gain is the cumulative difference between the high and low points on a hike. It is calculated from measurements and information collected using a smartphone application as well as from USGS topographic maps, landowner maps, and Google Earth.

The estimated time in hours and minutes is also based on the author's personal experience and includes time for sightseeing, snack and rest breaks, occasional side trail exploration, and a quick swim when possible. Consider your own pace and desires when planning a trip.

Information is included about the relevant USGS maps, about trail maps specific to the hike as available from the landowner or managing agency, and about the particular map reference in the DeLorme *Maine Atlas and Gazetteer,* which covers the area. The atlas is a useful and highly recommended resource for navigating Maine's roads and byways. The trail maps printed in this book will help guide you along your hikes. Useful as they are, it is wise to also take an official trail map with you. Trail maps are often—but not always—available online, at the trailhead, or at the visitor center or park entrance station. Download a trail map to your smartphone or take a photo of the map posted at the trailhead when possible for convenience and to save paper.

The directions explain how to reach the trailhead by car and, for some trips, by public transportation. GPS coordinates for trailhead parking lots are also included. When you enter the coordinates into your vehicle's device, it will provide driving directions. Whether or not you own a GPS device, it is wise to consult a road atlas such as DeLorme's before leaving your home and in transit. This section also indicates the number of parking spaces, availability and location of toilets, and whether an information kiosk is found at the trailhead.

The boldfaced summary that follows provides the basic highlights of what you will see during your hike.

In the trail description, you will find instructions on where to hike, the trails on which to hike, and where to turn. You will also learn about the pertinent natural, human, and geologic history to be found along your hike, as well as information about flora, fauna, and any landmarks and other objects you will encounter.

Each trip description concludes with several short sections. More Information provides contact information for the land management agency or organization for the property you will be hiking, access times and fees, and particular rules and regulations. The Nearby section includes information on fun activities to consider after the hike, including museums, historical sites, and other places of interest, as well as the availability of eateries, shops, entertainment, and lodging. The More Hiking section details additional hiking opportunities in the area that you may wish to explore on this or future trips, including the name and contact information for the relevant land management agency or organization. The Did You Know? section provides a fun and interesting factoid for most—but not all—hiking trips.

An appendix of helpful information—including local recreation organizations, camping resources, and contacts for other recreational opportunities—may be found online at outdoors.org/bookupdates.

TRIP PLANNING AND SAFETY

THE HIKING TRAILS ALONG THE MAINE COAST VARY WIDELY from easy forest paths to moderate oceanfront rambles to strenuous mountain treks. Most of the described hikes will provide an uncommon measure of solitude, while on a handful you will almost always see at least a few people. Perhaps only in the Camden Hills or Acadia might you encounter enough other hikers to consider the hike crowded. If you are looking for organized hikes, check with AMC Maine Chapter, local hiking groups and land trusts, parks, and preserves for scheduled outings.

Most of the hikes follow well-marked and signed trails, although this can certainly change over time. Expect to encounter wet and slippery sections of trail complete with rocks, roots, and mud, plus potentially hazardous ledges and clifftops, river and stream crossings, and ocean surf.

Weather, fatigue, injury, a lost trail—all can put you and your hiking companions at risk. Therefore, even for easy hikes of short duration, be sure to carry enough clothing, water, food, and emergency items should you have to spend extra time or even an overnight in the woods for any reason. You will be more likely to have a safe and enjoyable hike if you plan ahead and take proper precautions. Before heading out for your hike, consider the following:

- Select a hike that suits everyone in your group. Match the hike to the abilities of the least capable person in the group. If anyone is uncomfortable with the weather or is tired, turn around and return to complete the hike another day.
- Plan to be back at the trailhead before dark. Before beginning your hike, determine a turnaround time. Don't diverge from it, even if you have not reached your intended destination.
- Check the weather. The weather along the Maine coast is highly variable, so be prepared for windy, wet, and foggy conditions at any time of year. Wind

chill is an added concern in winter. Compared with inland locations, the climate is generally cooler along the immediate coast during the warmer months and milder in wintertime. Significant storms—including heavy winter snowfalls, spring rainstorms, and tropical storms in late summer and fall—may cause flooding, potentially dangerous ocean tides, and other hazards. When exploring the rocks and beaches and other areas along the coast, be sure to check tide tables in advance and keep an eye on the water at all times. If you are planning a ridge or summit hike, start early so that you will be off the exposed area before the afternoon hours when thunderstorms most often strike, especially in summer.

- Bring a pack with the following items:
  - ✓ Water: Two quarts per person is usually adequate, depending on the weather and the length of the trip. On extended day hikes, consider carrying some method of water purification so you can refill your water bottles en route.
  - ✓ Food: Even if you are planning just a one-hour hike, bring some high-energy snacks such as nuts, dried fruit, or snack bars. Pack a lunch for longer trips.
  - ✓ Map and compass: Be sure you know how to use them. A handheld GPS device may also be helpful, but it is not always reliable.
  - ✓ Headlamp or flashlight, with spare batteries
  - ✓ Extra clothing: waterproof/breathable rain gear, synthetic fleece or wool jacket, hat, and mittens or gloves
  - ✓ Sunscreen
  - ✓ Bandanna
  - ✓ First-aid kit, including adhesive bandages, gauze and tape, nonprescription pain relievers, moleskin, and personal prescription medications at a minimum
  - ✓ Pocketknife or multitool with a blade
  - ✓ Waterproof matches and a lighter
  - ✓ Trash bag
  - ✓ Toilet paper and hand sanitizer
  - ✓ Whistle
  - ✓ Insect repellent
  - ✓ Sunglasses
  - ✓ Cell phone: Be aware that cell phone service is unreliable in rural areas. If you do have a signal, use the phone only for emergencies to avoid disturbing the trail experience for other hikers. Note: In some coastal locations near Canada your cell phone may ping off the Canadian

towers, causing you to incur international roaming charges. Modify your cell phone plan accordingly ahead of time or keep your phone turned off in these areas.

✓ Trekking poles (optional)

✓ Binoculars (optional)

✓ Camera (optional)

- Wear appropriate footwear and clothing. Wool or synthetic hiking socks will keep your feet dry and help prevent blisters. Comfortable, waterproof hiking boots will provide ankle support and good traction. Avoid wearing cotton clothing, which absorbs sweat and rain and contributes to an unpleasant hiking experience. A synthetic or wool base layer (T-shirt, or underwear tops and bottoms) will wick moisture away from your body and keep you warm in wet or cold conditions. Synthetic zip-off pants that convert to shorts are popular. To help avoid bug bites, you may want to wear synthetic pants and a long-sleeve shirt.

- Comfortable shoes or boots that have good tread and have been broken in are essential. Gore-Tex or similar waterproof material is a bonus for the wet and muddy coastal trails. Ice creepers are necessary for good traction from late fall through early spring.

- If you hike ahead of the rest of your group, wait at all trail junctions until the others catch up. This avoids confusion and keeps people from getting separated or lost.

- If you see downed wood that appears to be purposely covering a trail, it probably means the trail is closed or has been redirected for some reason.

- If a trail is muddy, walk through the mud or on rocks, never on tree roots or plants. Waterproof boots will keep your feet comfortable, and staying in the center of the trail will help prevent erosion.

- Inform someone you trust about your itinerary and expected return time. If you see a logbook at a trailhead, be sure to sign in when you arrive and sign out when you finish your hike.

- Take precautions against deer ticks, which can transmit the dangerous Lyme disease, such as wearing long, light-colored pants, wearing socks, keeping to the trail, avoiding high grass, and using repellent. Check your clothes, skin, and hair for ticks after you complete your hike.

- Poison ivy is always a threat when hiking. To identify the plant, look for clusters of three very shiny, dark-green leaves that shine in the sun but are dull in the shade. If you do come into contact with poison ivy, wash the affected area with soap as soon as possible.

- Wear two items of blaze-orange clothing in hunting season. For specific dates of Maine hunting seasons (deer, moose, wild turkey, and other game), contact the Maine Department of Inland Fisheries & Wildlife at maine.gov/ifw or 207-287-8000.
- Biting insects such as mosquitoes, blackflies, deer flies, and no-see-ums are present during late spring and summer months. These can be a minor or significant nuisance, depending on seasonal and daily conditions. A variety of options are available for dealing with bugs, ranging from pump and aerosol sprays and lotions that include the active ingredient N,N-Diethyl-meta-toluamide (commonly known as DEET), which can potentially cause skin or eye irritation, to more skin-friendly products containing picaridin, citronella, or eucalyptus. Head nets, which often can be purchased for less than a can of repellent, are useful during especially buggy conditions.
- Always exercise care to observe all rules and regulations that have been designed to protect the land itself, the wildlife that makes its home there, and the rights of landowners. Treat all trails and property with great respect, as if the land were your own. This might require cleaning up after others less thoughtful. Hikers may sometimes share designated trails with other users, like mountain bikers, ATV riders, and horseback riders. There is room for enjoyment for all in the Maine outdoors, so please be courteous. Where dogs are allowed, owners should keep their pets under control at all times, whether by leash or voice control.
- Cars parked at trailheads can be the target of break-ins, so valuable items should never be left inside your vehicle while you are off hiking.
- Should an emergency situation arise that cannot be safely handled by your group, call 911 to alert authorities and initiate a search and rescue if warranted.

Always anticipate the unexpected on the trails of the Maine outdoors. Be safe and have fun.

LEAVE NO TRACE

The Appalachian Mountain Club (AMC) is a national educational partner of Leave No Trace, a nonprofit organization dedicated to promoting and inspiring responsible outdoor recreation through education,  research, and partnerships. The Leave No Trace program seeks to develop wildland ethics—ways in which people think and act in the outdoors to minimize their impact on the areas they visit and to protect our natural resources for future enjoyment. Leave No Trace unites four federal land management agencies—the U.S. Forest Service, National Park Service, Bureau of Land Management, and U.S. Fish and Wildlife Service—with manufacturers, outdoor retailers, user groups, educators, organizations such as AMC, and individuals.

The Leave No Trace ethic is guided by the following seven principles:

1. **Plan Ahead and Prepare.** Know the terrain and any regulations applicable to the area you're planning to visit, and be prepared for extreme weather or other emergencies. Small groups have less impact on resources and on the experiences of other backcountry visitors.

2. **Travel and Camp on Durable Surfaces.** Travel and camp on established trails and campsites, rock, gravel, dry grasses, or snow. Good campsites are found, not made. Camp at least 200 feet from lakes and streams, and focus activities on areas where vegetation is absent. In pristine areas, disperse use to prevent the creation of campsites and trails.

3. **Dispose of Waste Properly.** Pack it in, pack it out. Inspect your camp for trash or food scraps. Deposit solid human waste in catholes dug 6 to 8 inches deep, at least 200 feet from water, camps, and trails. Pack out toilet paper and hygiene products. To wash yourself or your dishes, carry water 200 feet from streams or lakes and use small amounts of biodegradable soap. Scatter strained dishwater.

4. **Leave What You Find.** Cultural or historical artifacts, as well as natural objects such as plants and rocks, should be left as found.

5. **Minimize Campfire Impacts.** Cook on a stove. Use established fire rings, fire pans, or mound fires. If you build a campfire, keep it small and use dead sticks found on the ground.

6. **Respect Wildlife.** Observe wildlife from a distance. Feeding animals alters their natural behavior. Store your rations and trash securely.

7. **Be Considerate of Other Visitors.** Be courteous, respect the quality of other visitors' backcountry experience, and let nature's sounds prevail.

AMC is a national provider of the Leave No Trace Master Educator course. AMC offers this five-day course, designed especially for outdoor professionals and land managers, as well as the shorter two-day Leave No Trace Trainer course, throughout the Northeast. For Leave No Trace information contact the Leave No Trace Center for Outdoor Ethics, 800-332-4100 or 302-442-8222; lnt.org. For a schedule of AMC Leave No Trace courses, see outdoors.org/education/lnt.

1

YORK COUNTY

THE YORK COUNTY SECTION INCLUDES the entirety of the southernmost county in Maine, which comprises a land area of 1,271 square miles. The county is bounded by New Hampshire, Oxford and Cumberland counties, and the Atlantic Ocean.

Established in 1636 when Sir Ferdinando Gorges received a patent from King Charles I of England for all the land along the coast of Maine from the Piscataqua River to the Kennebec River, York County is the oldest county in Maine and one of the oldest in the United States. When the Massachusetts Bay Colony claimed southern Maine in 1650, York County was split into three counties in 1760, with the new counties of Cumberland and Lincoln occupying the land from just south of the Scarboro River northeast to the Kennebec River. A section in the northern portion of York County was separated in 1805 to form part of Oxford County.

From Portsmouth Harbor, the Maine–New Hampshire state line and the western boundary of York County follow the Piscataqua River north to Eliot and then to the Salmon Falls River, where the stately pines and hemlocks of Vaughan Woods Memorial State Park are found (Trip 2). Across the north of York County, the Ossipee River then flows east to Cornish, where it joins the Saco River, which continues east, south, and then east again to the hamlet of

Bonny Eagle in Hollis. The town lines of Buxton, Saco, and then Old Orchard Beach are the delineation, ending at Grand Beach and the Gulf of Maine.

Along the coast, a string of beautiful sand beaches are punctuated by a series of scenic coves and harbors, points, capes, and rocky necks ranging from Saco Bay to Biddeford Pool to Cape Arundel, and from Cape Neddick to Gerrish Island on the east side of Portsmouth Harbor near Kittery Point. In summer, throngs of vacationing visitors flock to fun-in-the-sun places like Old Orchard, Ferry, Hills, Fortunes Rocks, Goose Rocks, Goochs, Kennebunk, Parsons, Drakes Island, Wells, Moody, Ogunquit, Short Sands, Long, Seapoint, and Crescent beaches. If anywhere in Maine gets truly crowded in summertime it's the coastal corridor between I-95/US 1 and the ocean. Three of Maine's famed lighthouses are found along this stretch of coast, including Wood Island Light off Biddeford Pool, Goat Island Light off Cape Porpoise, and Nubble Light off Cape Neddick. Trails at Rachel Carson National Wildlife Refuge at Cutts Island in Kittery (Trip 1) explore its wildlife-rich salt marsh and estuary habitats, oak and pine forests, and old field uplands. The Wells Reserve at Laudholm Farm in Wells (Trip 4) is a federal estuary research center on 2,250 acres of diverse coastal habitat that is home to 7 miles of trails. Acres of peaceful oak and pine woods and rocky outcrops at Edwin L. Smith Preserve in Kennebunkport (Trip 5), owned by the Kennebunkport Conservation Trust, hide remnants of the devastating Great Fire of 1947. The Saco Beach Loop (Trip 6) meanders through the forested environs of Ferry Beach State Park before striking north on the namesake beach, and connects trails of the extensive Saco Bay Trails system.

Away from the coast, York County maintains a distinctly rural character, with its pretty farmlands and forests, meadows and stone walls, low hills and historical small towns and villages. A string of good-size hills and mountains range in a south-to-north line through the interior from York to Cornish, including Mount Agamenticus and its sister peaks Second and Third hills (Trip 3). Bauneg Beg Mountain Conservation Area sports the only major hilltop in the area without a communication tower on its summit (Trip 7), a tribute to the work of the Great Works Regional Land Trust. North of Ossipee Hill and its historical firetower, Clark and Hoosac mountains exceed 1,300 feet in elevation, the highest summits in the county. The Francis Small Heritage Trust has preserved more than 1,000 acres in these Sawyer Mountain Highlands, including Sawyer Mountain (Trip 8) itself.

Several preserves owned by The Nature Conservancy, as well as a number of state wildlife management areas and experimental forests and dozens of other land trust properties of varying acreage, are scattered about York County.

TRIP 1
RACHEL CARSON NATIONAL
WILDLIFE REFUGE

Location: Kittery, ME
Rating: Easy
Distance: 1.8 miles
Elevation Gain: 40 feet
Estimated Time: 1.5 hours
Maps: USGS Kittery quad; *Maine Atlas and Gazetteer*, Map 1 (DeLorme); *Cutts Island Trail* (RCNWR)

Walk through upland oak and pine forests, tidal estuaries, and salt marshes in a wildlife refuge named for Rachel Carson, the renowned biologist, author, and environmentalist.

DIRECTIONS

From I-95/Maine Turnpike, Exit 2, drive south onto ME 236 about a quarter-mile to a rotary and the junction with ME 103, passing beneath US 1 en route. Begin mileage count. Continue south onto ME 236/103. At 0.7 mile from the rotary, where ME 236 bears right toward Kittery village, stay straight on ME 103. Soon, pass the entrance to Portsmouth Naval Shipyard on the right, located on Seavey Island in the Piscataqua River at the mouth of Portsmouth Harbor. Cross over Spruce Creek to reach the entrance to Fort McClary State Historic Site on the right at 2.0 miles. Ahead on ME 103, at 3.6 miles from the rotary, turn right onto Cutts Island Lane and follow this across the bridge over Chauncey Creek. The trailhead is on the left immediately beyond the bridge, where there is parking along the road for about six cars. *GPS coordinates: 43° 5.266′ N, 70° 40.535′ W.*

TRAIL DESCRIPTION

The eleven geographic areas of the Rachel Carson National Wildlife Refuge (RCNWR), which range along 50 miles of the Maine coast from Kittery to Cape Elizabeth, protect a wide variety of habitats important to migratory birds and other wildlife, including tidal estuaries, salt marshes, barrier beaches and dunes, coastal meadows, rocky coast, and forested uplands. The 5,600-acre refuge, established in 1966 with assistance from the state of Maine, is managed by the U.S. Fish and Wildlife Service. Originally known as the Coastal Maine

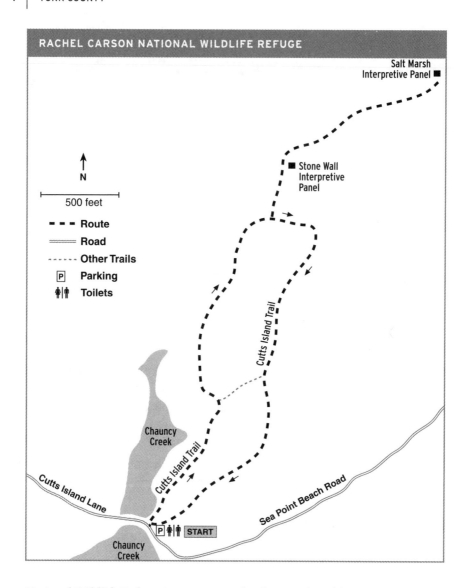

RACHEL CARSON NATIONAL WILDLIFE REFUGE

Salt Marsh
Interpretive Panel ■

N

500 feet

- - - Route
═══ Road
------ Other Trails
P Parking
Toilets

■ Stone Wall
Interpretive
Panel

Cutts Island Trail

Chauncy
Creek

Cutts Island Trail

Cutts Island Lane

Sea Point Beach Road

P START

Chauncy
Creek

National Wildlife Refuge, it was renamed in honor of world-renowned marine biologist, environmentalist, and author Rachel Carson in 1969.

The Brave Boat Harbor Division of RCNWR in Kittery encompasses 750 acres of salt marsh and estuary habitat as well as oak and pine forests and old field uplands in and around Brave Boat Harbor, Cutts Island, and Raynes Neck. The Cutts Island Trail system meanders 1.8 scenic miles through this diverse landscape.

Just beyond the gate are an information kiosk and vault toilets. From here, follow the wide Orange Loop Trail, which is blazed with round orange-and-

Wildlife-rich salt marshes, like this one along Chauncey Creek, help protect the coastline from storms and erosion, trap sediments, cycle nutrients, and serve as nurseries for fish.

silver markers. The trail soon narrows as it follows the east side of Chauncey Creek, which separates both Cutts and Gerrish islands from the mainland. At the junction with Blue Shortcut, bear left. Just beyond, a short spur leads left to a view of the salt marsh. Saunter through mixed woods that feature some impressive old white and red oak, white pine, and sweet birch trees.

After a boardwalk, reach a spur trail on the left that leads 0.3 mile to an overlook. Follow the spur trail to an interpretive sign, "New England Stone Walls." The old stone wall just ahead, like many thousands across New England, may have marked a farm's property boundaries and kept grazing livestock from straying.

Continuing on beneath the canopy composed primarily of beech and oak, the land narrows and salt marshes can be seen through the trees on both sides of the trail. Step off the trail to either side and walk to the edge of the woods for unobstructed views up and down Chauncey Creek.

The spur ends with a view north over the salt marshes to the waters of Brave Boat Harbor at an interpretive sign, "Salt Marshes in Southern Maine." Remain on the viewing platform to protect the fragile environment beyond. Salt marshes like this one are the transitional zones between the land and salty or brackish waters, and teem with wildlife that feed on the nutrients carried in on the twice-daily tides. Salt marshes help protect the coastline from storms and erosion, trap sediments and cycle nutrients, and function as nurseries for fish.

Retrace your steps to return to the main loop trail. At the junction, turn left to continue. Pass by more big pine, oak, and sweet birch trees. Cross several bog bridges to reach a nice hemlock grove. The wide path ascends a low rise, then crosses a slope with views downhill through the trees to a marsh.

Pass the final interpretive sign, "Forest Life," then follow the left edge of a ravine. After passing the east end of Blue Shortcut, the trail meanders nearly to the edge of a salt marsh on the left. In the woods just up from the marsh is a huge red oak that is close to 5 feet in diameter. It's worth a few moments to explore this old soldier of a tree.

Beyond, the trail trends easily downhill back to the start.

DID YOU KNOW?

After completing a graduate degree in biology at Johns Hopkins University in Baltimore, Rachel Carson began her career in 1936 with the U.S. Bureau of Fisheries, the precursor to the U.S. Fish and Wildlife Service, where she worked as a researcher, writer, editor, and biologist until 1952. Carson's most important work, the groundbreaking book *Silent Spring*, documented the deleterious effects of the unrestrained use of post-World War II chemical pesticides such as DDT. For this she is credited with launching the contemporary environmental movement in America.

MORE INFORMATION

Rachel Carson National Wildlife Refuge (fws.gov/refuge/rachel_carson, 207-646-9226). The Cutts Island Trail system is open year-round for foot traffic only from sunrise to sunset. Dogs are not allowed. Hunting is allowed by permit only. The Cutts Island Trail map is available for download. Refuge headquarters in Wells is open Monday though Friday 8 A.M. to 4:30 P.M. Contact RCNWR for information about additional hiking trails in the refuge.

NEARBY

Fort McClary guards the Piscataqua River at the entrance to Portsmouth Harbor in Kittery Point. This fort is the most recent of a number of fortifications that have stood on this site for more than 275 years. Named after New Hampshire native Major Andrew McClary, who died at the Battle of Bunker Hill in the Revolutionary War, the fort preserves important evidence of military history and changes in military architecture and technology. The site was manned during five wars but saw minimal conflict. Fort McClary is open daily from Memorial Day to September 30. A small fee is charged. More info: parkslandlands.com, 207-384-5160.

TRIP 2
VAUGHAN WOODS
MEMORIAL STATE PARK

Location: South Berwick, ME
Rating: Easy
Distance: 2.2 miles
Elevation Gain: 131 feet
Estimated Time: 1.25 hours
Maps: USGS Dover East quad; *Maine Atlas and Gazetteer*, Map 1
(DeLorme); *Map of Vaughan Woods Memorial State Park* (Maine DACF)

**Hike through great stands of century-old white pines and hemlocks
that thrive alongside a mile of protected Salmon Falls River frontage.**

DIRECTIONS

From the intersection of ME 4 and 236 in South Berwick, drive south on ME
236. At 1.0 mile, turn right (south) onto Brattle Street (small sign for park).
In another 0.8 mile, where the road curves sharply left (just past a sign for
Hamilton House), Brattle Street becomes Oldfields Road. Continue an additional 0.2 mile to the park entrance on the right. Continue past the parking
lot immediately on the left, down through the field to the end of the park road,
another 0.1 mile, where there is trailhead parking for about a dozen cars. *GPS
coordinates: 43° 13.040′ N, 70° 48.501′ W.*

TRAIL DESCRIPTION

More than 3 miles of wide, well-used trails crisscross the park-like forests of
Vaughan Woods Memorial State Park, a 250-acre tract on the Salmon Falls
River, offering hikers hours of exploration and a window into the natural and
human history of the area.

Elizabeth Vaughan bequeathed the park to the state in 1949 to be kept "in
the natural wild state as the Vaughan Woods Memorial." The Maine Department of Agriculture, Conservation, and Forestry, Bureau of Parks and Public
Lands now manages it. Vaughan and her mother, Emily Tyson Vaughan, a
wealthy Bostonian who purchased the property in 1898, cared for the land for
decades, allowing the forest to prosper and grow back from old pasture and
brushland. The pair restored the nearby Hamilton House, built by merchant
Jonathan Hamilton in 1785. Today, stands of century-old white pines and hem-

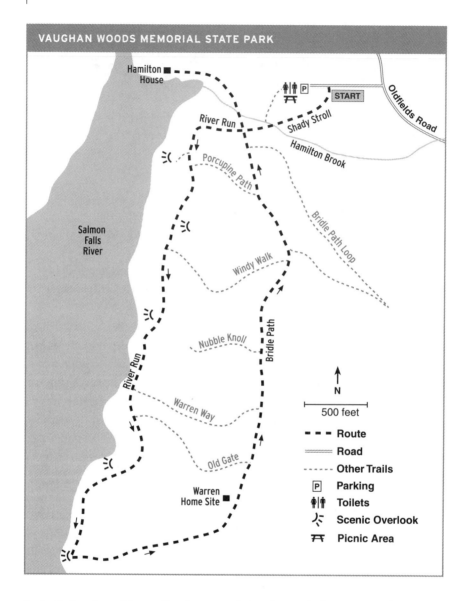

VAUGHAN WOODS MEMORIAL STATE PARK

locks thrive alongside a mile of protected riverfront, the home to an abundance of bird and animal life. The Hamilton House is a National Historic Landmark.

In the woods along the front edge of the trailhead parking lot are a number of picnic tables with grills. Opposite the parking lot are a playground, picnic pavilion, and pit toilets. An information kiosk is located at the far end of the lot; another kiosk is found at the head of the lot and the start of Shady Stroll.

Enter the woods on Shady Stroll and walk downhill. Cross a bridge over Hamilton Brook and quickly come to a four-way trail intersection. Proceed

Hamilton House on the Salmon Falls River was built by merchant Jonathan Hamilton in 1785 and is a National Historic Landmark open to the public.

straight ahead on River Run. You'll loop back later onto Bridle Path, which enters from the left. The trail to the right leads off the property to Hamilton House. At the first overlook, the Hamilton House View, you'll see the stately house just across the inlet and will reach the first of five benches on the route.

River Run travels south along the Salmon Falls River and passes five side trails on the left that connect with Bridle Path, the upper leg of the loop hike; shorten your walk by taking any of them.

River Run also crosses a series of ravines on bridges and remains well above the river level most of the way. At several places, it's possible to scramble down the bank to get an unimpeded view, but if you wait until Cow Cove, the trail meanders right down to the water's edge. Local legend holds that in 1634, a ship named *Pied Cow* sailed upriver into this cove to land the first cows in the area.

Signs of civilization are all but absent along this semi-wild stretch of river. The Salmon Falls River forms a natural state boundary with New Hampshire from Great East Lake to the Piscataqua River. Named for the once abundant salmon, the river was an important transportation route for early settlers and the lumber industry. The river also powered the very first sawmill in America, built in nearby York in 1623.

At the park boundary at Trail's End, the path turns left (east), away from the river, and River Run becomes Bridle Path. This trail leads easily up the hillside to the old home site of James Warren, who settled on a 50-acre lot here in the early 1600s. Warren, a Scot loyal to the king in the English Civil War, was captured by Oliver Cromwell and imprisoned. His only hope was to come to America as an indentured servant. At the conclusion of his indentures, Warren was given this lot, a common practice in those days.

The forest canopy along the ridgeline is more mixed, with oak and hickory trees among the softwoods, and crumbling stone walls delineating old property lines. Well-kept trail signs mark the side connecting trails and the main way, which ends at the original junction. At this point, turn right to return to the parking lot or hike straight ahead for another 0.2 mile to visit the Hamilton House.

DID YOU KNOW?

Since Colonial times, the fields near the park entrance along Oldfields Road have been known as the "oldfields." Here, American Indians used fire to manage wildlife habitat and clear the land for growing corn, beans, and squash. Using a rotating system, they allowed portions of the land to revert to berries, brush, and forest, while clearing other adjacent areas.

MORE INFORMATION

Vaughan Woods Memorial State Park (parksandlands.com, 207-490-4079 [summer park season], 207-624-6080 [off-season]). The park is open year-round from 9 A.M. to 7 P.M. There is a small daily entrance fee.

NEARBY

Elizabeth Vaughan also gifted the adjacent 160-acre property, which included the Hamilton House and its gardens, outbuildings, fields, and farmlands to Historic New England (historicnewengland.org), the oldest and largest regional heritage organization in the nation. Hamilton House is open Wednesday through Sunday from June 1 to October 15. Tours (fee) are available on the hour from 11 A.M. to 4 P.M. The grounds and small visitor center are free.

MORE HIKING

The Mount Agamenticus Conservation Region encompasses more than 10,000 acres of coastal woods and hills in southern York County, representing the largest intact parcel of coastal forest between Acadia National Park in Maine and the Pine Barrens in New Jersey. The large area of undeveloped land and abundant wetlands combine to provide habitat for dozens of rare, threatened, and endangered species. For more information and a trail map, visit agamenticus.org or call 207-361-1102.

THE KING'S PINES

It is no coincidence that Maine is nicknamed the Pine Tree State. The eastern white pine has played an important role in Maine's economy for more than 400 years, with its straight, lightweight, and strong wood highly valued as lumber for houses, furniture, and a variety of other products. In 1895 the Maine legislature designated the pine cone and tassel as the state flower, and in 1945 the white pine became the official state tree.

The white pine, the tallest tree in eastern North America, can reach 130 feet in height, 3 to 5 feet in diameter, and live more than 200 years. In the Colonial America of the 1600s and 1700s, virgin white pines were abundant, many growing as tall as 230 feet in Maine and around New England. These massive pines were not only prized for lumber in colonial America but also as masts for sailing ships by Britain, which had long before depleted its own forests.

To maintain supremacy over the seas, the British Navy depended upon a reliable supply of these huge white pines. Recognizing this significant asset in the New World, the Broad Arrow Policy of 1691 decreed that all white pines 24 inches or larger in diameter that grew within 3 miles of any navigable waterway were the exclusive property of the King of England, to be harvested and used solely by the British Navy.

Each such white pine was blazed with the mark of the Broad Arrow, a vertical hatchet slash topped by two more slashes that formed an inverted V. The term King's Pine originated from this colonial policy. Fines of 100 pounds sterling were levied on any colonist who dared cut or destroy the protected trees. Surveyors were appointed to manage the lands and mast agents hired to represent British interests. Captain George Tate of Portland served as the senior mast agent for the British Navy, overseeing the cutting and shipping of white pines from Maine to England.

American colonists, angry that they could not reap profits from the trees on their own lands, saw this policy as part of the increasing tyranny of the British Crown. Colonists rebelled by obliterating the Broad Arrow mark on the King's Pines and marking smaller pines instead. In further defiance, they would then fell the mast trees and sell them on the black market. The American Revolution finally ended the British monopoly on white pine.

TRIP 3
MOUNT AGAMENTICUS
CONSERVATION REGION

Location: York, ME
Rating: Moderate
Distance: 3.9 miles (round-trip)
Elevation Gain: 620 feet
Estimated Time: 3.0 hours
Maps: USGS York Harbor; *Maine Atlas and Gazetteer*, Map 1
(DeLorme); *Mount Agamenticus Trail Map* (Mount Agamenticus
Conservation Region)

**Experience this summit's beauty and history amid the largest intact
parcel of coastal forest between Acadia National Park and the New
Jersey Pine Barrens.**

DIRECTIONS
From I-95/Maine Turnpike, Exit 7 in York, drive east 0.2 mile to the junction
of US 1. Turn left onto US 1 and proceed north for 4.0 miles to Cape Neddick,
a hamlet of York. Immediately across from Flow's Hot Dogs (low, red roadside
building on the right) turn left onto Mountain Road. Follow this road northwest for 1.5 miles to a junction where Chases Pond Road merges from the
left. Turn right at the stop sign and continue another 2.6 miles on Mountain
Road, reaching the trailhead parking lot on the right, adjacent to the start of
the Mount Agamenticus summit access road. There is space for twelve cars. A
picnic table, portable toilet, and information kiosk are adjacent to the lot. *GPS
coordinates: 43° 13.020′ N, 70° 41.532′ W.*

TRAIL DESCRIPTION
The Mount Agamenticus Conservation Region (MACR) encompasses more
than 10,000 acres of coastal woods and hills in southern York County. Because
of its location, the mountain's environment is a unique mixing ground for a
number of southern and northern plant and animal species at the limits of
their ranges, including dozens of rare, threatened, and endangered species.
Nine rare natural communities exist here, including vernal pools, oak-hickory
forests, and floating kettle-hole bogs. Species that require a lot of land, such as
moose, bobcat, and bear, also make their home here.

The region—which is a cooperative of seven public, quasi-public, and non-profit landowners, including Great Works Regional Land Trust, Maine Department of Inland Fisheries & Wildlife, The Nature Conservancy, the towns of York and South Berwick, the York Land Trust, and the York Water District—offers a wide variety of recreational opportunities, from hiking and mountain biking to ATV and equestrian use. This trip uses portions of nine different trails to explore the region and the summits of Mount Agamenticus and Second Hill.

Ring Trail leaves from an information kiosk and donation tube just into the woods beyond the right corner of the parking lot. Follow the wide, white-blazed path to a junction where Ring Trail splits; turn left at the junction to follow this route clockwise. In 200 feet, cross the auto road (parking for two cars here), passing the first of a series of interpretive signs that are found along Ring and Witch Hazel trails.

Hike easily through a mixed forest of red and white oak, beech, hemlock, and pine. Pass Blueberry Bluff Trail on the right. Continue around the west side of the mountain to a viewpoint on the left. Ahead, Wintergreen Trail enters from the left.

Reach the junction with Fisher Trail on the right at about the 0.75-mile mark. Turn right onto Fisher Trail and ascend easily on switchbacks. The summit fire tower and communications tower come into view above as the trail breaks out into the open.

The trail meanders upward through the slash and stumps of a restoration project conducted in 2012 to return the summit area to young forest and shrubs, important habitat for American woodcock, Blanding's and spotted turtles, and New England cottontail.

At a bench, Fisher Trail joins Big A Trail, a mile-long trail that circumnavigates the summit of the mountain. Follow Big A Trail up and around to the left side of a pole barn and lean-to. Head straight for the rail fence and stone steps just ahead. At a gate on the old fire tower service road, look right to see the summit parking lot. A large information kiosk, an observation deck and the old Big A ski lodge are straight ahead. Seasonal portable toilets are immediately to the left, while a fire tower is a short distance beyond the toilets.

The fire tower is not open to the public, but the interpretive panels at its base are worth a visit. They recall David Hilton, who lead the effort to man with volunteers this fire tower as well as those nearby on Mount Hope and Ossipee Hill, in Sanford and Waterboro, respectively, after the state closed them to save in money in 1991.

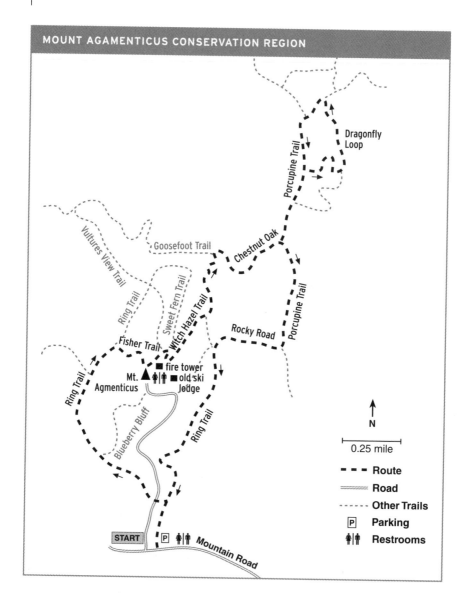

MOUNT AGAMENTICUS CONSERVATION REGION

Dragonfly Loop

Porcupine Trail

Vultures View Trail

Goosefoot Trail

Chestnut Oak

Ring Trail

Sweet Fern Trail

Witch Hazel Trail

Porcupine Trail

Rocky Road

Fisher Trail

fire tower

Mt. Agmenticus

old ski lodge

Ring Trail

Ring Trail

Blueberry Bluff

N

0.25 mile

- - - Route
=== Road
----- Other Trails
P Parking
Restrooms

START P Mountain Road

Mount Agamenticus was the site of the first U.S. Forest Service fire tower, built in 1918. It was removed in 1938 and a replacement tower was constructed in 1944. This tower stood until 1981, when the existing tower was delivered to the mountain by helicopter. The tower is owned by the state of Maine and is occasionally staffed by volunteers from the York Fire Department.

Return to the toilets, then hike up across the grassy field to the observation deck that marks the summit of Mount Agamenticus, signed "First Hill, elevation 692 feet." Begin your viewing by looking southward over the sea of pine trees to the Atlantic Ocean 6 miles to the southeast and then turning slowly clockwise to take in the magnificent 360-degree panorama. The vista includes Nubble Light on Cape Neddick, Boon Island Light, the Isle of Shoals, Cape Ann in Massachusetts, Chase Pond and Foley Pond, the Piscataqua River and Little Bay in New Hampshire, Bauneg Beg Mountain (Trip 7), Mount Hope and the Tatnic Hills, and the Kennebunk Plains.

Information posted at the kiosk just below the deck reveals the rich history of the mountain and its many firsts, from the name Captain John Smith gave the mountain when he explored the area in the early 1600s, to the legend that martyred Micmac chief St. Aspinquid is buried atop the mountain, to more modern notes, including the summit's use during World War II and more. The large brown Learning Lodge (open 11 A.M. to 3 P.M. on weekends from Memorial Day to Columbus Day), now an educational facility and headquarters for the MACR and its conservation programs, was once the summit lodge for the Big A Ski Area, which operated from 1964 to 1974. Several trails on the north side of the mountain follow the former ski slopes.

Walk northwest past the lodge and across the large grassy summit field to a second observation deck for vistas that range from Blue Job, Belknap, and Shaw mountains in New Hampshire's Ossipee Range north to Mount Chocorua, Green Mountain, and the Presidential Range in the White Mountains. Northeast in Maine is Bauneg Beg Mountain and the Tatnic Hills.

Walk northeasterly from the observation deck, heading for the rusting remains of an old T-bar lift tower and snow groomer. Turn left here onto Big A Trail and descend the former lift line. Soon, Vulture's View Trail departs left, and in another 100 feet, Sweet Fern Trail leaves to the left. Stay right and continue on Big A Trail.

In 50 feet, turn left onto Witch Hazel Trail, which soon leaves the cleared summit area and enters the forest, here composed of beech, chestnut oaks, white oaks, and hemlocks. Pass to the right of a huge, 250-year-old hemlock known as Big Hemi, and soon reach a junction with Ring Trail. Turn left here onto the Ring Trail and descend via switchbacks to the junction of three trails.

At this junction, Ring Trail goes left, Goosefoot Trail goes straight ahead, and Chestnut Oak Trail goes right. If you'd like, take a moment to walk a few feet left onto Ring Trail to the base of the old ski area T-bar. To continue, turn right onto Chestnut Oak Trail. Wind down the backside of Mount Agamenticus, pass the red blazes of a property line, contour along, then drop down to the junction with Porcupine Trail.

Turn left onto Porcupine Trail toward Second Hill. Cross a small brook and wander ahead through a forest of chestnut oaks, with their deeply furrowed

Remnants like this old T-bar lift line of the former Big A Ski Area, which operated from 1964 to 1974, can still be seen on the slopes of Mount Agamenticus.

bark and distinctive leaves. Because chestnut oaks produce a tremendous heat when fired, these hardwoods were extensively cut to fuel the charcoal industry in the 1800s and early 1900s. At a sign that reads "Porcupine," a trail on the right leads to private property. Continue straight ahead on Porcupine Trail through chestnut oaks and hemlocks. Ahead, in a small clearing with a cairn amid a grove of white pines, reach the junction with Second Hill Trail.

Turn right onto Second Hill Trail and follow it up the park-like hillside. Climb through several large ledge outcrops, bearing left and up to reach a short spur leading left to a granite bench and a viewpoint and a gnarly jack pine. Continue 100 feet past the jack pine to reach a small clearing with a view looking up at the Learning Lodge atop Mount Agamenticus.

Return to the main trail and in 50 feet, look left for a short spur to the open area atop Second Hill and a sign that reads, "Second Hill Summit, 555 feet." The sign faces away from the trail, so it's difficult to notice. Many hikers miss the true summit of Second Hill for this reason.

From the Second Hill summit, Ridge Trail continues straight along the ridge, with occasional views through the trees to Third Hill. Pass a sign for "New Trail" as you hike along the ridgeline following white blazes. Dip down, then traverse before descending off the ridge in earnest. Cross a low spot on a short footbridge to reach a signed junction, where an unmarked trail leads left and white blazes lead right.

Turn left at the sign to follow the unmarked trail and quickly reach its junction with Porcupine Trail. Turn left onto Porcupine Trail and follow it along the western base of Second Hill. Pass the cairn and clearing at the base of the trail up Second Hill. From here, retrace your steps along Porcupine Trail to its junction with Chestnut Oak Trail. Bear left to continue on Porcupine Trail. Cross a brook on stones, then hike a long, straight stretch of trail over exposed bedrock on a high shelf of the mountainside.

At the junction, turn right onto Rocky Road Trail and follow it to a boardwalk with a vernal pool on the left. Beyond, climb the wide, rocky, and eroded path up the slope to its junction with Ring Trail. Hairpin Turn Trail goes straight here, but you'll turn left to continue on Ring Trail.

Descend, then contour along the slope through young stems of beech and a scattering of pines. Ahead, bear left under a phone/power line. Ahead, with the summit access road and a parking pullout in sight, turn sharply left to continue on Ring Trail. Pass the initial Ring Trail junction and soon reach the base of the mountain and the trailhead parking lot on Mountain Road.

DID YOU KNOW?

There are a number of spellings and meanings for Agamenticus: Accominta is the name given by native people who lived near the York River, while Akukumigak is a Chippewa expression referring to "the place where land and water meet." Agamenticus or Accominticus is the name of small tribe of Penacooks that lived in a village at or near the present day town of York. The Mount Agamenticus summit was the site of the first radar tower in the country, built in the early 1940s at the time of World War II. In 1977–78, the mountain was the first release site for the reintroduction of wild turkeys in Maine. The mountain was also an important landmark for early mariners along the Maine coast.

MORE INFORMATION

Mount Agamenticus Conservation Region (agamenticus.org; 207-361-1102). The area is open year-round from dawn to dusk. Dogs are allowed on-leash.

NEARBY

The popular beach towns of Kennebunkport, Kennebunk, Wells, Ogunquit, and York are just a few miles east of Mount Agamenticus, with a wide range of entertainment, shopping, dining, and lodging possibilities (mainebeaches association.org).

TRIP 4
WELLS RESERVE AT LAUDHOLM

Location: Wells, ME
Rating: Moderate
Distance: 4.2 miles (loop)
Elevation Gain: 50 feet
Estimated Time: 3.0 hours
Maps: USGS Wells; *Maine Atlas and Gazetteer,* Map 3 (DeLorme); *Wells Reserve Trail Map* (Wells National Estuarine Research Reserve)

Meander along the trails of a historical 2,250-acre protected area with a diversity of ecologically important estuarine habitats.

DIRECTIONS
From the junction of ME 9 and US 1 in Wells (1.5 miles east of I-95/Maine Turnpike Exit 19) drive north on US 1/ME 9 for 1.5 miles. Turn right onto Laudholm Farm Road and drive 0.5 mile. Turn left onto Skinner Road and soon after, turn right at the gate for Wells Reserve. The public parking lots for visitors are just 0.2 mile ahead and offer dozens of spaces. From the upper parking lot, proceed to the welcome kiosk and deposit the admission fee. Walk the paved path to the renovated barn; public restrooms are located just inside. Bear right at the barn past the old water tower and icehouse to reach the visitor center located in the historical Laudholm farmhouse. Several trails leave from this beautiful spot. *GPS coordinates: 43° 20.304′ N, 70° 33.054′ W.*

TRAIL DESCRIPTION
The Wells National Estuarine Research Reserve, as it is officially known, is an oasis of tranquility just a short distance from the busy US 1 coastal corridor. This beautiful property—a restored saltwater farm known as Laudholm to many—encompasses 2,250 acres of diverse wildlife habitat, from grasslands and woodlands to salt marshes, dunes, and sandy beach, and spans the estuaries of the Webhannet River, the Little River (fed by the Merriland River and Branch Brook), and the Ogunquit River.

The Wells facility is one of 28 such National Estuarine Research Reserves in the US that work to expand the knowledge of coasts and estuaries through research and monitoring, education and training, and stewardship and conservation. The reserve is supported by the nonprofit Laudholm Trust.

Estuaries form where ocean salt water mixes with fresh water from inland rivers. These incredible mixing grounds are some of the most dynamic and productive ecosystems on the planet. Estuaries like the three found at the Wells Reserve provide critical habitat for a variety of plant and animal life, help protect human communities from flooding, serve as buffers against coastal storms, and filter pollutants from the fresh water before it empties into the ocean.

The Laudholm farmhouse contains the visitor center and a series of exhibits describing the changes in the coastal landscape of southern Maine from the time of the last glaciation 14,000 years ago to the present day. Maps and information are also available when the center is open (10 A.M. to 4 P.M. Monday through Saturday and noon to 4 P.M. on Sunday, from Memorial Day through Columbus Day, and weekdays the remainder of the year. The center is closed December 24 through March 31). Seven miles of hiking allow visitors a variety of options for exploring this unique and important coastal land. This trip combines a portion of all nine reserve trails. Start your walk from the front of the visitor center.

Looking out toward the gazebo, bear right around the building and walk to an interpretive sign in the field, which describes some of the wildlife to be seen in this area during the daytime and at dusk. Go right of the sign and cross the field to the road; Muskie Trail begins across the road. Proceed on the raised dirt path through the alder and gray birch swamp. Cross a drainage to enter a field on a boardwalk. Look for cranberries and Labrador tea to either side of the path through here. To the left there are views back to the farm complex.

Follow the wide, grassy trail along the edge of the field past the honeysuckle and barberry. Enter the woods again at a boardwalk and boundary marker for the Rachel Carson National Wildlife Refuge (Trip 1). Pass a bench on the left, then trace a route through shrubs at the lower edge of the field, where an interpretive sign describes the importance of shrublands for wildlife.

In the woods once again, a sign describes the importance of vernal pools, temporary water bodies born of spring rains and snowmelt that function as breeding and feeding grounds for wood frogs, mosquitoes, fingernail clams, fairy shrimp, and other wildlife. Large red oaks dominate the woods, and white pines are sprinkled throughout. Pass a massive old pasture pine before arriving at the junction with Pilger Trail (bench).

Turn right onto Pilger Trail and pass a sign describing the migration routes of ducks and geese. Continue to the overlook at the edge of a salt marsh along the Webhannet River, where a viewing platform with benches makes for a fine

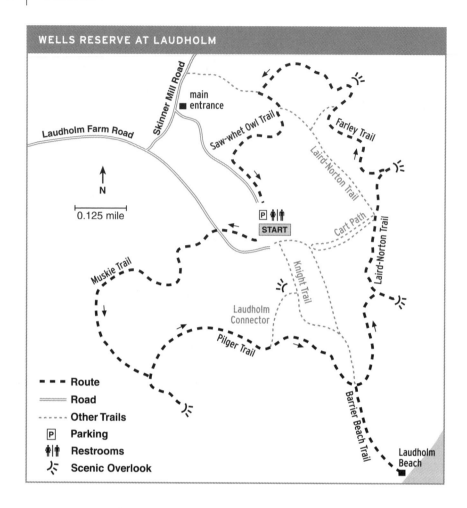

WELLS RESERVE AT LAUDHOLM

Skinner Mill Road

main ■ entrance

Laudholm Farm Road

Saw-whet Owl Trail

Farley Trail

Laird-Norton Trail

N

0.125 mile

P ♦|♦ START

Cart Path

Laird-Norton Trail

Muskie Trail

Knight Trail

Laudholm Connector

Pilger Trail

Barrier Beach Trail

Laudholm Beach

- - - Route
═══ Road
----- Other Trails
P Parking
♦|♦ Restrooms
⊱ Scenic Overlook

spot to sit still and watch for wildlife. A sign describes how a healthy salt marsh is replenished with important sediments by the twice-daily tides.

The extensive salt marshes stretching from Kittery to Cape Elizabeth attracted European settlers to this area. Since 1641 only four families have owned and worked Laudholm Farm: the Boades, Symonds, Clarks, and Lords. These denizens raised cattle, cultivated farm crops, tended orchards, and, later, raised sheep and produced dairy products.

From the overlook, double back on Pilger Trail to its junction with Muskie Trail, then continue on Pilger Trail through an area thick with highbush blueberries. Ahead, break out into the open and hike along the shrubby edge of a field. Reach a bench at the junction of Laudholm Connector, which diverges left to connect with Knight Trail. Remain on Pilger Trail and enter the shrubby woods ahead. Follow the wide, grassy path through an old apple orchard then through a grove of aspens and red maples, cherries and birch. This trail ends at Barrier Beach Trail, where a sign describes the four types of wetlands found in the Wells Reserve: red maple swamp, vernal pool, freshwater marsh, and salt marsh. Laird-North Trail starts directly opposite.

Turn right here onto Barrier Beach Trail and follow the wide dirt road toward Laudholm Beach, the roar of the not-too-distant surf unmistakable from this point. Cross a salt marsh on a causeway to arrive at a sign on the left describing seven different wildlife habitats found along the coast of Maine.

Pass around the gate just beyond, then proceed through a neighborhood of summer and year-round homes. Ahead, a footbridge leads over the fragile dunes to the sands of Laudholm Beach, where the extensive view ranges from Kennebunkport in the northeast to Ogunquit in the southwest.

To continue the hike, return on Barrier Beach Trail to the junction of Laird-Norton Trail. Turn right onto Laird-Norton Trail and follow the extensive boardwalks, with a red maple swamp on the left and a salt marsh on the right.

Ahead, a spur trail on the right leads to a viewpoint overlooking the salt marshes at the mouth of the Little River and beyond to Laudholm Beach. A sign describes the various natural features of this estuarine environment, while a second sign explains why estuaries are some of the most productive ecosystems on the planet and why they are important to wildlife and people.

American Indians lived, or visited seasonally, along the Maine coast beginning several thousand years ago, subsisting on the bounty of shad, eel, alewife, and salmon. In winter they hunted beavers, otters, moose, bears, and caribou, while in summer they feasted on fish and shellfish from the ocean. Cattails, salt hay, and wild plants were used for weaving, medicine, and food.

As you proceed farther along the edge of the salt marshes along the Merriland and Little rivers, look out across the expanse of salt marsh meadows, which are protected from the ocean by barrier beaches.

Laird-Norton Trail threads through an area thick with leafy, green skunk cabbage before reaching the junction with Cart Path on the left and a gate immediately to the right. Standing facing the gate, walk 50 feet left to the signpost. Ahead, in the field just beyond the edge of the woods, is a second trail junction. Here, a second arm of Cart Path goes to the left, Farley Trail departs to the right, and Laird-Norton Trail continues straight ahead.

Turn right onto Farley Trail and follow the wide, grassy path across the field into the woods. Soon, a spur leads right to an overlook on the margin of the salt marsh, where a sign explains how wildlife uses the estuary for food, shelter, and reproduction. A second sign describes the complex food web of a salt marsh. After the overlook, hike to a bench overlooking a field, then bear right along its edge. Reenter the woods at a corner of the field and proceed through the pine and spruce woods. Pass by Farley Connector on the left to arrive at another overlook with a long view eastward to the ocean. A sign describes the importance of forest along streams and rivers.

By the late 1970s, Laudholm Farm had fallen into a state of disrepair and pressure to develop the farmland into home sites became acute. In response, local residents formed the nonprofit Laudholm Trust. They acquired the property and adjacent lands with the support of the National Oceanic and Atmospheric Administration, the U.S. Fish and Wildlife Service, the Maine Coastal Program, the Maine Department of Conservation, and other key stakeholders. The reserve was dedicated in 1986.

Ahead on Farley Trail, the park-like forest of tall pines, large oaks, and yellow birches leads out to yet another field. Follow along the field edge, then cross it to reach the junction with Laird-Norton Trail.

Turn left onto Laird-Norton Trail, then just ahead turn right onto Saw-whet Owl Trail. In this final stretch of woods, pass two more interpretive signs. The first describes the process of succession whereby a field like the one you see here turns into a mature forest over time. The second sign describes the many ways wildlife large and small use the forest for food, shelter, and reproduction.

Beyond a cabin used for environmental education, reach the entrance road and the final interpretive sign describing forest types found in the reserve. Turn left and follow the road a short distance to the main parking lots.

DID YOU KNOW?

The name Laudholm was given to the farmstead in the early 1900s. The word "laud" means praise, while the suffix "holm" means meadow.

MORE INFORMATION

Wells National Estuarine Research Reserve (wellsreserve.org; 207-646-1555). The reserve is open year-round from 7 A.M. to sunset. No dogs or smoking allowed. Fees are charged from Memorial Day weekend to Columbus Day only.

NEARBY

A series of sandy beaches from Ogunquit north to Saco offers plenty of opportunities for fun in the sun (mainebeachesassociation.org). Lower Village in Kennebunk and Dock Square and Ocean Avenue across the Kennebunk River in Kennebunkport offer a pleasant diversion of shops, restaurants, and waterfront strolling (kennebunkport.org).

TRIP 5
EDWIN L. SMITH PRESERVE

Location: Kennebunkport, ME
Rating: Moderate
Distance: 8.7 miles
Elevation Gain: 280 feet
Estimated Time: 4.5 hours
Maps: USGS Biddeford; *Maine Atlas and Gazetteer*, Map 3 (DeLorme), *Edwin L. Smith Preserve* (Kennebunkport Conservation Trust)

Combine five trails for a pleasant loop hike through one of the largest blocks of undeveloped forestland on the southern Maine coast.

DIRECTIONS
From I-95/Maine Turnpike, take Exit 25 in Kennebunk and drive east on ME 35 for 1.8 miles to downtown Kennebunk. At the junction of ME 35, ME 9A, and US 1, turn left (north) onto US 1. At 3.1 miles, turn right (east) onto Old Post Road. At 3.9 miles, where Old Post Road bears left, continue straight ahead on Sinnott Road. Quickly, turn left onto Lombard Road at 4.0 miles and follow this to Log Cabin Road at 4.8 miles. Turn onto Log Cabin Road to reach the Seashore Trolley Museum at 4.9 miles. Just beyond, at 5.0 miles, turn left onto Goose Rocks Road and take this to Guinea Road at 5.7 miles. Turn left here to reach the Edwin L. Smith Preserve trailhead parking lot on the left at 5.8 miles. The parking area is marked by a large granite sign and has space for five to six cars. *GPS coordinates: 43° 25.122′ N, 70° 27.798′ W.*

TRAIL DESCRIPTION
The 1,400-acre Edwin L. Smith Preserve in the northeast corner of Kennebunkport comprises a sizeable chunk of one of the largest remaining blocks of undeveloped land along the Maine coast between Kittery and Brunswick. Owned and managed by the Kennebunkport Conservation Trust, the Smith property is home to five hiking trails offering 12 miles of woods walking through a wildlife-rich landscape of granite ridges, oak and pine forests, and pocket vernal pools. Blanding's and wood turtles, foxes, owls, red-shouldered hawks, minks, bobcats, fishers, deer, coyotes, and black bears make their home here. This hike combines all or part of each of the preserve's trails for an interesting circuit that reaches into every part of the Edwin L. Smith.

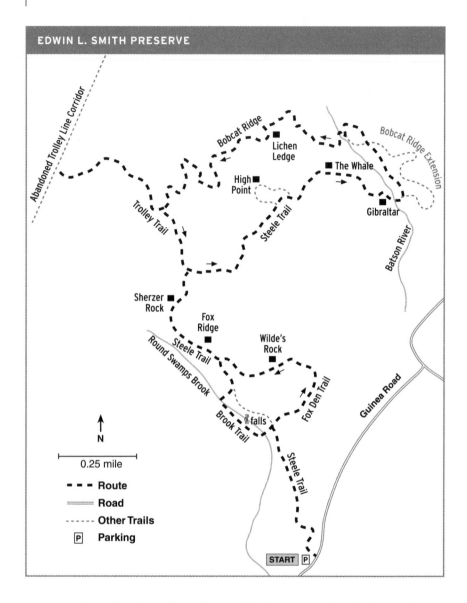

EDWIN L. SMITH PRESERVE

From the trailhead, Steele Trail immediately crosses a footbridge and enters the woods. The yellow-blazed trail parallels Guinea Road for a short time before bearing away to the left (west) onto a wide track. The old road, bounded by stone walls at several points, passes a number of granite outcrops as it proceeds deeper into the forest.

After a little over 0.5 mile, blue-blazed Brook Trail departs to the left. In 50 feet, turn right onto green-blazed Fox Den Trail. Beyond a big rock and downed telephone pole, the trail slips through highbush blueberry, laurel, and witch hazel shrubs. Where a private trail continues straight ahead, Fox Den Trail takes a sharp left and becomes a narrow footpath.

It doesn't take long to notice the color map signs and numbered posts (there are eighteen posts in all) at trail intersections. The trust erected this excellent way-finding system in the name of safety due to the large size of the property and extensiveness of the trail network.

Soon after a footbridge, reach a stone wall and Wilde's Rock on the right. Meander through a series of granite outcrops and cross another footbridge to rejoin Steele Trail. Just ahead, the large mound of rocks to the right of the trail is known as Fox Ridge. Beyond, pass between two mounds of rock to reach Sherzer Rock on the left.

During the unusually dry October of 1947, a series of forest fires along the coast of Maine from Mount Desert Island to York County blazed out of control for more than a week, burning more than 200,000 acres of woodland and razing nine communities. In Kennebunkport, a great wall of fire 8 miles long burned across the town, destroying 200 homes and dozens of woodlots, including this property. Realizing the fire-decimated land had no value now, the owners of these woodlots in Kennebunkport salvaged what timber they could and then stopped paying taxes on the properties, which reverted to town ownership and eventually became part of the town forest. Though little evidence of the Fire of 1947 is left here, the memories and accounts of that terrible event remain.

In 2002, Kennebunkport voters overwhelmingly approved the transfer of 741 acres of town forest to the Kennebunkport Conservation Trust. The trust later purchased the Steele property, adding 400 acres. Another half-dozen abutting and interior parcels totaling 300 acres have since been acquired, bringing the Edwin L. Smith Preserve to its current total acreage.

Continuing on, Steele Trail makes several switchbacks to arrive at an old trail on the left, which is blocked. Turn right here, zig around a blowdown, and jog easily downslope to meet red-blazed Trolley Trail.

Turn right to continue on Steele Trail, which follows an old woods road here through a thick grove of white pines. Where a private trail leads straight ahead, bear left to stay on Steele Trail, now a narrow pathway once again. The rolling and winding trail soon reaches a footbridge over a branch of the Batson River. Beyond, an obscure and easily missed trail on the left loops around to High Point—at 219 feet, it is the highest point in Kennebunkport—before rejoining Steele Trail just ahead.

Cross one wide and one narrow footbridge in close succession, then scamper over several low rises. At a large ledge outcrop, avoid a shortcut on the left;

instead continue around and up the rock on a switchback. Cross the top of the ledge, then make a winding descent to a large, blocky glacial erratic on the left known as Gibraltar.

Beyond, switchback down the slope to enter the thick woods along the Batson River, a small creek just 3 to 4 feet wide at this point. The river, which flows 6 miles south and east to empty into the Atlantic Ocean at Goose Rocks Beach, is home to a native brook trout population. Cross the river on a long footbridge. Continue along the north side of the river on a wide trail through a dark wood of hemlock and birch. Ahead, not far after a footbridge, reach the end of Steele Trail at a junction. Here, Bobcat Ridge Trail Extension bears to the right, while Tote Road continues straight ahead.

Follow Tote Road to a junction with the other end of Bobcat Ridge Trail Extension and Bobcat Ridge Trail. Turn left (west) to follow white-blazed Bobcat Ridge Trail left on switchbacks to a footbridge where you recross the babbling Batson River. Bobcat Ridge Trail was built for both mountain biking and hiking, and for the next 2.0 miles you'll follow the many twists and turns of this fun and interesting pathway as it climbs up, over, and around a series of ledges that form the wooded spine of Bobcat Ridge.

Several miles of woods roads existed on the Edwin L. Smith property, built after the 1947 fires. In just the past few years, however, small groups of volunteers have painstakingly built the existing system of multiuse trails, with more trails planned.

Cross the Log Bridge over a muddy area, then meander through the pines to Lichen Ledge. After a stretch of ridge-top walking atop the semi-open rocks of Bobcat Ridge, make several gentle ups and downs through the red pines before reaching the junction with Trolley Trail.

Turn right onto red-blazed Trolley Trail and follow the wide track easily along to the Long & Winding Bridge over a branch of Goff Mill Brook. Beyond, where an old road enters from the right, bear left and soon reach the end of the trail at the old Atlantic Shore Line trolley corridor, now a long, sandy tunnel through the trees.

From the old trolley line, retrace your steps back along Trolley Trail to Bobcat Ridge Trail junction. From there, continue on Trolley Trail to cross a wide footbridge. Ahead, bear right off the old road onto a narrow footpath, which quickly leads to the junction with Steele Trail.

Recrossing Fox Ridge, pass the junction with Fox Den Trail on the left and soon reach Brook Trail on the right. Take blue-blazed Brook Trail over Round Swamps Brook and follow along its south bank through a glen, passing several pleasant cascades en route. From a high point above the brook, drop down and cross the waterway again to rejoin Steele Trail.

Turn right and follow Steele Trail south back to the trailhead.

DID YOU KNOW?

The Atlantic Shore Line was the second-longest electric trolley line in Maine, providing passenger and freight service from 1900 to 1949 on 87 miles of track connecting fourteen communities around York County.

MORE INFORMATION

Kennebunkport Conservation Trust (kporttrust.org; 207-967-3465). A trail map is available for download.

NEARBY

The Seashore Trolley Museum is the oldest and largest electric trolley museum in the world, housing a fascinating collection of more than 250 mass transit vehicles, most of them trolleys. Visit the museum and store, three car-barns, restoration shop, and other exhibits seven days a week from 10 A.M. to 5 P.M., Memorial Day through Columbus Day. The museum is also open on weekends in May and October (trolleymuseum.org; 207-967-2712).

MORE HIKING

Elsewhere in Kennebunkport, enjoy several miles of trails at Emmons Preserve and Tyler Book Preserve (kporttrust.org: 207-967-3465). The neighboring Kennebunk Land Trust has a variety of trails across eight preserves, including 2.5 miles of hiking in the 625-acre Alewive Woods (kennebunklandtrust.org; 207-985-8734). Managed by The Nature Conservancy, the Kennebunk Plains Wildlife Management Area, Kennebunk Plains Preserve, and Wells Barrens Preserve protect 3,200 acres of sandplain grasslands and early successional forest habitat, offering miles of foot travel possibilities (nature.org; 207-729-5181).

THE GREAT FIRES OF 1947

Devastating forest fires raged across Maine in October of 1947, burning nearly 206,000 acres in 200 different locations from York County to Mount Desert Island. Wildfires greater than 100 acres affected 35 Maine communities, burned major portions of seventeen of these towns, and completely razed nine of them. More than 2,600 structures were destroyed and 10,000 people were injured, but fortunately the fires claimed only sixteen lives. The incredible conflagrations caused many millions of dollars of damage. It's little wonder why 1947 is often remembered as "the year Maine burned."

Several factors contributed to the great fires of 1947. Excessive slash—downed trees and branches—remained on the ground, left by a hurricane in 1938 and a severe snowstorm in 1945. Also, 1947 was a "cone year," when the coniferous trees produced an abundant supply of seed-filled cones. And while the winter of 1946-47 saw a normal amount of snowfall, the summer season that followed saw a pronounced lack of rain, unusually high temperatures and low humidity, which combined to dry out the accumulated wealth of fuel in the woods and the living growth. By early October, these drought conditions had turned Maine into a tinderbox. Inadequate forest fire prevention and control systems also contributed to the seriousness of the fires; no formal plan had existed to combat the large number or scope of forest fires as few could ever have ever imagined a situation so dire at the time.

On October 7, the Maine Forest Service received reports of numerous small fires, which were subsequently extinguished. Over the next week, however, concern mounted as fires were reported over an ever larger geographic area. By mid-October colossal fires fanned by gusty winds were sweeping through a whole host of York County towns, while on Mount Desert Island, wind-driven fires were incinerating great swaths of Acadia National Park and the summer cottages, grand old hotels, and homes of Bar Harbor. For several weeks, thousands of volunteer firefighters, military personnel, ordinary citizens, and many others from Maine and well beyond courageously battled the fires. By month's end, the blazes were finally declared under control amid a change in weather and most welcome rains. It was mid-November before the worst fire disaster in Maine's history was pronounced completely out.

Wildfire Loose: The Week Maine Burned by Joyce Butler provides an excellent account of the October 1947 fires.

TRIP 6
SACO BEACH LOOP

Location: Saco, ME
Rating: Easy
Distance: 4.1 miles
Elevation Gain: Minimal
Estimated Time: 2.0 hours
Maps: USGS Biddeford; *Maine Atlas and Gazetteer,* Map 3 (DeLorme); *Saco Beach Loop* (Saco Bay Trails)

Stroll along a sandy beach, hike through mixed woods and past salt marshes, and visit a rare tupelo swamp on this wonderfully diverse loop hike.

DIRECTIONS
From I-95/Maine Turnpike, Exit 36, proceed east on I-195. At 1.0 mile, take Exit 2A (Saco, US 1). At the bottom of the ramp, turn right onto US 1 and drive south into downtown Saco. At the junction of US 1 and ME 9 (traffic light) at 1.9 miles, continue straight ahead on ME 9. Just ahead at the second traffic light, turn left (east) onto ME 9 (Beach Street). At 2.8 miles, Beach Street becomes Ferry Road. At 4.8 miles, turn left (north) onto Bayview Road (sign for Ferry Beach State Park). Reach the entrance gate for Ferry Beach State Park on the right at 5.1 miles. Continue on the park road to the entrance station at 5.6 miles (pay fee) and soon after, reach two large parking lots with capacity for 100 cars. At the east end of the lots are an information kiosk, toilets, changing rooms, and the start of this hike; the park's main trailhead is 50 feet north on the edge of the upper lot. *GPS coordinates: 43° 28.536′ N, 70° 23.196′ W.*

TRAIL DESCRIPTION
Ferry Beach State Park is a 117-acre gem in Maine's state park system. It features more than 1.5 miles of white sand beach fronting on the Atlantic Ocean and a pleasant network of five foot trails that offer 1.4 miles of hiking through mixed woods, including a rare tupelo swamp and a freshwater pond. By combining four of the park's trails plus a walk along Ferry Beach with three trails in the Saco Bay Trails system (Atlantic Way, Plymouth Trail, and Vines Trail) as well as several short sections of paved road, you can enjoy a wonderfully diverse 4-mile loop hike.

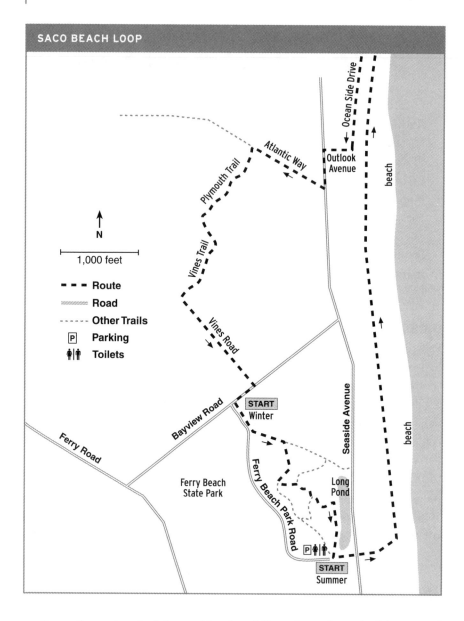

SACO BEACH LOOP

Ocean Side Drive

Outlook
Avenue

beach

Atlantic Way

Plymouth Trail

Vines Trail

N

1,000 feet

- - - Route
≈≈≈ Road
------ Other Trails
P   Parking
🚹🚺 Toilets

Vines Road

Bayview Road

START
Winter

Ferry Road

Seaside Avenue

beach

Ferry Beach
State Park

Ferry Beach Park Road

Long
Pond

P 🚹🚺

START
Summer

beach

From the east end of the parking lot, follow the wide trail of fine gravel eastward toward the beach, immediately passing a water fountain, bench, and cold shower on the left. Just beyond is an interpretive sign detailing several interesting facts about the park.

A few feet ahead, reach a four-way junction. The side path on the left leads 200 feet to the shore of Long Pond and two benches for enjoying the view.

Ferry Beach is part of a 7-mile arc of sandy beach that ranges from Camp Ellis to Pine Point on Saco Bay, the longest continuous stretch of beach in Maine.

From the junction, continue straight ahead through the concrete tunnel under Seaside Avenue (ME 9). The wooden walkway beyond leads through a gnarled grove of pitch pines, then a sandy path slices through the dunes to Ferry Beach.

Ferry Beach is part of a 7-mile arc of beach extending from the mouth of the Saco River at Camp Ellis north to Old Orchard Beach and on to Pine Point Beach at the mouth of the Scarborough River, making it the longest continuous stretch of beach in Maine. The expansive view from Ferry Beach ranges over the entirety of Saco Bay, from Fletcher Neck in Biddeford Pool to the south to Prouts Neck in Scarborough to the north.

Take a good look out at Wood Island Light just off Fletcher Neck before turning left (north) and walking up the beach amid the sounds of squawking gulls and rhythmic surf; the pebbles, shells, and driftwood; and the occasional piece of human-made detritus washed ashore. Pass summer cottages and year-round homes atop the dunes to your left. Beachgoers are asked to kindly stay off the dunes and respect private property. The famous Old Orchard Beach Pier, a fixture on the Maine coast that has been entertaining tourists since 1898, comes into focus ahead as you stroll on.

At 1.5 miles, pass a timber retaining wall on the left and, soon, the first of several public access paths connecting points along Ocean Side Drive to the beach. About 200 feet past the last house (a gray two-story cottage) and before you reach Goosefare Brook, head left up to the dune grass and look for the narrow opening of a footpath leading west. Follow this path away from the beach to the end of Ocean Side Drive. The path emerges onto the pavement behind the gray cottage at the two-car garage of a white cottage. Continue south through the neighborhood on Ocean Side Drive to its end, passing Cottage, Shore, Palmer, and Dune avenues. Where Ocean Side Drive ends, turn sharply right onto Outlook Avenue and proceed a short distance to Seaside Avenue (ME 9).

Turn left and walk along the edge of the road for 0.1 mile, exercising caution as there are no shoulders. Just past a yellow fire hydrant at the end of a driveway, cross the road to the Atlantic Way trailhead, where there is a turnout and parking for two or three cars.

Pass through a gap in the fence and in 50 feet reach an information kiosk. The land ahead traversed by the trail is part of the Rachel Carson National Wildlife Refuge (RCNWR), which encompasses 5,300 acres over eleven geographic units ranging from Kittery to Cape Elizabeth.

Cross an arm of Goosefare Brook on an old causeway to reach a bench and footbridge over a concrete culvert in a ditch. In the woods beyond, reach the junction with Plymouth Trail on the left. Take Plymouth Trail and follow the occasional splotches of red paint marking the trail to quickly arrive at another junction. Proceed straight, past Plymouth Drive to the right, to Vines Road through the mixed forest of oaks and pines.

At the next junction, Link Trail departs right. Turn left to remain on Vines Trail and soon cross an arching footbridge over a creek in hemlock woods. After a second arched bridge over a wet area, pass a boundary sign for RCNWR. Ahead, pass to the left of a red house and soon reach the pavement of Vines Road. Cross the street to follow the sidewalk a short distance left to Bayview Road.

At the junction of Vines Road and Bayview Road, turn right and walk 0.1 mile to the entrance of Ferry Beach State Park. Walk along the park road, and in a few hundred feet, turn left off the road and into the woods on red-blazed Red Oak Trail (no sign).

Follow wide Red Oak Trail through the oak and pine forest. At an unmarked junction ahead, bear right onto white-blazed White Oak Trail and continue the easy going on level ground. Cross a small creek on a footbridge and just after, come to another junction. Turn left here onto Witchhazel Trail to follow along the creek.

At the next junction, with a footbridge to the left and a bench on the right, proceed straight ahead on blue-blazed Tupelo Trail and quickly reach a wetland on the left. At the Y junction beyond, Greenbriar Trail leaves right. Continue to the left on Tupelo Trail to arrive at an interpretive sign on the left describing the tupelo swamp you are about to enter. Rare at this latitude, the medium-sized tupelo or black gum trees are easily identified by their light brown, deeply fissured bark and short horizontal branches. The fruit of the tupelo is an important food source for migrating birds and the heavy, hard, cross-grained wood made it a popular material for making wooden implements.

Trundle along the long and curving boardwalk through the swamp, noting not only the tupelos but the abundance of highbush blueberries and winterberry. Beyond the boardwalk, pass an information kiosk on the left and then a picnic table and short path to Long Pond, a scenic freshwater tarn that borders Seaside Avenue. Note the small beach and bench at the north end of the pond.

Continue along the west side of Long Pond, then cross a boardwalk to reach a T junction. Turn left here onto White Oak Trail, and cross another boardwalk with a large trail map sign on the left to arrive at the paved trailhead parking lot and the end of the hike.

DID YOU KNOW?

Three centuries ago, long before the advent of roads, beaches were important as overland travel routes for people from as far away as Boston. A ferry crossing connecting Hills Beach and Camp Ellis at the mouth of the Saco River nearby served these early beach travelers, thus giving Ferry Beach its name.

MORE INFORMATION

Ferry Beach State Park (parksandlands.com; 207-283-0067 [in season], 207-287-3200 [off season]). The park is open from April 1 through October 31. Visitors are welcome to use the park in the off-season, but must park outside the gate on Bayview Road. There is a daily entrance fee. Download a trail map of Saco Beach Loop from Saco Bay Trails at sacobaytrails.org/beachloop.shtml.

NEARBY

Old Orchard Beach has been a popular summer vacation destination for beachgoers for more than a century, offering miles of beautiful sand beach and ocean swimming; a wide range of amusements and entertainment, including arcade games, miniature golf, carnival rides, classic beach food, and a variety of music; plus the iconic 100-year-old Old Orchard Beach Pier (oldorchardbeachmaine.com; 207-934-2500).

MORE HIKING

The Saco Bay Trails network includes more than 20 miles of hiking and walking on 25 trails in Saco, Biddeford, and Ocean Park (sacobaytrails.org).

TRIP 7
BAUNEG BEG MOUNTAIN
CONSERVATION AREA

Location: North Berwick, ME
Rating: Easy
Distance: 1.5 miles
Elevation Gain: 340 feet
Estimated Time: 1.0 hour
Maps: USGS Sanford; *Maine Atlas and Gazetteer*, Map 2 (DeLorme); *Bauneg Beg Mountain Conservation Area* (Great Works Regional Land Trust)

Hike a short, scenic loop over two forested peaks, the only major mountaintops in southern York County without any communications towers on top.

DIRECTIONS

From the second, or northerly, intersection of ME 9 and ME 4 in North Berwick, drive north on ME 4. At 2.1 miles, turn left (west) onto Boyle Road. At 3.4 miles, beyond its junction with Valley Road, Boyle Road becomes Ford Quint Road. Continue on Ford Quint Road to Fox Farm Hill Road, at 6.8 miles. Turn left (northwest) onto Fox Farm Hill Road and proceed to the trailhead parking area (sign) on the left at 7.2 miles from North Berwick. A short driveway leads to a gravel lot with space for five to six cars. *GPS coordinates: 43° 23.658' N, 70° 46.914' W.*

TRAIL DESCRIPTION

Bauneg Beg Mountain rises inconspicuously above the rural outskirts of North Berwick. Driving to the trailhead, the mountain and its three peaks aren't readily distinguishable until you're nearly upon them. Perhaps that's because the mountain is the only major summit in southern York County without a communications tower on its top. Despite the mountain's low profile, a 25-minute hike via Bauneg Beg Trail to 850-foot Middle Peak's craggy ledges reveals distant views to Pleasant Mountain, the White Mountains, and the Atlantic Ocean.

Bauneg Beg Mountain is part of the 89-acre Bauneg Beg Mountain Conservation Area, which is owned and managed by Great Works Regional Land

Trust. The trust assembled the preserve from three parcels of land purchased in 2000 and 2001. The land on North Peak is owned by the town of North Berwick, a 9-acre parcel that nicely complements the Bauneg Beg Mountain land. The trails on both properties were built with help from the Maine Conservation Corps and are maintained by dedicated local volunteers.

Bauneg Beg Trail starts to the right of the information kiosk at the back of the parking area. Follow a series of bog bridges through a corridor of young hardwoods beneath a canopy of pines and hemlocks. Where an old trail enters from the left, bear right and head up the slope. The path soon levels off before entering a dense stand of pines. Reach the junction with North Peak Loop on the right at just over 0.25 mile into the walk. Continue straight ahead on Bauneg Beg Trail through a lovely hemlock grove to a second junction.

Here, Linny's Way leads right to the summit via Devil's Den. Bear left to continue the hike via Ginny's Way, which swings around the south side of Middle Peak. Occasional white blazes mark the trail as you climb a shallow ravine dotted with hemlocks. After a short rise the trail bears sharply right up the southeast ridge to reach the junction with Tom's Way, which leads 0.5 mile southwest to Bauneg Beg Hill Road. If time allows, make this pleasant out-and-back walk for a little extra enjoyment.

A scant 150 feet beyond the Tom's Way junction, reach the north-facing summit ledges atop Middle Peak. The view includes the low summit of North Peak, part of Sanford in the center of the scene, the forested lowlands east of town to the right, and the multiple communications towers on Mount Hope to the left. The vista stretches more than 50 miles north to Mount Washington on a clear day. Through a narrow window in the trees to the west are the Blue Hills of southeastern New Hampshire. The name Bauneg Beg (pronounced like "Bonny Beg") has caused its share of confusion over time. According to Steve Pinkham's *Mountains of Maine: Intriguing Stories Behind Their Names*, Bauneg Beg was once thought to be of Scottish origin. But historian Fannie Hardy Eckstorm determined it to be derivative of the Wabanaki word *Bannebeaugue*, which means "spread out" and "still water." The name may describe Bauneg Beg Pond at the mountain's eastern base, essentially a part of the Great Works River, which is wide and slow moving.

From the summit the trail bears left (northwest) and down to reach a second area of open ledges with similar views as above. Follow the edge of the ridge to an unmarked (as of 2014) junction. Bear sharply right onto Linny's Way to descend into the rocks of Devil's Den. Scamper down a narrow passage in the rocks beneath the impressive rock overhangs of the summit ledges.

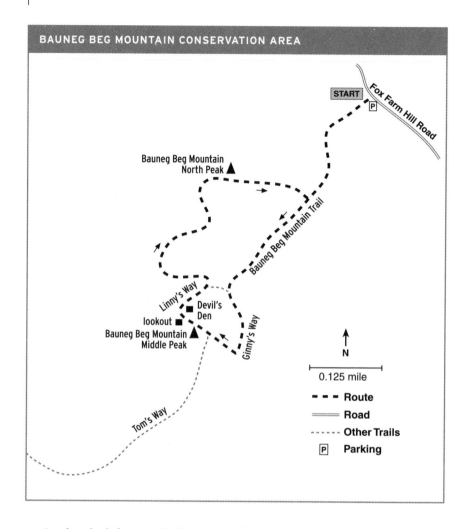

BAUNEG BEG MOUNTAIN CONSERVATION AREA

START

Fox Farm Hill Road

Bauneg Beg Mountain
North Peak ▲

Bauneg Beg Mountain Trail

Linny's Way

Devil's
Den

lookout ■

Bauneg Beg Mountain ▲
Middle Peak

Ginny's Way

N

0.125 mile

- - - Route
═══ Road
----- Other Trails
P Parking

Tom's Way

In a hemlock forest at the base of the descent, reach the junction with North Peak Loop and a sign pointing right to Ginny's Way. Continue straight on North Peak Loop, first on the level, then down an easy slope. Ahead, the trail passes through the shallow valley between the two peaks, crosses a streamlet, and then makes a wide arc on a switchback. At a white arrow painted on a tree, bear sharply left and climb easily through mixed hardwoods.

Just after a sharp right turn marked by a double blaze, arrive at a junction with a spur trail on the right, which leads 75 feet to an open ledge topped with a cairn and a view southward (in fall and winter) to Middle Peak and the rocks of Devil's Den. Back on the trail, meander on through a passage in a stone wall and emerge from the woods on the semi-open rocks atop North Peak, with limited views west over the treetops. Turn sharply right to walk across the low summit, marked by a large cairn.

Beyond, the trail crosses the stone wall again and reenters the woods. After another stone wall it is easy walking through the forest marked by young beech in the understory and white pines in the canopy. North Peak Loop soon reaches the junction with Bauneg Beg Trail. Turn left here to return to the car in about 0.3 mile.

DID YOU KNOW?

Two tiny ski areas once operated on Bauneg Beg Mountain. From 1938–1958, the Bauneg Beg Ski Club ran a rope tow with a 250-foot vertical drop, an open slope, and Devil's Den Trail. From the mid-1990s until around 2007, the Legere family ran Bauneg Beg Ski Trails, a 110-foot vertical slope just south of the former area.

MORE INFORMATION

Bauneg Beg Mountain Conservation Area is open year-round from dawn to dusk. The parking lot is not plowed in winter. A trail map is available from the Great Works Regional Land Trust (gwrlt.org; 207-646-3604).

NEARBY

The noted author Sarah Orne Jewett (1849–1909) lived near South Berwick her entire life. Jewett is perhaps best known for her work *The Country of the Pointed Firs*, which captured the isolation and hardship of life in the fishing villages along the Maine coast. The Sarah Orne Jewett House Museum and Visitor Center in South Berwick showcases the family's life and treasures in the two adjacent homes they occupied on Portland Street in the center of town. Open Friday through Sunday from June 1 to October 15, tours are available on the hour from 11 A.M. to 4 P.M. There is a small admission fee.

MORE HIKING

The Great Works Regional Land Trust has protected nearly 5,200 acres since 1986, many of which have hiking trails open to the public (gwrlt.org; 207-646-3604). Nearby, the Kennebunk Plains Wildlife Management Area (maine.gov/ifw; 207-287-8000), and the Kennebunk Plains and Wells Barrens preserves (The Nature Conservancy, nature.org; 207-729-5181) protect 3,500 contiguous acres of sand plain grasslands, pine barrens, and blueberry barrens and provide many more miles of walking.

TRIP 8
SAWYER MOUNTAIN HIGHLANDS

Location: Limerick and Limington, ME
Rating: Easy
Distance: 3.0 miles (round-trip)
Elevation Gain: 680 feet
Estimated Time: 2.0 hours
Maps: USGS Limerick; *Maine Atlas and Gazetteer*, Map 4 (DeLorme);
Sawyer Mountain Highlands (Francis Small Heritage Trust)

**Hike to the top of Sawyer Mountain through the largest unfragmented
block of undeveloped land in York and Cumberland counties.**

DIRECTIONS

From the post office at the junction of ME 5 and ME 11 in the village of Limerick, drive north on ME 11 for 0.9 mile. Just after the boat launch and outlet
dam on Sokokis Lake, turn left onto Emery Corner Road. Follow this for 0.8
mile to a four-way intersection, where Quarry Road goes left and Pickerel
Pond Road goes right. Proceed straight through the intersection to continue
on Emery Corner Road. In another 1.2 miles, Coffin Hill Road diverges right;
here, bear sharply left onto Sawyer Mountain Road to reach Emerys Corner
in another 0.5 mile. Continue straight on the dirt-surfaced Sawyer Mountain
Road, while paved Lombard Hill Road goes left and dirt Shaving Hill Road
goes right. In another 0.6 mile, Nason Corner Road diverges left; continue
straight ahead on Sawyer Mountain Road to reach the gravel trailhead parking
lot (space for ten to twelve cars) on the right in another 0.3 mile. If you reach
a town turnaround in sight of a red barn on a hill up to the right, you've gone
just a little too far. (Note: during spring mud season the parking lot is closed,
requiring hikers to park along the roadside.) *GPS coordinates: 43° 44.226' N,
70° 45.912' W.*

TRAIL DESCRIPTION

The Francis Small Heritage Trust owns Sawyer Mountain Highlands, a parcel
of 1,472 contiguous acres on Sawyer Mountain in Limerick and Limington.
The property is part of the largest unfragmented block of undeveloped land in
York and Cumberland counties, and part of a plan to conserve 2,000 acres and
create a greenway stretching from the New Hampshire border east to Sebago

Lake. Sawyer Mountain Highlands was assembled by the trust from seventeen different parcels purchased between 1996 and 2011. The land is open to public use and enjoyment for a variety of recreational pursuits. More than 5 miles of trails thread through the hilly terrain, which is home to stands of old growth red oak, hemlock, sugar maple, and beech. This trip combines Smith Trail, old Sawyer Mountain Road, and a short spur trail for a lovely hike featuring a series of old stone walls and the remains of a historical homestead along the way to the summit of 1,213-foot Sawyer Mountain .

Smith Trail (sign) leaves from the right-hand corner of the lot. Immediately pass a sign warning of deer ticks. Hike uphill through oaks and pines on a wide track. Notice the trail markers as you go, small blocks of wood with the outline of a turtle carved into them and painted yellow. This "sign of the turtle" is the mark of Captain Sandy, also known as Chief Wesumbe, of the Newichewannock Abenaki.

Ahead, bear left up a ridge, which climbs next to a stream that flows out of a rocky ravine. The trail soon levels off and bears right to cross the stream. Proceeding on a contour, the path follows an old jeep trail fringed with bright green mosses. The woods here are composed of good-size oaks, tall pines, and some maple and ash. The trail bears left off the jeep track onto a foot path (arrow) and climbs up and left below a ridge of mossy boulders. After the angle eases, the path proceeds through park-like woods.

Swing up and right through a hemlock grove. Note the huge, ancient oak 25 feet to the right of the trail. Part of the trunk has broken and fallen to the ground but the old soldier still thrives. Just beyond, at a pass of sorts, bear left. Occasional bits of orange tape mark the trail as it ascends easily up the slope. Bear sharply left (arrow), then pass through a gap in a stone wall.

Meander through the young stems of beech and birch amid an overstory of hemlocks and pines. Pass through another stone wall, then continue along on a wide, level stretch past a stand of pines. After a third stone wall, look for the decaying stumps that tell a story of the heavy timber harvesting that took place here a half-century ago. Trend gently downhill, pass through a fourth stone wall, and then quickly reach the junction with old Sawyer Mountain Road (sign). Before making the right turn and continuing toward Sawyer Mountain, look for the old stone foundations directly ahead in the woods across from the junction. The foundations, cellar holes, and well are the remnants of the old Sawyer family farmstead, first settled by Deacon William Sawyer and his son John in 1794. Poke around the impressive extent of the structures as evidenced by the many stone outlines, including the walls of what were the livestock

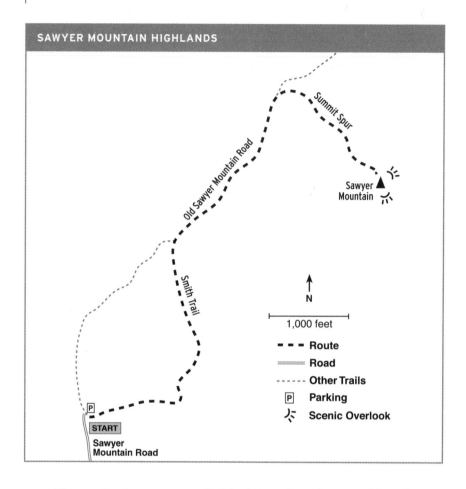

SAWYER MOUNTAIN HIGHLANDS

Summit Spur

Old Sawyer Mountain Road

Sawyer Mountain ▲

Smith Trail

N

1,000 feet

- - - Route

═══ Road

----- Other Trails

P Parking

Scenic Overlook

P

START

Sawyer
Mountain Road

pens. The area has been pretty well picked clean, but a few rusted barrel staves still remain among the leaves.

Back on the road, head north uphill. Cross a low spot with a wet area to the right and a stream to the left. Beyond, ascend a short section of eroded road over rocks and slabs of bedrock. Continue on the wide, rocky road to the crest of the hill, where the trail levels off. Pass a persistently muddy spot in the road by veering in and out of the stone wall on the left. Ahead, follow a rock wall and line of pines as the road winds around the base of the summit cone.

Reach the spur trail to the summit (sign) on the right at the height-of-land. The old Sawyer Mountain Road continues straight ahead 1.5 miles to a trail-head on Cape Road (ME 117) in Limington. Ascend from this point on the wide trail over rocks and pine needles through the park-like woods. Look for the name "LULU" carved in a trailside rock. Lulu was the daughter of Autien Sawyer, the last of the family to farm on the mountain in the early 1900s.

The vista south and west from the top of Sawyer Mountain takes in the lowlands of York County and the hills and mountains of southwestern Maine and southeastern New Hampshire.

Reach a crest then descend slightly. Pass a viewpoint on the right just past a clump of pines. The trail dips a little more just ahead, rises again, then levels off. The summit sign is just ahead, stuck in a pile of rocks to the right of the trail. Immediately to the right of the sign is a path to a viewpoint south and west.

As Sawyer Mountain is visible from the ocean, the summit was once the site of a whale oil light that guided ships safely into Portland Harbor in the eighteenth century. In 1884, the U.S. Geological Survey erected a 15-foot stone monument on the site, which was later destroyed by lightning. Scattered stones from the tower still remain.

The main trail continues left of the summit sign to a fine flat rock and a level, grassy clearing, where it ends. A view northeast reveals Sebago Lake, the second-largest and deepest lake in Maine. To the south and west, beyond the pines, views stretch over the lowlands of York County, including the fire-tower on Ossipee Hill, and the hills and mountains of southwestern Maine and southeastern New Hampshire. A feint trail continues a short distance south-east from the summit through the park-like woods past a boulder to views east to Portland on Casco Bay, a worthwhile detour if so desired.

To return, retrace your steps to the trailhead.

DID YOU KNOW?

Francis Small (1625–1714), the namesake of the trust, was a fur trader and landowner and is said to have owned the largest amount of land of any person who has ever lived in Maine. In 1668, Small operated a trading post in what is now Cornish, a few miles northwest of Sawyer Mountain, at the confluence of the Ossipee and Saco rivers and the crossroads of three major American Indian travel routes, the Sokokis Trail (now ME 5), the Ossipee Trail (now ME 25), and the Pequawket Trail (now ME 113).

Abenaki tribesmen who owed debts to Small plotted to kill him to avoid payment. However their chief, Wesumbe (also known as Captain Sandy), warned Small in time to foil the plan, but not before Small's home was burned to the ground. To compensate for the loss, Chief Wesumbe sold Small 20 square miles of land in the area, which came to be known as the Ossipee Tract. The tract was bounded by the Saco, Great and Little Ossipee, and Newichewannock (later Salmon Falls) rivers. Today that area includes the towns of Limerick, Limington, Cornish, Newfield, and Parsonsfield, and the very area where the Francis Small Heritage Trust works to conserve land. In return for the land, Small paid Chief Wesumbe 2 large Indian blankets, 2 gallons of rum, 2 pounds of powder, 4 pounds of musket balls, and 20 strings of beads.

MORE INFORMATION

Francis Small Heritage Trust (fsht.org; 207-221-0853).

NEARBY

The Willowbrook Museum in Newfield is a nineteenth-century village featuring two historical farmhouses and barns; a replica schoolhouse and bandstand; a millpond; horse-drawn sleighs, carriages, and trades wagons; an 1849 Concord stagecoach; an 1894 carousel; gas engines; and exhibits of various trades and tools (willowbrookmuseum.org; 207-793-2784).

MORE HIKING

Explore the length of the old Sawyer Mountain Road north to Cape Road (ME 117) in Limington. From the Limerick trailhead, short side trips can be made to a gorge and cascading waterfall. A few miles north of the Sawyer Mountain Highlands are pleasant trail networks on Douglas Hill in Sebago and Mount Cutler in Hiram. Trails for both of these areas are described in the AMC *Maine Mountain Guide*.

2

CASCO BAY

THIS SECTION ENCOMPASSES the Greater Portland and Casco Bay portion of Cumberland County south of Sebago Lake, and includes the entirety of thirteen municipalities and parts of five others. Named for William, Duke of Cumberland, a son of England's King George II, Cumberland County was founded in 1760 from a portion of what was then York County, Massachusetts.

With 66,000 residents, Portland is the largest city not only in Cumberland County but in Maine and serves as the state's most important urban center. The metropolitan area of Greater Portland is home to more than 250,000 people, almost one-fifth of Maine's population. Abenaki called the area "Machigonne," meaning great neck, an apt description of the Portland peninsula. George Cleeve and Richard Tucker's fishing and trading village, established in what is now Portland in 1633, became the first permanent European settlement in the Casco Bay region.

Casco Bay comprises 200 square miles of estuaries, islands, and ocean ranging from Two Lights in Cape Elizabeth to Cape Small in Phippsburg, and is the dominant natural feature along this part of the Maine coast. The 986 square miles of the greater Casco Bay watershed are drained by thirteen major rivers, including the Fore, Presumpscot, Royal, and New Meadows, as well as eleven major lakes, including Long Lake and Sebago Lake, Maine's deepest and second-largest inland body of water.

The area in this section is bounded on the south by the town lines of Scarborough and Gorham. The line turns northeast to run through the rural forests and farmlands on the outskirts of Gorham, Windham, Gray, and North Yarmouth as far as Pownal. The section boundary then zigs and zags, following the Freeport and Brunswick town lines to the Androscoggin River. At Cooks Corner the southeast-flowing river joins Merrymeeting Bay, an expansive freshwater bay where six rivers meet, including the Kennebec River. From Merrymeeting Bay, the section boundary bears southeast to Bath, then south along the New Meadows River. The river continues south to divide Great Sebascodegan Island in Harpswell from the Phippsburg Peninsula, eventually emptying into Casco Bay.

From this point west to Dyer Point in Cape Elizabeth and the iconic Portland Head Light—built in 1791 by order of General George Washington and the oldest lighthouse in Maine—the undulating shoreline of Casco Bay is deeply indented by a series of long peninsulas, necks, islands, bays, and sounds between Harpswell and Freeport. The coastline of Freeport, Yarmouth, Cumberland, and Falmouth gives way to myriad islands offshore, including Cousins; Littlejohn; Great and Little Chebeague; Long; Great and Little Diamond; Peaks; and Mackworth islands. The urban environs of the cities of Portland and South Portland are divided by the Fore River and Portland Harbor. South and west of Cape Elizabeth, the coastline extends to Prouts Neck, passing Willard, Crescent, Higgins. and Scarboro beaches. The Scarboro River drains the smaller Nonesuch, Libby, and Dunstan rivers and Mill and Cascade brooks.

Major conservation land in this southern portion of Cumberland County includes the Scarborough Marsh Wildlife Management Area, which is bisected by the 65-mile-long Eastern Trail (Trip 9); a unit of the Rachel Carson National Wildlife Refuge; Maine Audubon nature sanctuaries at Gilsland Farm and Mast Landing; and state parks and public lands at Scarboro Beach, Crescent Beach, Mackworth Island (Trip 12), Wolfe's Neck Woods (Trip 13), Pineland, and Bradbury Mountain (Trip 14). The region is also home to numerous land trust parcels, thanks to nonprofit groups like Portland Trails, South Portland Land Trust, Falmouth Land Trust, Royal River Conservation Trust, Freeport Conservation Trust, Brunswick-Topsham Land Trust, Harpswell Heritage Trust (Trip 15), and others.

In the fabulous Portland Trails network covering Falmouth, Portland, Westbrook, South Portland, and Cape Elizabeth, the extent of urban pathways totals more than 70 miles and includes the Forest City Trail (Trip 11) and the Spring Point Shoreway (Trip 10), both of which connect scenic locales and green spaces with built environments for a wonderful walking experience.

TRIP 9
EASTERN TRAIL/
SCARBOROUGH MARSH

Location: Scarborough, ME
Rating: Easy
Distance: 4.2 miles
Elevation Gain: Minimal
Estimated Time: 2.0 hours
Maps: USGS Prouts Neck; *Maine Atlas and Gazetteer*, Map 3
(DeLorme); *Eastern Trail Guide*, Map 6 (ETA)

Meander along an old railroad corridor turned multiuse trail through the wildlife-rich environs of Maine's most extensive salt marsh.

DIRECTIONS

From I-95/Maine Turnpike, Exit 42 in Scarborough, proceed a short distance to Payne Road. Cross Payne Road and continue on Haigis Parkway for 1.5 miles to the junction of US 1/ME 9. Turn right and drive south on US 1/ME 9. At 3.1 miles, ME 9 and US 1 diverge. Turn left onto ME 9 (Pine Point Road) and proceed southeast. Pass the Scarborough Marsh Audubon Center at 3.9 miles. Reach the trailhead parking lot for the Eastern Trail (sign) on the left at 4.3 miles. The dirt lot has space for at least twelve cars. *GPS coordinates: 43° 33.673′ N, 70° 22.175′ W.*

ShuttleBus operates intercity bus service between Biddeford, Saco, Old Orchard Beach, Scarborough, and Portland (shuttlebus-zoom.com; 207-282-5408), making six round-trips on weekdays, five round-trips on Saturday, and five round-trips on summer Sundays (June 15 through September 15 only), passing the Pine Point Road trailhead en route.

TRAIL DESCRIPTION

The Eastern Trail is a 65-mile nonmotorized greenway extending from Bug Light on Casco Bay in South Portland to Strawbery Banke on the Piscataqua River in Portsmouth, New Hampshire. The trail is a work-in-progress, a connected series of off-road and on-road sections, with the goal over time to bring as much of the trail off-road as possible. It is being assembled along the old Eastern Railroad Corridor, which operated from 1842 until 1945, when the Boston & Maine Eastern Railroad ended train service between Kittery and

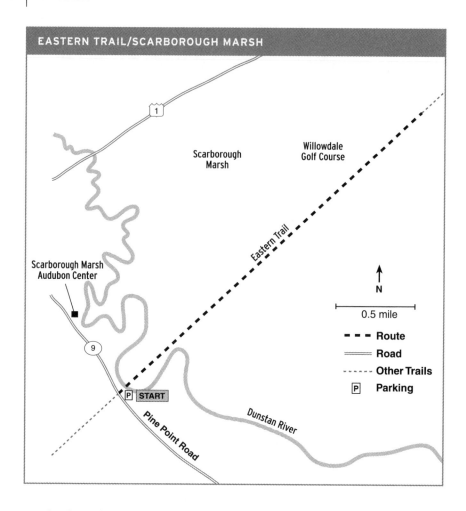

EASTERN TRAIL/SCARBOROUGH MARSH

1

Scarborough Marsh

Willowdale Golf Course

Eastern Trail

Scarborough Marsh Audubon Center

9

N

0.5 mile

- - - Route

Road

----- Other Trails

P Parking

P START

Pine Point Road

Dunstan River

Portland. Portland Gas Light purchased much of the abandoned right-of-way in 1965 and installed a natural gas pipeline. New Hampshire-based Unitil acquired the gas line and most of the right-of-way in 2008.

In 1998, the Eastern Trail Alliance was formed around the concept of a trail from Scarborough to Saco along this rail bed. By the early 2000s, the larger vision of the Eastern Trail caught on with the support of the twelve Maine towns along the potential route. Today, 30 percent of the trail is completed and off-road, with the Eastern Trail Alliance and the Eastern Trail Management District working together to advocate for, maintain, and build the trail. The trail also forms a portion of the 2,900-mile East Coast Greenway, a planned, nonmotorized trail from Florida to Maine, much of it along similar abandoned rail corridors.

This popular section of the Eastern Trail crosses the largest salt marsh in Maine. The expansive 3,200-acre Scarborough Marsh Wildlife Management Area (WMA), owned and managed by the Maine Department of Inland Fisheries & Wildlife, includes 2,700 acres of salt marsh, five tidal rivers, several smaller streams, freshwater marsh, tidal flats, and 200 acres of wooded uplands. The estuarine environment of the marsh, where salt water mixes with fresh water, provides a critically important resting, feeding, and breeding ground for an abundance of bird, animal, and aquatic life.

This out-and-back hike between Pine Point and Black Point roads begins from the trailhead kiosk at the far end of the parking lot (posted map). Be sure to pack your binoculars and camera for this wildlife-rich walk.

Proceed northeast on the wide, straight path. Soon, cross the pedestrian bridge over the Dunstan River. The span was constructed and opened to the public in 2004. Across the open space of the marsh, houses on Pine Point can be seen far to the right, while off to the far left is the traffic of US 1. The thick layer of peat forming the river banks is the result of decomposed grass and other materials accumulated over time to depths as great as 15 feet. The tall grass along the river is cord grass, while farther back on the slightly higher ground is salt hay. Early settlers grazed their cattle on the salt hay and used the cord grass to thatch their rooftops. As you walk, be on the lookout for a wide variety of birds, including sandpipers, willets, ibis, egrets, great blue herons, mallards, black ducks, ospreys, hawks, and gulls.

Ahead at a lone red oak, the river curves sharply away toward Pine Point, Prouts Neck, and the ocean at Saco Bay. Few signs of civilization are visible amid the forest fringes around the marsh.

The shallow ponds in the marsh are called salt pannes. Unconnected to the tidal streams, these ponds rely on rain and very high tides for their water supply. The weathered wooden poles are known as staddles. Farmers of olden days would harvest the salt hay and pile it high against these wooden posts until the marsh froze and horse-drawn carts could come and retrieve it. Staghorn sumac and aspens line the trail route here. Beyond is a bench next to a leaning birch; a second bench lies ahead amid some maples and oaks.

At 0.8 mile, the Eastern Trail reaches the wood line, marked by the yellow posts of Granite State Gas. Pass several cattail swamps on the left and oak woods on the right. Ahead, the path passes a Scarborough Public Works facility on the left, and two Unitil natural gas pipe enclosures on the right. In a forest of large red oaks, a side road enters on the left; keep straight here. Just ahead is a bench on the left on the edge of a pretty pond. A window out to the marsh proper is to the right of the trail; cross over a culvert for a view to Pine Point.

Pass by several greens and tees of the Willowdale Golf Course on the left, a pond, and then a farmhouse. The marshes along the Nonesuch River are visible through the woods to the right of the pathway. After another bench, cross over a drainage culvert, then sidle past more of the lovely golf course property. Up ahead, pass the gated road of a subdivision. A telephone line shares the trail route. Pass through a yellow gate. A sign reads, "Shared Roadway Ahead," and another sign indicates that this is the Scarborough Marsh WMA. The hike ends here. Retrace your steps to return to your car.

DID YOU KNOW?

Scarborough Marsh accounts for 15 percent of the total salt marsh area in Maine. American Indians aptly named it *Owascoag*, or "Land of Many Grasses."

MORE INFORMATION

The Eastern Trail is open for year-round recreational use. Dogs should be kept on-leash to protect nesting wildlife. The 28-page, full-color *Eastern Trail Guide* covers the entire on- and off-road trail network. The spiral-bound guide is available for purchase; a PDF file may be downloaded for free from the Eastern Trail Alliance (easterntrail.org; 207-284-9260).

NEARBY

The Scarborough Marsh Audubon Center is located just north of the Eastern Trail crossing on Pine Point Road. The center is open from Memorial Day through Labor Day, providing canoe rentals daily from 9 A.M. to 4 P.M., perfect for further exploration of Scarborough Marsh. The center also features interpretive exhibits, guided walks, and a nature store. A fascinating self-guiding nature trail begins across Pine Point Road (maineaudubon.org/find-us/scarborough-marsh; 207-883-5100 April through September; 207-781-2330 x213 October through March).

MORE HIKING

Nearly six miles of the Eastern Trail traverse the town of Scarborough, including sections worth exploring both north and south of the described hike. The Scarborough River Wildlife Sanctuary a short distance south of the Eastern Trail crossing on Pine Point Road offers 1.5 miles of hiking trails (healthy mainewalks.com). The Scarborough Land Trust has miles of wonderful hiking at Fuller Farm, Broadturn Farm, Libby River Farm, Sewall Woods, Frith Farm, and other properties (scarboroughlandtrust.org; 207-289-1199).

EAST COAST GREENWAY

The East Coast Greenway is one of the most ambitious long-distance trail projects underway in the United States, with the ultimate goal of forming a continuous 2,900-mile transportation and recreation route, a public right-of-way for people-powered users linking Key West, Florida, with Calais, Maine. The East Coast Greenway will provide the 45 million Americans who live within the counties traversed by the trail convenient access to a safe and pleasant place for exercise, escape, even commuting to and from work; a close-to-home resource for friends and family to walk, hike, run, bike, horseback ride, skate, ski, bird-watch, and fish. Advocates are working hard to piece together existing and planned multiuse trails through urban, suburban, and rural areas up and down the Eastern Seaboard, utilizing waterfront areas and parklands, abandoned railroad corridors and canal towpaths, and other on- and off-road connections as necessary. Work on the East Coast Greenway began in 1991, when a small group of cycling and long-distance hiking enthusiasts met in New York City to form the nonprofit East Coast Greenway Alliance. Today the greenway is 29 percent complete, with 834 miles of trail now off-road. Some 100 trails along the route are now part of the greenway and officially marked and signed as such.

In Maine, 381 miles of the East Coast Greenway traverse an amazing variety of coastal landscapes as it crosses the state from Kittery to Calais. Nearly 35 percent of this distance is now off-road. Major sections of the greenway in Maine include Eastern Trail (Trip 9), South Portland Greenway, Beth Condon Memorial Pathway, Androscoggin River Bike Path, Topsham Trail, Lisbon Trail, Kennebec River Rail Trail, Downeast Sunrise Trail (Trip 45), the Moosehorn National Wildlife Refuge (Trip 48), and the Calais Waterfront Walkway. The Maine DOT produces the helpful guide *Explore Maine by Bike: Maine's East Coast Greenway*, which is available online at exploremaine.org/bike/eastcoastgreenway. Contact the East Coast Greenway Alliance at greenway.org or 919-797-0619.

TRIP 10
SPRING POINT SHOREWAY

Location: South Portland, ME
Rating: Easy
Distance: 2.4 miles, one way
Elevation Gain: Minimal
Estimated Time: 1.5 hours
Maps: USGS Portland East; *Maine Atlas and Gazetteer,* Map 3 (DeLorme); *Trails, Parks & Open Spaces: Portland, Maine and Surrounding Communities* (Portland Trails); South Portland Land Trust Trail Map (South Portland Land Trust).

Walk this historical pathway along a spectacular stretch of Casco Bay that features beaches, forts, lighthouses, museums, and scenic island and harbor views.

DIRECTIONS

To the starting trailhead: From the junction of ME 77 and Broadway in South Portland, continue straight on Broadway and drive 0.2 mile. Here, ME 77 goes right; remain on Broadway for another 1.1 miles to its intersection with Preble Street. Turn right onto Preble Street and follow it 0.4 mile to Willow Street. Turn left onto Willow Street and proceed 0.2 mile to the paved parking lot for Willard Beach on the right, where there is space for 55 cars. The trail to the beach starts from the cul-de-sac just ahead. *GPS coordinates: 43° 38.508' N, 70° 13.656' W.*

To the ending trailhead: From the intersection of Broadway and Preble Street, continue north on Broadway for 0.2 mile to a T junction. Here, Benjamin Pickett Street goes right, but you'll turn left onto Breakwater Street. At 0.3 mile, the road bears sharply right and becomes Madison Street. At 0.7 mile, reach the entrance to Bug Light Park on the right. An abundance of parking is a short distance ahead. *GPS coordinates: 43° 39.199' N, 70° 14.114' W.*

The South Portland Bus Service (Route 21) serves points close to the beginning and end of this hike, Monday through Saturday (southportland.org; 207-767-5556).

TRAIL DESCRIPTION

The Spring Point Shoreway, established in 1978, encompasses 21 acres on Casco Bay from Fisherman's Point and Willard Beach to Bug Light Park, and includes part of the Southern Maine Community College (SMCC) campus, Spring Point Ledge Lighthouse, and Fort Preble.

From the parking lot, walk 100 yards right to the cul-de-sac at the end of Willow Street. The building ahead has a snack bar, restrooms, and showers, which are open to the public during the summer beach season. Take the sandy trail to the right of the building past the playground out to Willard Beach.

Once on the 4-acre sand-and-pebble beach, note the rocky Fisherman's Point off to the right, which forms the southern boundary of Simonton Cove. Beyond the point out in the thoroughfare is Cushing Island. To the right of Cushing is Ram Island Light; to its left and farther out is the bulk of Peaks Island. Left of Peaks, the smaller island is House Island, and beyond it are Little Diamond and Great Diamond islands. Turn left to walk north along the beach. Homes line the beach edge, and ahead you can see the buildings of SMCC. Founded in 1946, the school occupies an 80-acre campus on the scenic edge of Casco Bay, which includes Fort Preble and the Spring Point Ledge Lighthouse; both are visible to the right of the campus complex.

Pass the end of Beach Street, a beach access point, and a set of wooden steps before arriving at a second wooden staircase. Go left up this staircase to join a paved pathway. Turn right here and follow along the fence. Pass by a portion of the Shoreway Arboretum, which is maintained by SMCC and includes a variety of salt-tolerant trees and shrubs, including a Swiss Stone Pine. Ahead are several benches and a picnic shelter housing two tables, along with a plaque dedicated to members of the Civilian Conservation Corps.

At a viewpoint beyond are two interpretive markers. The first describes several species of birds and how migrating songbirds often get stranded here. The second describes the sweet-smelling, leathery, green bayberry shrubs in front of you; explains how food, cover, and a mix of open and vegetated areas are important to wildlife; and tells all about the barnacles found on the rocks below.

Pass behind the SMCC Computer and Electronics Center to reach an observation deck with a posted map of all the Casco Bay islands. You can see Fort Scammel on House Island; this was the only one of the Casco Bay forts to fire a shot and be fired upon in battle (in early August of 1813).

Pass by a parking lot on the left to arrive at another viewpoint with two interpretive markers, one on the settlement history of Ferry Village and the other on shipbuilding, which notes that before the Civil War there were more than 30 active shipyards in South Portland. With an observation deck and the earth mounds and granite walls of Fort Preble just ahead, proceed left up the stairs and then north along the promenade, where there are wonderful

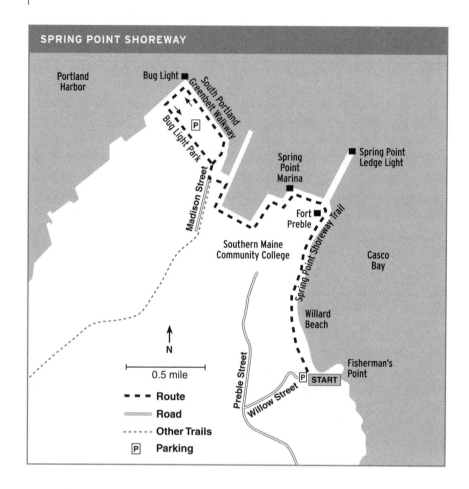

SPRING POINT SHOREWAY

Portland Harbor

Bug Light

South Portland Greenbelt Walkway

Bug Light Park

P

Madison Street

Spring Point Ledge Light

Spring Point Marina

Fort Preble

Spring Point Shoreway Trail

Southern Maine Community College

Casco Bay

Willard Beach

N

0.5 mile

Preble Street

Willow Street

P START

Fisherman's Point

- - - Route

═══ Road

------- Other Trails

P Parking

views of Spring Point Ledge Lighthouse and the long breakwater leading to it. Benches line the path, which winds over the top of the fort.

Fort Preble began as Fort Hancock, a temporary structure built during the Revolutionary War. In 1808, the fort was expanded and named after Commodore Edward Preble. Fort Preble saw continuous use from the War of 1812 through World War II before being deactivated in 1947.

At an old gun emplacement, turn right and descend the stairs. A marker describes Fort Gorges, which can be seen prominently ahead out in Casco Bay. Built on Hog Island Ledge between 1858 and 1871, the fort, which was never finished, was meant to supplement Fort Preble and Fort Scammel in protecting the entrance to Portland Harbor.

A small blue-green building at the base of the stairs serves as a snack shack and ticket booth in summer, when a small fee is charged to visit Spring Point Ledge Lighthouse. Turn right here to reach the circular pathway. Just before is

Constructed in 1875 and modeled after an ancient Greek monument, Bug Light occupies a commanding spot at the entrance to Portland Harbor.

a plaque on the left dedicating the Spring Point Shoreway, and an interpretive marker describing the history of Spring Point Ledge Lighthouse (built in 1897) and the breakwater (built in 1951). The lighthouse was the scene of many shipwrecks and groundings on the west side of the main shipping channel in and out of busy Portland Harbor. Originally owned and operated by the U.S. Coast Guard, the light was transferred to the Spring Point Ledge Light Trust in 1998, and the following year, it was opened to the public for the first time. The Coast Guard retains control of the light and fog signal.

To reach the lighthouse, bear left onto the circular path, then left again up the steps and over the fort wall to the breakwater. Hike carefully over the beautiful pink-granite blocks out to the light, the only caisson-style lighthouse in the US that is accessible by land and one of the few lighthouses in Maine open to the public for tours during summer weekends. Circle the light and enjoy the wonderful close-up view of the harbor, the bay, and the islands. Look south for a fabulous view of Portland Head Light. Commissioned by George Washington in 1787, the light is one of the most visited and photographed spots in Maine.

Return to the mainland at the blue-green shack and turn right to continue the journey. Pass several campus buildings on the left, with a series of benches on the right. Go through a parking area, then Lighthouse Circle. Just beyond, bear right toward the pier, then left onto a footpath at the art studio. Proceed along the edge of campus on Osprey Lane.

At an observation deck with a picnic table, two interpretive markers detail the brief revival of shipbuilding in South Portland. Another series of panels at the Liberty Ship Memorial provides additional context.

Turn left and walk the path along the chain-link fence of the Breakwater Marina. Ahead at a sign for "Greenbelt Walkway," go right through a gap in the fence and then make your way across the marina. Pass the function room of Joe's Dockhouse, and just beyond, Joe's Boathouse restaurant, a fine place to duck in for a meal and beverage.

Pass by a brick stanchion marking the Spring Point Marina, and with condos to the left and the marina slips to the right, continue along to Marina Drive. Turn right to follow along the opposite side of the marina. Beyond the gray-and-white marina building, avoid the entrance to the Portland Pipeline Corporation, Maine Terminal Pier 2, by turning left onto Cushing Court. Follow this a short distance to Madison Street.

At Madison Street, turn right and follow the sidewalk to the entrance of Bug Light Park. Pass through a gap in the wooden rail fence and pass between the park sign and a placard of rules. The paved path continues through a corridor of scraggly Scots pines out to the water. The trails of Bug Light Park are part of the South Portland Greenbelt Walkway, a continuous 6-mile urban path connecting the park to the western edge of the city.

With the oil terminal pier to the right and Fort Gorges directly ahead, turn left and walk to the Liberty Ship Memorial, marked by the skeletal hull of a Liberty ship and a series of interpretive panels. The shipyards that once occupied this 140-acre parcel included 60 buildings and had the capacity to build thirteen ships at a time with the help of some 30,000 workers. Between 1941 and 1945, the yards turned out an incredible 266 cargo vessels, 30 ocean-class vessels for the British Navy, and 236 liberty ships for the U.S. Navy. The 9-acre Bug Light Park was established in 1996 and the memorial erected in 2001.

Striding on, Bug Light is just ahead, with the Eastern Promenade of Portland in the distance. Spot Mackworth Island out in the bay off to the right. Pick up the walkway to Bug Light on the right, past the long parking lot, with an open, grassy promenade to the left and the skyline of downtown Portland beyond.

The spur leads a short distance to the elegant light, officially known as the Portland Breakwater Lighthouse, and an expansive view across the bay as far as Cousins Island in Yarmouth. Constructed in 1875, the light was modeled on an ancient Greek monument and built with cast-iron plates. The light was dubbed "Bug Light" because of its diminutive stature.

From the light, double back to the main walkway and continue along the Fore River, with the grassy fields on the left and oil storage tanks directly ahead. Just before the boat launch, turn left up the steps and take the path across the windswept promenade. The straight path ends at the road up ahead, where you'll turn right then quickly left to complete the hike at the entrance to Bug Light Park. Just before the end, pass the brick edifice of the Cushing Point Museum and South Portland Historical Society, which houses a fascinating history of shipbuilding (sphistory.org; 207-767-7299).

If you've spotted a car at Bug Light Park, you're all set. If not, return to the original trailhead by catching a bus or by walking Madison Street, Breakwater Drive, Pickett Street, Fort Road, and Preble Street back to Willow Street, a distance of about 2.0 miles.

DID YOU KNOW?

A spring once flowed from the shoreline bank near the high-tide mark at Spring Point, thus its name. The original American Indian name for Spring Point was *Purpooduck*, meaning "place that conspicuously juts out into the water and is little frequented."

MORE INFORMATION

South Portland Land Trust (southportlandlandtrust.org). City of South Portland, Parks & Recreation Department (southportland.org; 207-767-7650). Dogs are allowed on Willard Beach during the summer season (May 1 to September 30) only from 7 A.M. to 9 A.M. and 7 P.M. to 9 P.M. Outside of these dates, dogs are allowed on the beach from 6 A.M. to 9 P.M.

NEARBY

Guarding the entrance to Portland Harbor in Cape Elizabeth is Portland Head, said to be the most photographed lighthouse in the world. Built of rubblestone and completed in 1791, the lighthouse is the oldest in the state. Today, the light is automated and the former lightkeeper's house is a maritime museum. Portland Head Light is part of Fort Williams Park, a popular 90-acre public park that is home to old military batteries and the Goddard Mansion (capeelizabeth .com/visitors/home.html). Just south of the light is Two Lights State Park and its 41 acres of rocky headlands, and the adjacent Crescent Beach State Park, a mile-long arc of sandy beach (parksandlands.com).

MORE HIKING

Trails, Parks & Open Spaces: Portland Maine and Surrounding Communities is an excellent map and guide to 31 trails totaling more than 70 miles of hiking, plus a host of open spaces and parks (trails.org; 207-775-2411).

TRIP 11
FOREST CITY TRAIL

Location: Portland, ME
Rating: Strenuous
Distance: 10.0 miles, one-way
Elevation Gain: 260 feet
Estimated Time: 5.5 hours
Maps: USGS Portland West; *Maine Atlas and Gazetteer*, Maps 3 and 4 (DeLorme), *Parks & Open Spaces* (Portland Trails)

This 10-mile hike links the many wild places and green spaces and historic neighborhoods of Portland, Maine's largest city.

DIRECTIONS

From Maine Turnpike/I-95, Exit 46, in Portland, turn left onto Skyway Drive and go 0.2 mile to ME 22/Congress Street. Turn right onto Congress Street and drive 0.2 mile. Turn left onto Blueberry Road and follow it 0.2 mile to its end, marked by a guardrail across the road. There is space here for six to eight cars. An information sign just to the right of the parking area marks the start of Forest City Trail, which coincides with Stroudwater Trail for the first 1.3 miles. *GPS coordinates: 43° 39.288′ N, 70° 19.998′ W.*

The METRO bus (Route 5) offers limited service along this section of Outer Congress Street. Call ahead to be sure of scheduled times (gpmetrobus.net, 207-774-0351).

To spot a car at the end of the hike, take Maine Turnpike/I-95 to Exit 53. From the exit, turn right (south) onto Auburn Street (ME 26/100) and drive 1.0 mile. Turn left onto Summit Street. In 0.4 mile, turn left onto Curtis Road then turn right onto Overset Road in 0.3 mile. Follow Overset Road to its end 0.1 mile ahead, where there is trailhead parking for three to four cars and a kiosk describing the Presumpscot River Preserve. *GPS coordinates: 43° 43.194′ N, 70° 16.902′ W.*

Numerous local taxi services offer an easy way back to your car. By bus, take METRO Route 3 to Westgate Shopping Center and then transfer to the Route 5 bus for the second leg to the corner of Blueberry Road and Congress Street.

TRAIL DESCRIPTION

Forest City Trail follows a sinuous 10-mile route across Portland from the southwest corner of the city near Westbrook to its northern edge on the boundary with Falmouth. The route combines numerous individual trails while navigating a diverse landscape of natural beauty and wealth of human history, from the quiet of the wild places and green spaces to the sights and sounds of the urban streets and residential areas.

The trail is the brainchild of Tom Jewell, a Portland native, lawyer, trails advocate, and one of the founders of Portland Trails, a nonprofit urban land trust. Jewell led a walk every spring from Stroudwater to the Presumpscot and eventually decided to formalize the route, which was officially opened to the public in 2011. Portland Trails has been building trails and connecting open spaces, neighborhoods, and schools in Greater Portland for recreation and transportation since 1991. Forest City Trail forms the spine of the Portland Trails network, with its many other shorter trails serving as the arms. The network now exceeds 70 miles on 31 trails.

To the right of the Blueberry Road trailhead, follow an old road with broken pavement that leads to two brick buildings of the Portland Water District. The stack of a waste management facility rises to the left. Below, a sign for Forest City Trail marks the intersection with Stroudwater Trail. Bear right and walk past the building to pick up a footpath marked by white blazes. Climb the steps behind the parking lot of a manufacturing business, then proceed underneath the Maine Turnpike/I-95. Beyond, swing around the back side of a corporate parking garage, then bear left into the woods (sign). Cross a ravine on a bridge, then walk along the back side of the large outdoor parking lot. With a retaining wall to your right, bear left again into the woods.

Hike east along the placid waters of the winding Stroudwater River, traversing a low area on boardwalks. After a gas pipeline corridor, enter a stand of tall white pines. The trail swings around a shallow ravine, passes three benches, and crosses two gullies on footbridges and a stream on a boardwalk. After passing a private canoe rack, climb steps up to a paved trailhead parking lot next to a house on River's Edge Drive (parking for four cars).

Turn left and proceed to Congress Street, then turn left to follow the sidewalk along the busy road. Soon, the walkway crosses the Stroudwater River. Across the street is the historic Tate House. Built in 1755, it was home to George Tate, a British Royal Navy captain in charge of the felling and shipment of King's Pines, tall white pines claimed exclusively by the King of England for

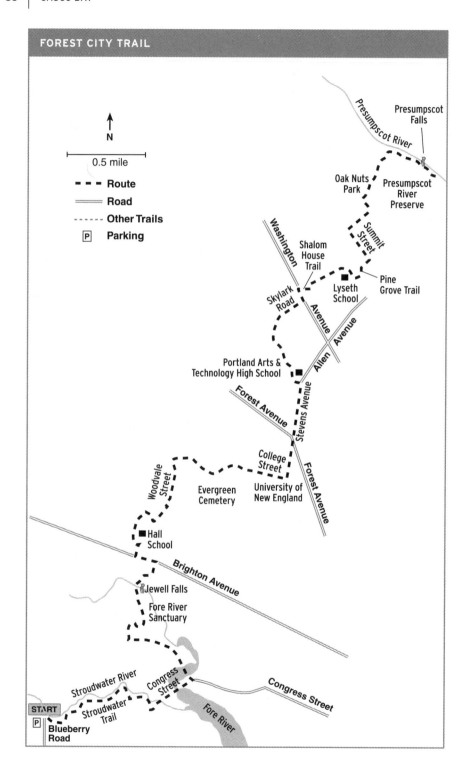

FOREST CITY TRAIL

N

0.5 mile

- - - Route
=== Road
----- Other Trails
P Parking

Presumpscot River

Presumpscot Falls

Oak Nuts Park

Presumpscot River Preserve

Washington

Shalom House Trail

Summit Street

Skylark Road

Avenue

Lyseth School

Pine Grove Trail

Allen Avenue

Portland Arts & Technology High School

Forest Avenue

Stevens Avenue

College Street

Forest Avenue

Woodvale Street

Evergreen Cemetery

University of New England

Hall School

Brighton Avenue

Jewell Falls

Fore River Sanctuary

Stroudwater River

Congress Street

Congress Street

Fore River

START

P Blueberry Road

Stroudwater Trail

With the removal of the old Smelt Hill Dam in 2006, Presumpscot River Falls and 7 miles of its namesake river were restored to their free-flowing state for the first time in more 250 years.

use as masts for the Royal Navy's sailing ships. The house, now a museum, is the oldest standing publicly accessible structure in Portland.

Soon after crossing Westbrook Street at a traffic light, pass the Stroudwater Baptist Church and several commercial buildings as you stride in historic Stroudwater. Founded in 1757 by Colonel Thomas Westbrook, the village was the site of a mastyard and shipyards. To the right along the Fore River is the Portland International Jetport and a bridge over I-295.

After the bridge over the Fore River, pass the 1685 Stroudwater business complex. At a sign just ahead, bear left off the pedestrian way into the Fore River Sanctuary, an 85-acre property owned and managed by Portland Trails. Pass a spur trail leading to a trailhead parking area and follow the path down to the salt marsh and a trail kiosk next to the Stroudwater Boat Basin, where maintenance boats for the Cumberland & Oxford Canal were once moored.

The canal, opened in 1832, connected Portland Harbor with Sebago Lake and on to Long Lake in Harrison. The canal used 28 locks to carry boats along the 38-mile route between sea level at the Fore River and Long Lake, 272 feet higher. A feat of engineering, the canal was 34 feet across on the surface of the water, 18 feet at the bottom of the water, and 4 feet deep. Horses on the tow path pulled the boats in either direction. The flat-bottomed canal boats had blunt bows, square sterns, and a draft of three feet. When heading downstream to market they were full of lumber and agricultural products; return trips carried manufactured goods back upstream. A six-cent toll was charged by each lock keeper en route; passengers paid a half-cent per mile. Railroads forced the canal operation into bankruptcy in 1857. It closed in 1870 but remained in use into the twentieth century.

Follow the tow path of the old canal to the steel footbridge over the Fore River. Beyond the bridge, the trail passes an information kiosk, then remains on the tow path for 0.5 mile, with the extensive salt marsh always on the right.

Cross three foot bridges on the hawthorn-lined pathway. Ahead at a bench, the trail bears sharply right over a footbridge. Cross over the head of the marsh, pass under a powerline, then stay straight at a trail junction.

Up the steps and into the woods beyond, swing around a point of land through mature hemlocks and pines, then cross a section of salt marsh on a footbridge with a railing. And its end, go right then quickly left. Atop a rise, turn right at a junction and proceed downslope to a long plank bridge. Turn left after the bridge to quickly arrive at the tracks of the old Mountain Division Railroad. Abandoned in 1983, the rail line once connected Portland to St. Johnsbury, Vermont, 131 miles to the northeast through the White Mountains. Parts of the rail line farther north near Sebago Lake have been converted to a rail-with-trail.

Climb the far bank to reenter the woods. At a signpost ahead, a trail leads right to parking at Capisic Street. Stay straight on the wide trail through the oak woods. At the next signpost, a trail leads left to parking at Rowe Avenue. Here, stay straight again.

Amid the tall pines and hemlocks, descend into a ravine and pass by a pocket salt marsh before reaching the cascading Jewell Falls. The land around Portland's only natural waterfalls was donated to Portland Trails by Tom Jewell. Climb up the stone steps on the left side of the falls past a granite bench to reach the footbridge over the top of the falls. Cross the bridge and follow the wide trail north to the end of Hillcrest Avenue, where there is a sign and parking.

Follow Hillcrest Avenue out to the busy intersection of Capisic Street and Brighton Avenue. Turn left and follow the sidewalk west along Brighton Avenue through the Nasons Corner neighborhood. At a pedestrian crosswalk, cross over Brighton Avenue. On the other side, turn left and walk for 150 feet to a trail signpost.

Turn right onto Lomond Street and walk along the dirt lane. Pass around a barrier and soon reach the corner of Riggs Street. Turn left here to enter the park-like woods of large oak trees. Emerge onto a sidewalk and follow it past the rear of Hall Elementary School. Pass the basketball courts and ball field to reach Hall School Fitness Trail.

At a signpost just ahead, turn right into the woods and then left at a granite bench to descend into a ravine. After a footbridge and an observation deck, swing around the school building to its entrance drive and follow the sidewalk left out to Warwick Street in the Sagamore Village neighborhood, which was built by the federal government in 1943 to satisfy a housing shortage during World War II, when Portland Harbor was part of a booming defense industry. Follow Warwick Street left over Capisic Brook, then past junctions with Sunset and Starlight streets. At the intersection of Warwick and Glen Haven streets, turn left onto Glen Haven and then quickly turn right onto Woodvale Street, passing Glen Haven West.

At a white fence on the right, Ledges Trail enters the woods. Avoid this and stay on Woodvale Street to the cul-de-sac; enter the woods at a sign for Evergreen Cemetery. The wide trail soon passes the other end of Ledges Trail. Beyond, the path merges with a cemetery road. Continue right on the road. Beyond, another road enters from the right. Continue straight on the cemetery road.

At about the 5-mile mark, pass by a silver gate to enter Evergreen Cemetery proper. Pass by a single-chain gate. Turn left at a second gate to walk between the duck ponds; waterfowl and other bird life are often present. The 239-acre Evergreen Cemetery is the largest cemetery in Maine and the second largest publicly owned space in Portland. Established in 1854, the garden-style cemetery was designed by Charles H. Howe as a rural landscape of winding paths, ponds, footbridges, a Gothic-style chapel, and funerary art and sculpture. The cemetery is a wildlife oasis and home to geese and ducks, pheasants and swans, blue herons, turtles, fox and mink, deer, and even moose. Walking trails were first established here in the 1970s.

Reach a paved parking area, then continue ahead into the woods on a footpath. At a junction with a yellow-blazed trail, go straight. Pass through a grove of hemlocks to emerge along the edge of the cemetery. Head upslope on an eroded track, then stay left at the top to follow along a fence line.

Leave the cemetery at a big maple tree, reaching a gated drive on the left. Turn right to follow the drive, then turn left and quickly right around the University of New England's Ginn Hall. Follow the brick sidewalk on College

Street through the center of campus along the common to Stevens Avenue and turn left. In about 0.5 mile, continue past the intersection with Bishop Street to reach the busy intersection of Stevens, Forest, and Allen avenues. A myriad of eateries are found in this area, a good place to stop for a more formal trail lunch. Cross the railroad tracks and proceed to McDonald's, then cross Forest Avenue at the pedestrian crosswalk directly in front of the restaurant. On the opposite side, bear right by a sandwich shop to continue your hike north on Allen Avenue. Cross another set of railroad tracks (restaurant across the street), then pass by Ruby Lane and Plymouth Street (blinking yellow light).

At a signpost on the left just before the sign for the Portland Arts and Technology High School (PATHS), leave Allen Avenue by turning left onto a paved walkway. Follow the walkway—also part of 26-mile Sebago-to-Sea Trail connecting Sebago Lake to Casco Bay—through campus, crossing a road to reach a cul-de-sac in front of the main entrance to PATHS. Bear left around a little yellow playhouse, then right between the parking lot and school. At the far end of a greenhouse, bear left around a Forest City Trail kiosk to enter the woods. Beyond a field, reenter the woods at a signpost and soon cross a creek on a plank bridge.

Approach a gray house, go left out to a cul-de-sac, then right, down the sidewalk on Skylark Road. Beyond Hennessy Street, reach Washington Avenue. Cross and turn left to follow the avenue north for a short distance. At a signpost and brown picket fence, bear right off the sidewalk to follow along the fence-shrub-wood line. This section of the route is known as Shalom House Trail. Ahead, at the corner of a parking lot, bear left into the woods for 100 feet, then out to Croquet Lane.

Follow Croquet Lane right to Auburn Street. Cross and follow the entrance road into Lyman Moore Middle School. Continue on to Harrison Lyseth Elementary School, passing left and then right around the rear of the building. Walk along the edge of the parking lot past basketball courts to a playground. In the middle of the playground, turn left to follow a paved walk between houses. At Bramblewood Drive, turn left. Cross Summit Street and turn left to walk along it, passing by an impressive line of large Norway spruce trees. This is the North Deering neighborhood, the northernmost in Portland, and home to some of its oldest surviving houses, many of which went unscathed through four terrible fires that over the centuries ravaged other parts of Portland.

Pass Pinelock Drive and soon reach a trail kiosk at a stone wall, granite bench, and metal gate at the entrance to Oat Nuts Park. The park is a former 1930s-era subdivision of tiny lots, the deeds to which could be found in boxes of Oat Nuts cereal. The city later reclaimed the parcels and created a public park. Follow the trail through the forest of oaks and pines on a gentle gradient leading to a creek. After a footbridge, bear sharply left along the creek. Ahead, after a sharp right, cross under a powerline to enter Presumpscot River Preserve, which protects 48 acres along the river corridor.

Follow the creek down the ravine, passing a spur on the left to trailhead parking at the end of Overset Road (Note: the route doubles back to this trailhead). Reach the banks of the Presumpscot River and the junction with Presumpscot River Trail. Turn right here to follow the beautiful river corridor to its end at Presumpscot River Falls 0.5 mile ahead. As the roar of the looming falls becomes noticeable, pass a portage warning sign. Two high points directly above the falls provide nice views of the river. Ahead, the trail drops 50 feet to river level just below the falls at the site of the old Smelt Hill Dam (interpretive sign) and the official end of Forest City Trail. Maine's first dam was built here in 1731. Although the dam provided hydropower for more than 250 years, it also blocked passage for a variety of searun fish, including alewives, smelt, shad, Atlantic salmon, herring, and striped bass. Damaged by a flood in 1996, the dam was finally removed in 2006, restoring the last 7 miles of the 26-mile long river to its natural free-flowing state.

To complete the hike, follow Forest City Trail back upriver 0.5 mile, then turn left and take the trail uphill to the spur leading right out to the trailhead parking lot at Overset Road.

MORE INFORMATION

Portland Trails, (trails.org, 207-775-2411). Dogs are allowed on Forest City Trail route, with varying restrictions: a maximum 25-foot leash in Stroudwater Park and Evergreen Cemetery proper; unleashed but under voice command in Hall School Woods, the PATH campus, and the undeveloped wooded part of Evergreen Cemetery; and on an 8-foot leash on city streets.

NEARBY

Portland's vibrant urban center has endless possibilities for sightseeing, entertainment, shopping, dining, and lodging. Check with the Convention and Visitors Bureau of Greater Portland (visitportland.com, 207-772-5800) for all there is to see and do.

TRIP 12
MACKWORTH ISLAND

Location: Falmouth, ME
Rating: Easy
Distance: 1.5 miles
Elevation Gain: 60 feet
Estimated Time: 45 minutes
Maps: USGS Portland East; *Maine Atlas and Gazetteer,* Map 5 (DeLorme); *Trails, Parks & Open Spaces: Portland, Maine and Surrounding Communities* (Portland Trails)

This easy trail circumnavigates the island with far-reaching views of the islands and lighthouses of Casco Bay and Portland Harbor.

DIRECTIONS

From I-295, Exit 10, drive east on Bucknam Road to its junction with US 1 in Falmouth. Turn right (south) onto US 1 and follow it 2.0 miles to Andrews Avenue and a blue-and-white sign for Governor Baxter School for the Deaf. Turn left (east) and drive 0.7 mile, first through a neighborhood, then over the causeway leading to the island. Stop at the white gatehouse, where the attendant will direct you into the parking lot on the right. *GPS coordinates: 43° 41.357′ N, 70° 14.111′ W.*

By bus, take METRO Route 7 (Falmouth Flyer) to the stop at the corner of US 1 and Andrews Avenue (gpmetrobus.net; 207-774-0351). Walk southeast on Andrews Avenue to the trailhead.

TRAIL DESCRIPTION

The 100-acre Mackworth Island is owned and managed by the state of Maine. In 1946, Mackworth Island was donated to the state by Governor Percival Proctor Baxter (who also famously purchased the lands around Katahdin that helped establish Baxter State Park in 1931) to be used for public purposes and "as a sanctuary for wild beasts and birds." The island houses the Governor Baxter School for the Deaf (not open to the public), which occupies eleven buildings on 15 interior acres. A copy of the self-guiding trail brochure, *Mackworth Island: Human Influence on a Coastal Island,* may be borrowed from the gate attendant. This out-of-print publication by the Bureau of Parks and Lands details the interesting natural and human history of the island and the many sights you'll see along your walking route. (Obtain a copy to keep by contacting the BPL office at Bradbury Mountain State Park at 207-688-4712.) Please be sure to return the brochure after your hike.

At the far end of the trailhead parking lot is an information kiosk with a posted map. A pit toilet is nearby. Walk past the kiosk to quickly connect with the perimeter trail and turn left (east).

Just before you reach a small brick building (Portland Water District), stairs on the right lead down to the shore. Continue ahead along the edge of a lawn on the wide gravel path. With the Baxter School across to your left, bear easily downhill to the right into the trees.

At a swinging bench, enjoy extensive views over Casco Bay to the Eastern Promenade of Portland; the entrance to Portland Harbor; Spring Point Ledge Light in South Portland; and Little Diamond, Great Diamond, Peaks, House, and Cushing islands. The unmistakable stone structure on Hog Island Ledge is Civil War-era Fort Gorges, now a public park.

On the trail ahead, look closely for the orange-colored bark of the spindly Scots pines. The forest canopy on the island also includes red and white pines, white and Norway spruce, tamaracks, red oak, and a mix of other hardwoods.

At a gnarled Scots pine, the trail passes the edge of a ballfield before reentering the woods and passing beneath the drooping branches of Norway spruce. A short distance beyond is a stone pier built during the Civil War, when the island was operated as Camp Berry of the Union Army. Steps on either side of the pier lead to the beach. Walk out for views north to Cousins Island (the smokestack is part of a power plant there) and Great and Little Chebeague and Long islands. To the south is a good view of Portland Head Light on Cape Elizabeth. Completed in 1791 at the direction of George Washington, the lighthouse is the oldest in Maine, and one of the most photographed.

Pass by another swinging bench and a park bench to reach stone steps leading down to a sand-and-gravel pocket beach; explore the intertidal zone for periwinkles, green crabs, barnacles, rockweed, clams, and mussels. Straight ahead are the Calendar Islands, including The Brothers, Clapboard, Sturdevant, Basket, and Cousins islands.

Farther north, the trail passes an unusual cemetery, reached by either of two short side trails on the left. Buried in the circular stone pen are Percival Baxter's beloved pets: fourteen Irish setters and his horse Jerry Roan. Not far ahead, in a plantation of red and white pines, is the Mackworth Island Community Village of fairy houses, tiny structures on the forest floor constructed of natural materials found on-site. The fairy village, a popular spot with children, was established by local families and exists by permission.

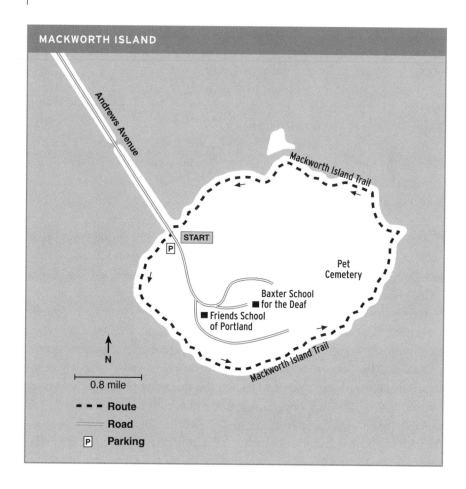

MACKWORTH ISLAND

Andrews Avenue

Mackworth Island Trail

START

P

Pet
Cemetery

Baxter School
■ for the Deaf
■ Friends School
of Portland

Mackworth Island Trail

N

0.8 mile

- - - Route
——— Road
P Parking

The trail passes two more park benches before swinging around to the west side of the island to cross a footbridge. The causeway leading to Mackworth comes into view before the path jogs inland around a ravine. Old farm fields open up to the left as the trail weaves through the pines along the shore. Immediately beyond an old mill pond is the gatehouse, and ahead, the parking lot. Just below, one final set of stairs leads to a long, curving beach.

DID YOU KNOW?

Mackworth Island is named after Arthur Mackworth, who was given possession in 1631 by Sir Ferdinando Gorges, an early English Colonial entrepreneur and founder of the province of Maine. For centuries prior to the arrival of the Europeans, the island was home to the Wabanaki, "the People of the Dawnland."

From the Civil War-era stone pier on Mackworth Island, hikers can enjoy extensive views of the Casco Bay islands, including Cousins, Long, and Great and Little Chebeague.

MORE INFORMATION

Mackworth Island (parksandlands.com; 207-688-4712) is open year-round from dawn to dusk. Owing to its close proximity to Portland, the island is a very popular spot for walkers and runners, especially on weekday evenings and weekends. There is parking for only twenty cars, and when the lot is full, please turn away and return at another time or find a parking spot along the METRO bus line and ride the bus to within a mile of the trailhead. Maps are available through Portland Trails (trails.org, 207-775-2411).

NEARBY

The Portland Observatory atop Munjoy Hill on Congress Street is the only known historical maritime signal tower remaining in the US. Built in 1807, the distinctive 86-foot, brick-red tower offers spectacular views of Portland, its harbor, and the islands of Casco Bay. This National Historic Landmark, owned by the city and operated as a museum and historical site by Greater Portland Landmarks, is open from Memorial Day to Columbus Day (portlandland marks.org; 207-774-5561).

FAIRY HOUSES

Fairy houses along the Maine coast are fascinating little structures constructed by creative nature lovers of all ages, and one may be hidden at the base of a tree, under a fallen log, among driftwood on a beach, or in a crevice among the rocks. Built of natural materials found nearby and ranging in size from tiny lean-tos and small caves to elaborate mansions and large fortresses, fairy houses are meant to serve as homes and visiting places for fairies.

Fairy house builders may use sticks, twigs, dry grass, leaves, cones and nuts, pebbles and stones, seaweed and sea shells, bark and feathers to fashion their dwelling. However, the builders never use live plants like ferns, mosses, flowers, or the bark of live trees.

Some believe the Maine fairy house tradition dates to the working farms of the early 1900s, when traveling school teachers brought folk tales of fairies to the island communities, inspiring children and adults alike to build fairy houses to attract the enchanted beings to come and watch over their livestock and families during the long winter. Others think the tradition derives from the folklore of Europe, particularly Ireland, Britain, and Germany; perhaps some of the fairies there stowed away on ships and made their way to Maine by sea, remaining here because the damp, mossy forests and craggy headlands reminded them of their homes in the Old World.

Whatever the reason, the magic and allure of fairies and fairy houses has persisted, becoming ever more popular as children and adults alike seek to connect with nature and spend more time in the Maine outdoors. It's a simple and rewarding activity that captures the imagination and instills respect for the natural environment.

Sanctioned fairy house villages can be found on Mackworth Island in Falmouth (Trip 12), along the Cliff Trail in Harpswell (Trip 15), and at the Coastal Maine Botanical Gardens in Boothbay, where visitors not only may view them but are encouraged to build their own fairy houses. In the Cathedral Woods on Monhegan Island, visitors are asked not to build new fairy houses but rather simply enjoy those already in existence. The Coastal Maine Botanical Gardens holds an annual Maine Fairy Houses Festival in August, with fairy dances, crafts, storytelling, games, music, teas, and even a fairy parade (mainegardens.org).

TRIP 13
WOLFE'S NECK WOODS
STATE PARK

Location: Freeport, ME
Rating: Easy
Distance: 2.2 miles
Elevation Gain: 160 feet
Estimated Time: 1.5 hours
Maps: USGS Freeport; *Maine Atlas and Gazetteer*, Map 6 (DeLorme); *Wolfe's Neck Woods State Park Map* (Maine Department of Agriculture, Conservation, and Forestry, Bureau of Parks and Lands)

This loop hike features pleasant views of the Harraseeket River and a string of Casco Bay islands.

DIRECTIONS

From I-295, Exit 22, travel east on ME 136 for a half-mile to its junction with US 1 in Freeport. Turn right onto US 1 (Main Street) and proceed south through downtown for 0.2 mile to Bow Street (opposite L.L. Bean). Turn left onto Bow Street and follow it eastward. In 1.0 mile, Bow Street becomes Flying Point Road. Continue on Flying Point Road and in another 1.4 miles, turn right onto Wolf Neck Road (park sign). Follow this road for an additional 2.1 miles to the park entrance. Follow the park road to the entrance station (pay fee), and soon arrive at the first of three large parking lots on a loop at the end of the road. Altogether, there is parking for at least 60 cars here. Restrooms, a water fountain, a pit toilet, a picnic shelter, and a field with picnic tables are found off the easterly parking lot. The trailhead for the hike described is at the south end of the large westerly parking lot, the first lot encountered, where there is a large information kiosk. *GPS coordinates: 43° 49.290′ N, 70° 5.010′ W.*

TRAIL DESCRIPTION

Wolfe's Neck Woods State Park spans the breadth of the Wolfe's Neck Peninsula from the Harraseeket River in the east to Casco Bay in the west, encompassing 245 acres of mixed woods, rocky ocean shoreline, mudflats, and salt marshes. The park is named for Henry and Rachel Woolfe, who in 1733 became the first Europeans to permanently settle the land here. Early settlers like the Woolfes cleared the land for farming and pasturing, but over the centuries,

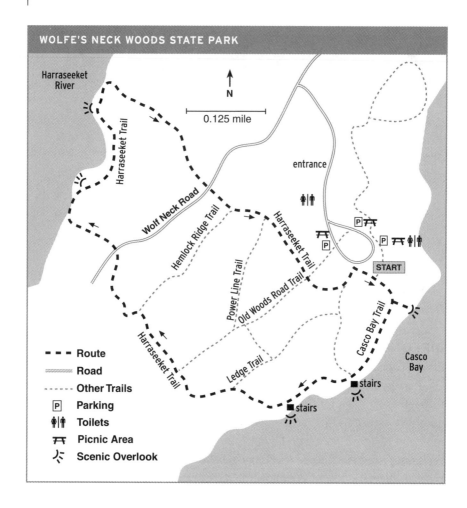

WOLFE'S NECK WOODS STATE PARK

Harraseeket River

N

0.125 mile

entrance

Harraseeket Trail

Wolf Neck Road

Hemlock Ridge Trail

Harraseeket Trail

Power Line Trail

Old Woods Road Trail

START

Casco Bay Trail

Casco Bay

Harraseeket Trail

Ledge Trail

stairs

stairs

- - - Route
=== Road
----- Other Trails
P   Parking
♀♂ Toilets
🔀 Picnic Area
⚡ Scenic Overlook

the woods have returned. The now heavily forested land was gifted to the state in 1969 by Eleanor and Lawrence M. C. Smith of Freeport, and in 1972, the park was opened to the public. A network of eight trails provide about 4 miles of walking opportunities. Ten interpretive signs describe the special natural features to enjoy.

This easy hike combines Casco Bay and Harraseeket trails for a lovely loop hike that reaches across the breadth of the peninsula. Begin to the left of the information kiosk (posted trail map) on the trail marked "to shore and Casco Bay Trail."

The wide trail passes a number of picnic tables before crossing a footbridge to intersect Casco Bay Trail. Turn right here to continue the hike, but first, take the short spur trail straight down the slope to the rocks and a pebble beach on

Just offshore from Wolfe's Neck Woods State Park on the Casco Bay side is Googins Island, a sanctuary for ospreys complete with a human-made nesting platform high in a white pine tree.

Casco Bay. Here, an interpretive sign describes some of the plant and animal life that lives in the rocky tidal zone.

Just offshore is Googins Island, a sanctuary for ospreys. Once endangered, the birds are now thriving due to the elimination of DDT and widespread habitat protection and restoration efforts. Look closely and you'll see the human-made osprey nesting platform high in a white pine tree and perhaps one of the adult birds, or maybe even one of the youngsters. To protect the ospreys, Googins Island is closed to human visitors.

Back at Casco Bay Trail, turn left to continue the loop hike. The path traces a route along the bay through pleasant woods of oaks, hemlocks, firs, spruce, and pines. At the next viewpoint, an interpretive sign describes some of the wildlife that makes its home in the bay, including the harbor seal, common eider, and mackerel. Wooden stairs lead to the shore for broad views of Flying Point and myriad islands, including Cousins Island, distinctive with its power plant stack reaching above the treeline. The trail leads easily ahead, crossing several footbridges and offering nearly continuous glimpses of the ocean waters through the trees.

At a beautiful stone patio and log bench 0.5 mile from the start of the hike, Casco Bay Trail ends and Harraseeket Trail begins. In case you've been scratching your head and wondering up to this point, an interpretive sign identifies the many islands and mainland points in sight. From left to right across the view horizon from Flying Point you'll see Bustins, Eagle, Little Bustins, French, Moshier, Little Moshier, Crab, Chebeague, Lanes, and Cousins islands. Take the wooden staircase down to the water for a closer view and enjoy.

Resume hiking on Harraseeket Trail, making a quick and easy ascent to intersect Ledge Trail on the right beneath two tall spruce trees and a big white pine. Beyond, crest the hill over occasional rocks and roots in the woods of big pines and young stems of red oak. Pass the gnarled branches of an old bull pine, and then descend to the junction with Old Woods Road Trail.

Just ahead on Harraseeket Trail, pass under a power line, cross a wet spot, then climb easily, crossing a stone wall. On a knoll among the spruce and pines, Hemlock Trail departs to the right. Continue left on Harraseeket Trail as it winds down the other side of the low hill. At its base, follow a section of rock sidewalk, and continue downslope through an impressive grove of mature spruce and pines.

At 1.0 mile, cross Wolf Neck Road and pass a "No Hunting" sign. Just beyond, a sign describes the hemlock woolly adelgid, an invasive insect that has infested and damaged the hemlock forest here. Visitors are asked to avoid contact with infested branches so as not to help spread the crawlers and thus the insect.

After a wet spot, the trail trends gradually downslope to the Harraseeket River. With the water in view, the path turns sharply right to follow along the river through woods of white birch, bigtooth aspen, and hemlock.

Beyond a shallow cove and its pebbly beach, occasional views through the trees reveal homes tucked in the woods above the far shore and sailboats moored on the river. Not long after crossing a ravine, reach a nice outlook atop a large rock ledge, with big views up and down the Harraseeket River, including the busy marina and boatyard in South Freeport.

Ahead, pass a huge boulder, and in a grove of mature hemlock, reach another open rock and viewpoint over the river.

The trail soon bears upslope and away from the river, crosses a series of bog bridges on level ground, and then rises again. It's easy going on the wide trail through stately pines and hemlocks.

Cross Wolf Neck Road and, in quick succession, pass by junctions with Hemlock and Power Line trails. After the power line, enjoy good walking on the hard gravel trail. Pass through the intersection with Old Woods Trail, and then hike over a nice section of rock sidewalk.

Where a spur of Casco Bay Trail enters from the right, turn left, and in 150 feet, reach the end of the loop hike at the westerly parking lot and trailhead kiosk.

DID YOU KNOW?

The Desert of Maine in Freeport is a 40-acre tract of land composed of fine-grained glacial silt hemmed in by a forest of pines. Years of poor farming practices, land clearing, and overgrazing led to soil erosion and the exposure of the underlying sand-like silt, which eventually overtook the former farmland. This unusual "desert" has been a popular tourist attraction since 1925.

MORE INFORMATION

Wolfe's Neck Woods State Park (maine.gov/wolfesneckwoods; 207-865-4465). Open daily from 9 A.M. to sunset from Memorial Day to Labor Day, although visitors are welcome during the off-season. There is a small daily entrance fee. Dogs are allowed on-leash. The park offers a regular schedule of guided nature walks, short talks, and activities, weather permitting. A trail map is available online.

NEARBY

Wolfe's Neck Farm is a nonprofit, 626-acre demonstration farm and educational resource center specializing in innovative and sustainable agricultural and natural resource practices that makes a fun visit for the whole family (wolfesneckfarm.org). The busy shopping district of downtown Freeport has a wide variety of restaurants and shopping outlets, anchored by the venerable outdoor retailer L.L. Bean (freeportusa.com).

MORE HIKING

Three miles of trails wind through the forest and estuarine habitats along the Little River at nearby Wolfe's Neck Farm (wolfesneckfarm.org). The Freeport Conservation Trust manages an extensive system of preserves and easements throughout the town, where seventeen trails provide more than 20 miles of hiking opportunities (freeportconservationtrust.org). Mast Landing Audubon Sanctuary features 3 miles of hiking bordering the Harraseeket River estuary (maineaudubon.org).

TRIP 14
BRADBURY TO PINELAND CORRIDOR
TRAIL AND BRADBURY MOUNTAIN STATE PARK

Location: Pownal, ME
Rating: Moderate
Distance: 4.2 miles (round-trip)
Elevation Gain: 860 feet
Estimated Time: 3.0 hours
Maps: USGS North Pownal; *Maine Atlas and Gazetteer,* Maps 5 and
6 (DeLorme); *Bradbury to Pineland Corridor Trail: Pownal Segments*
(Royal River Conservation Trust)*; Bradbury Mountain State Park:
Multi-Use Trail Map, West Side* (Maine Department of Agriculture,
Conservation, and Forestry, Bureau of Parks and Lands)

**Link the old feldspar mines on Tryon Mountain to the open summit
of Bradbury Mountain via this new corridor trail.**

DIRECTIONS
From I-295, Exit 22 in Freeport, proceed west on ME 136. In 0.1 mile, turn
left onto Pownal Road and follow it for 2.4 miles to its intersection with Ver-
rill Road. Here, Pownal Road becomes Elmwood Road. Continue straight
ahead on Elmwood Road for 2.0 miles to its junction with ME 9 (convenience
store on left, sign pointing right to Bradbury Mountain State Park). Continue
straight through the intersection, traveling another 2.3 miles on Elmwood
Road to Lawrence Road. Turn right onto Lawrence Road and follow it 0.9 mile
to the dirt trailhead parking lot on the left, where there is an information kiosk
and space for five to six cars. *GPS coordinates: 43° 54.833′ N, 70° 11.915′ W.*

TRAIL DESCRIPTION
When complete, the Bradbury to Pineland Corridor Trail will link the 800-
acre Bradbury Mountain State Park in Pownal with the 600-acre Pineland
Public Reserved Land, which spans New Gloucester, Gray, and North Yarmouth. These two large state-owned properties are 3 miles apart as the crow
flies, but 7 miles by way of the corridor. Begun in the late 1990s, the Bradbury
to Pineland Corridor will encompass 1,094 acres of easements and acquired
land. Project partners include the Royal River Conservation Trust, Casco Bay
Estuary Project, New England Mountain Bike Association, and the state of

Maine. This trip offers a nice introduction to the corridor, utilizing a portion of the new corridor trail on Tryon Mountain and linking to existing trails in the Bradbury Mountain State Park. A bronze marker set into a rock in the grassy park just to the right of the parking lot honors the Tryon family, whose roots in Pownal date back to 1800. Conservation of Tryon Mountain was made possible by the generosity of the Tryons.

The trail begins at a sign for Tryon Mountain on the opposite side of Lawrence Road about 100 feet south of the parking area. Follow an old woods road gently uphill, crossing over several erosion control bars. Amid the old field pines at the crest of the hill, reach a junction with a sign. Bear left here toward the quarry and the Tryon summit.

After a dip, pass to the right of a wet area to reach an old woods road and take a right; tailings from the quarrying operations are visible just to the left. Reach a spur on the left just ahead and take it to the historical feldspar quarries atop Tryon Mountain. Following green diamond markers, climb the bare slabs of the eroded road. Look for the quarried area just beyond an old bull pine on the left.

The road swings around to the top of the mountain. With a large grove of hemlocks on the right, look left to see a large quarry and the remains of cables used in the operation attached to a pine. Tailing piles of orthoclase feldspar are scattered about. Take the unmarked path around the largest of the quarry pits to see more cables and a spar pole. Exploration around the mountaintop will reveal numerous old quarry pits. Return to the spur junction and turn left to continue to Bradbury Mountain.

Descend to cross a beautiful stone wall. Ahead at a fork, where a faint trail goes right, continue left to follow the wide track through oaks and pines. Descend a moderate slope of crushed rock. Beyond, where the valley narrows, turn sharply right across a low, often wet area. *Note: This is an easy to turn to miss.* Turn up the other side of the valley to enter a hemlock grove. Take care, as markers are few and the path is not well defined. At a woods road, turn left to quickly reach the long wooden bridge over Thoit's Brook. State wildlife biologists have identified this area as important to wintering deer.

Soon after the bridge, bear left, then right onto a footpath. Wind up the slope to a stone wall that marks the northwestern boundary of Bradbury Mountain State Park and the junction with Boundary Trail, which traces a route around three sides of the park.

Turn right (southwest) onto orange-blazed Boundary Trail and climb the slope ahead. Soon, pass a bench on the left and continue striding on easy ground along the stone wall. Pass signs indicating the park is closed to hunting.

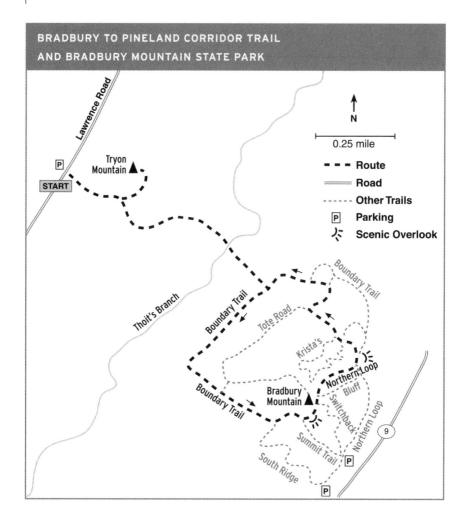

BRADBURY TO PINELAND CORRIDOR TRAIL AND BRADBURY MOUNTAIN STATE PARK

Lawrence Road

Tryon Mountain ▲

P

START

0.25 mile

N

- - - Route
═══ Road
····· Other Trails
P Parking
)≺ Scenic Overlook

Boundary Trail

Thoit's Branch

Boundary Trail

Tote Road

Krista's

Northern Loop

Bluff

Boundary Trail

Bradbury Mountain ▲

Switchback

Northern Loop

9

Summit Trail

P

South Ridge

P

Pass post 11, the first of numerous numbered posts you'll encounter in the park. The numbers correspond to the park trail map and denote trail intersections. Several stone walls meet at a corner; turn left here to continue along the park boundary. With post 12 on the left, clamber up the slab and the ridge beyond, then cross a long, wooden walkway. Pass post 13, then pass through a gap in a stone wall perpendicular to the one you've been following, padding through the quiet forest composed mostly of pine and hemlock.

Just shy of the 2.0-mile mark, reach the junction of South Ridge and Summit trails. A trail map is posted here. South Ridge Trail leads right down to a trailhead at the group camping area. Turn left to continue on Summit Trail. Climb over ledges and past a decaying bull pine, then ascend easily over the final stretch to the sweeping granite ledges of Bradbury Mountain's summit.

The open ledges on the summit of Bradbury Mountain are a popular spot for watching hawk migrations in spring and fall.

Step forward, past Summit Trail's departing path to the right, and enjoy the big view eastward to Casco Bay. Ranging from left to right, the vista includes Freeport (green water tower), Cousins Island (tall stack of a power plant), and the Portland skyline. The summit is a popular spot for watching the hawk migrations in spring and fall; an official hawk watch is conducted here from March 15 to May 15 each year, run by local birding enthusiasts. This summit has drawn people for centuries: Wabanaki camped on Bradbury Mountain, and in the early 1800s, the Cotton family created terraces here to grow grapes.

From the summit ledges, bear left and follow the wide track over the bedrock to the woods line. Here, Tote Road Trail departs to the left. Continue straight ahead following Northern Loop Trail's blue blazes.

Post 6 marks the junction with Switchback Trail. Just ahead, reach post 7, where red-blazed Bluff Trail leaves to the right.

Carry forward on Northern Loop Trail to the other end of Bluff Trail, marked by post 5. Take a short detour to the right here onto Bluff Trail to reach a fabulous outlook in about 150 feet. Retrace your steps to Northern Loop Trail and turn right. Trend easily downhill to pass Ski Trail (post 4) and then Tote Road Trail (post 3 and bench). Turn left here to leave Northern Loop Trail and continue the hike on Tote Road Trail.

Ski Trail is a reminder of early skiing days at Bradbury Mountain, when a row tow operated on the slopes of the mountain in the late 1930s and early 1940s, just one of many dozens of small ski mountains around Maine that have long since ceased operation.

White-blazed Tote Road Trail soon passes two junctions with Krista's Loop Trail, a mountain bike path (posts 19 and 20).

Beyond, contour across the mountainside to a junction with Boundary Trail (post 17). Go right on Boundary Trail and parallel a stone wall on the right. At post 16, turn left. Beyond this, take an unmarked and easy-to-miss sharp right turn. Fifty feet beyond the unmarked turn, reach post 10 and Boundary Trail proper. Turn left to follow a stone wall. Descend a short moderate pitch, then cross a brook on a short boardwalk to return to the junction of Boundary Trail and the trail to Tryon Mountain.

Turn right here and retrace your steps back to the trailhead on Lawrence Road.

DID YOU KNOW?

Bradbury Mountain was acquired by the federal government in 1939 and soon after became one of Maine's five original state parks, along with Sebago Lake, Aroostook, Mount Blue, and Lake St. George.

MORE INFORMATION

Royal River Conservation Trust (rrct.org; 207-847-9399); Bradbury Mountain State Park (bradburymountain.com: 207-688-4712). There is no fee to use the Bradbury to Pineland Corridor Trail, however, the state park charges a small day-use fee should you wish to reach the mountain from the east at ME 9. The state park offers camping at 35 sites, complete with picnic tables, fire rings, toilets, and hot showers.

NEARBY

The nonprofit Pineland Farms is a 5,000-acre working farm, business campus, and education and recreation venue in New Gloucester, where visitors can enjoy the market and welcome center and a variety of farm-fresh products and Maine-made merchandise, as well as some 18 miles of multiuse trails (pinelandfarms.org: 207-688-4539).

TRIP 15
HARPSWELL CLIFF TRAIL

Location: Harpswell, ME
Rating: Moderate
Distance: 2.5 miles
Elevation Gain: 280 feet
Estimated Time: 1 hour 45 minutes
Maps: USGS Orrs Island; *Maine Atlas and Gazetteer*, Map 6
(DeLorme); *Cliff Trail Map* (town of Harpswell)

**This scenic loop hike features lovely cliff-top views over tidal Long
Reach and a fairy house village.**

DIRECTIONS

From the junction of ME 24 (Bath Road) and ME 123 (Federal Street) in Bath,
just off US 1, drive south on ME 123 (now Bath Road) for 6.4 miles to a blinking yellow light. Here, turn left (east) onto Mountain Road. Cross the bridge
over Ewing Narrows at 7.1 miles, and soon reach the Harpswell Town Office
on the left at 7.7 miles, just opposite Harpswell Sound. Take the drive left of the
building to the far left corner of the lot behind the complex, where a portable
toilet, bike rack, and dog waste bin are located. The trail enters the woods just
beyond. Park anywhere here among the striped spaces. *GPS coordinates: 43°
48.876' N, 69° 56.592' W.*

TRAIL DESCRIPTION

Cliff Trail is located on 205 acres of Harpswell town property assembled in
three purchases between 1978 and 2002 and bounded by Strawberry Creek,
Henry's Marsh, Long Reach, and Mountain Road. Though originally intended
for affordable housing, municipal buildings, recreation, and conservation,
the land's ridges, cliffs, streams, and wetlands made the property unsuitable
for development. While the portion of land fronting on Mountain Road was
eventually developed, the remaining acreage was preserved for low-impact
recreation and wildlife habitat. Sometime after 2002, the original Cliff Trail
was extended to the northern tip of the property, bringing the loop to its
current 2.5-mile length. To begin, cross a short footbridge over a gully and
enter the woods. Pass a map box on the right (there may or may not be maps
available) and a sign describing fairy houses and applicable town ordinances

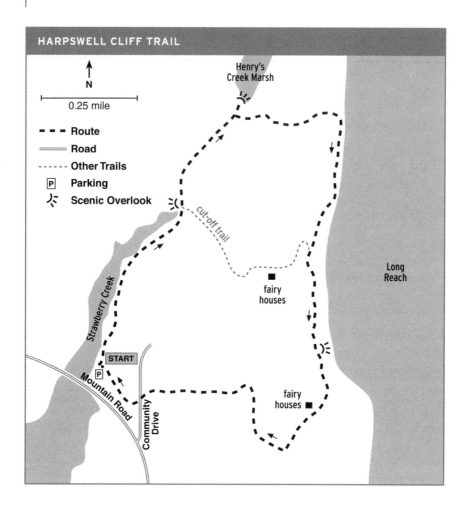

HARPSWELL CLIFF TRAIL

N

0.25 mile

- - - Route
=== Road
----- Other Trails
P Parking
Scenic Overlook

Henry's Creek Marsh

cut-off trail

Long Reach

fairy houses

Strawberry Creek

START

P

Mountain Road

Community Drive

fairy houses

relating to the property. Walk another 100 feet to a sign reading "Cliff Trail" that gives estimated distances for following the two loop options.

Hike through the spruce woods on the margin of Strawberry Creek, a tidal inlet that becomes a mudflat at low tide. After a viewpoint that offers a nice look up and down the creek, the soft trail through the quiet forest proceeds through a mixture of spruce, pines, cedar, and aspen.

Soon, cross a gully on a footbridge and just ahead, reach an old woods road (Old County Road) and a spur trail on the left leading to the head of Strawberry Creek. To the right, Old Road Trail (yellow blazes) leads 0.6 mile to Cliff Overlook on Long Reach and 1.5 miles back to the trailhead. Use this as a shortcut if needed.

Immediately beyond, cross a brook on a footbridge and reach another junction. A spur trail on the left leads 50 feet to Cascade Overlook, where the inlet brook pours over the rocks. At 0.7 mile, a spur to Henry's Creek Lookout on the left leads 150 feet to views over the salt marsh, a worthwhile detour. Swing around the head of Henry's Creek on bog bridges, then climb a slope between mossy ledges. Near the top of a ridge, bear sharply left to make the final climb to the reach the washboard spine of the ridge top. Cross over the ridge and descend toward Long Reach.

At the base of the descent bear sharply right, proceed on the level for a stretch, then drop down to just above the water. Now hike along the reach in an oak-and-pine forest, contouring along the slope with a few easy ups and downs and broad views of the long and narrow inlet. Because of the steep bank, access to the water is difficult and not recommended.

Climb a pine-needled slope and then a shallow gully to the east junction of Old Road Trail on the right (sign). One of two fairy house villages is a short distance down this shortcut. Explore it if you must, but another is ahead directly on the main loop trail.

Continue up the ridge line past a large rocky hump that temporarily blocks your view of Long Reach. Beyond, the trail traverses a steep slope, navigates in and out of another gully, and then proceeds high above the water on the crest of the spine with nice views below. Finally, a sign urges caution at Cliff Trail Overlook just ahead, where visitors are asked to please restrain dogs, watch children, and stay on the trail. Larger views open up before the trail mostly levels off to reach the overlook on the cliff-top ledge topped with young pines, juniper, and huckleberries 200 feet above the water.

Here are the best views yet up and down the 3.5-mile length of Long Reach. A small, unnamed island is just below, and in-season, clam diggers working hard for their daily catch can be seen in the mud flats at low tide. Directly across from your perch on the other side of the reach is the 93-acre Long Reach Preserve, a property of the Harpswell Heritage Land Trust as well as 233 contiguous acres of conservation easements. These lands are located on Great Island, called Erascohegan by the Abenaki, who also referred to Harpswell Neck to the east as "quick carrying place." The large, light-colored building in view far to the north beyond the reach is a hangar at the now-defunct Brunswick Naval Air Station. Other than that distant industrial object, the scene is one of lovely coastal wildness.

Moving on, hike along the top of the cliff edge, passing a steep gully slicing down through the rock wall to the water. Just past another warning sign for those traveling in the opposite direction, the trail bears away from Long Reach and soon arrives at the Fairy House Building Zone. Look closely in this area for myriad little structures built by visitors entirely of natural materials found on-site.

Ahead, cross a streamlet in the dark hemlock woods, pass the far boundary of the fairy house zone, and take a sharp right onto an old woods road. In 50 feet, bear left off the road (sign) and follow the footpath to the top of a knoll just shy of the town's high point. Descend, stride easily through the woods, and cross a shallow, wet valley on a footbridge. Another gentle downslope stretch brings you to the pavement and a trailhead sign directly across from the A. Dennis Moore Recycling Center and Transfer Station.

Turn left onto the road, then quickly right to pass in front of the facility. Look for a paved path leading off the road to the obvious town office building and take it. Walk to the side doors of the building, bear right around it, then cross the parking lot to your car.

DID YOU KNOW?

The town of Harpswell, incorporated in 1758, comprises a complex system of peninsulas and islands between Merepoint Bay and the New Meadows River that reach far out into Casco Bay. Altogether, the town has 218 miles of ocean-front coastline, the most of any municipality in Maine. The town has a long heritage of fishing, farming, and shipbuilding. Popular with tourists, Harpswell has also attracted many prominent individuals, including Harriet Beecher Stowe, Arctic explorer Robert E. Peary, and poet Edna St. Vincent Millay.

MORE INFORMATION

Town of Harpswell (harpswell.maine.gov; 207-833-5771). The Cliff Trail is open year-round from dawn to dusk. Dogs are allowed on-leash. A trail map entitled *Harpswell Guide to Outdoor Recreation* is available on the town of Harpswell website.

NEARBY

South on ME 24, the Bailey Island Bridge, which connects Bailey and Orr's islands, is the only cribstone bridge in the world. Some 10,000 tons of local granite were used to construct the open cribbing of the historical 1,150-foot bridge, allowing the tidal waters to ebb and flow freely while the bridge withstands heavy winds and waves. The Lobsterman's Statue, which depicts local fisherman H. Elroy Johnston, overlooks Jaquish Gut and Jaquish Island at Land's End on the southern tip of Harpswell. The nearby Land's End Gift Shop has been a Maine souvenir shopper's must-see for more than 50 years (maine gifts.com; 207-833-2313).

3
MIDCOAST

THIS SECTION INCLUDES THE ENTIRETY OF Sagadahoc, Lincoln, Knox, and Waldo counties, a land area of 1,806 square miles, and is bounded by Cumberland, Androscoggin, Kennebec, Somerset, and Penobscot counties; the Penobscot River; and the Atlantic Ocean from Penobscot Bay to Casco Bay. A plethora of land trusts and conservation groups have worked to preserve the natural beauty of this part of the Maine coast while building many miles of trails.

From the eastern margin of Casco Bay, the section is bounded by the New Meadows River as far as Bath, then by the Androscoggin River west and north to Lisbon Falls. The Cathance River Nature Preserve protects several miles of Cathance River frontage in the lower Kennebec River and Androscoggin River watersheds (Trip 16). The Whiskeag Trail in Bath, a collaborative project of the Kennebec Estuary Land Trust, Bath Trails, and others, is a pleasant country walk through the oft-wild and wooded outskirts of town (Trip 17). The Center Pond Preserve in Phippsburg is fine example of the many such conservation efforts of the Phippsburg land Trust (Trip 18).

The section boundary trends east to Pleasant Pond in Litchfield. It cuts north to the Sebasticook River at Peltona Bridge. Moving east and south around Troy to Jackson, the section encompasses Monroe and Winterport to Barrett's Cove on the Penobscot River, 8 miles south of downtown Bangor.

The section advances southward on the river, past Verona Island, the Penobscot Narrows Bridge and Observatory, and into Penobscot Bay. From here, the line is defined by the coast, which includes notable landmarks such as the big islands of Islesboro, North Haven, and Vinalhaven; the coastal towns of Camden and Rockland; and Port Clyde, all with a jumble of good-size hills and mountains as a backdrop. Trips in this part of the section include a swath of land, two reservoirs, and a river corridor (Trip 29) conserved by the Belfast Bay Watershed Coalition and the Belfast Water District. Farther south, the magnificent Camden Hills (Trip 28) are found along the western margin of Penobscot Bay, affording panoramic ocean vistas from many points. Extending far out into the blue waters of Megunticook Lake, the Coastal Mountains Land Trust's Fernald's Neck Preserve protects outstanding groves of old growth pines and hemlocks (Trip 27). The Georges Highland Path is an ambitious trail project spearheaded by the Georges River Land Trust; perhaps its most spectacular miles are those that traverse the cliffs and ledges of Ragged Mountain in Rockport (Trip 26) on lands protected by the Coastal Mountains Land Trust.

From Port Clyde south and west, a series of long, finger-like peninsulas interspersed with deep bays indent the undulating shoreline. The coast rounds Friendship to reach the myriad islands of Muscongus Bay, home to Eastern Egg Rock and a significant nesting colony of Atlantic puffins. Beyond Pemaquid Point and its lighthouse are Johns Bay, Christmas Cove, and the mouth of the Damariscotta River. Between Ocean Point, Cape Newagen, and the Cuckolds Light are Linekin Bay and the lovely Boothbay Harbor. Across the wide entrance to Sheepscot Bay is Georgetown Island. Offshore of Popham Beach and the mouth of the Kennebec River is Sequin Island and its famous light. Enjoy the bold oceanfront rocks at La Verna Nature Preserve in Bristol (Trip 22), compliments of the Pemaquid Watershed Association. Ten miles offshore, Monhegan Associates has conserved more than half of the ruggedly beautiful Monhegan Island (Trip 23). The Damariscotta River Association protects important habitat around Great Salt Bay (Trip 21). The Boothbay Region Land Trust showcases it conservation efforts with the Ovens Mouth Preserve in Boothbay (Trip 20). Reid State Park offers miles of beach roaming and ocean swimming, plus a network of forested trails (Trip 19).

The hilly rural interior of the Midcoast becomes mountainous as you travel north and east toward Penobscot Bay. In Jefferson, a 1,000-acre nature preserve and outdoor education facility protects the hills around Little Dyer Pond (Trip 25). Amid a jumble of forested hills in the Montville, Knox, Freedom, and Liberty area, the Sheepscot Wellspring Land Alliance has protected 1,500 acres and constructed a 25-mile network of trails (Trip 24).

TRIP 16
CATHANCE RIVER NATURE PRESERVE

Location: Topsham, ME
Rating: Moderate
Distance: 4.1 miles
Elevation Gain: 210 feet
Estimated Time: 2.5 hours
Maps: USGS Brunswick; *Maine Atlas and Gazetteer*, Map 6 (DeLorme); *Cathance River Preserve Trail Map* (Cathance River Education Alliance)

Hike along a spectacular stretch of the sinuous Cathance River through a nature preserve, where a cool forest walk leads past placid pools and roaring rapids.

DIRECTIONS

From the junction of ME 196 and US 201 in Topsham (0.7 mile east of I-295, Exit 31), drive east on ME 196 for 0.5 mile. At the sign for the Highland Green retirement community, turn left onto Village Drive and proceed into the complex. In 0.7 mile, pass the clubhouse of Highland Green Golf Course, and just ahead, reach Evergreen Circle and a sign for the Cathance River Nature Preserve. Turn right here and in 0.1 mile, where Redpoll Drive goes left, continue straight ahead on a dirt road. Follow this for 0.6 mile, turning left at a T intersection (sign) and then bearing right at a Y junction, to reach the trailhead parking lot on the left. There is space for three cars in the fenced-in area, with more nearby. A kiosk is located here. Heath Trail, the first trail of this hike, starts through the fence just to the left of the kiosk. *GPS coordinates: 43° 57.114′ N, 69° 56.831′ W.*

TRAIL DESCRIPTION

The Cathance River meanders for more than 16 miles from its source in the wooded hills of Litchfield through Bowdoin, Topsham, and Bowdoinham, where it empties into the waters of Merrymeeting Bay. En route, where the river bends sharply to the east, not far from I-295 and the busy downtown areas of Topsham and Brunswick, you'll find the Cathance River Nature Preserve, a 230-acre sanctuary of woods and wildlife. The preserve includes a wild and scenic section of the river, which drops an impressive 80 feet over 1.5 miles and constitutes an expert canoe run of Class III and IV whitewater.

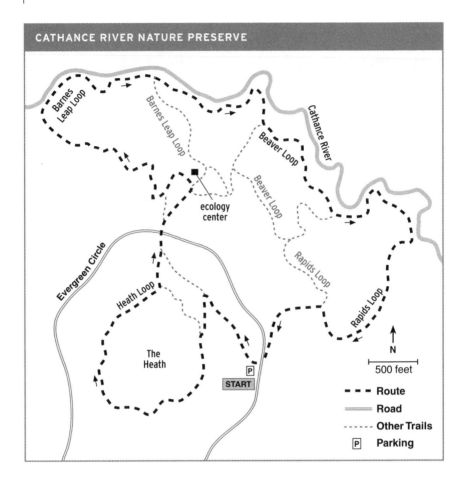

CATHANCE RIVER NATURE PRESERVE

In 2000, as part of the approval process for the Highland Green retirement community development, an agreement was forged between Central Topsham Associates, LLC, the developer, and a citizen's group called Topsham's Future. The agreement established the Cathance River Education Alliance (CREA) and the preserve along the Cathance River, which accounted for more than one-third of the total acreage of the planned campus. The Cathance River Nature Preserve is cooperatively managed by the Brunswick-Topsham Land Trust, Highland Green, and the CREA, whose mission it is to provide education and promote proper stewardship of the conservation land and the Cathance River. Five miles of well-blazed hiking trails meander through the preserve, each forming a loop. This hike covers a portion of four of the five trails, including the Heath, Barnes Leap, Beaver, and Rapids loops.

Heath Loop, marked by green blazes, leads through a semi-open stretch of mixed woods to a junction. The former trail to the right is closed, so turn left

Pancake ice, like that pictured in the Cathance River, can form on the outer bends in a river where accelerating water creates rotational shear force that grinds pieces of ice into smooth circles.

to quickly reach Heath Loop. Turn left onto the loop to circumnavigate the 30-acre heath clockwise. Partway along, the trail merges with a hardened, accessible path. Along this is a spur trail leading to a boulder and bench on the edge of the heath. Cross multiple bog bridges as you continue.

On the west side of the heath are several old quarry ponds, remnants of the feldspar mining in operation here from the mid-1800s into the 1950s. The mineral feldspar was important for making ceramics, pottery, abrasive soaps, and even false teeth. By the 1920s mills in Topsham were producing one-eighth of all the feldspar mined in the US and one-sixteenth of the world's entire production.

At the north end of the heath, turn left to leave the loop (sign for ecology center) and pass between several homes. Pass a former trail on the right and then a sign for Barnes Leap Loop. Cross Evergreen Circle, then take the steps down into the woods. Just ahead, where Barnes Leap Loop goes straight, bear right onto the dirt road (also Beaver Loop) and follow it to the ecology center, the obvious red building in the open area just ahead.

The ecology center, completed in 2006, was built to serve as a model of sustainability with a number of green-energy features, like photovoltaic panels on the roof, a wind turbine, special thermal insulation in the walls, and a wood pellet stove. The center is home to a variety of ongoing environmental education programs for children and adults alike. It is open to the public on the first Sunday of every month (seasonally) from 11 A.M. to 2 P.M.

From the kiosk in front of the center, take Barnes Leap Loop and soon reach a wooden viewing platform that looks out over the large vernal pool. Swing around the pool and cross a rocky ledge to reach a junction. Here, Vernal Pool Loop goes straight; turn right to remain on red-blazed Barnes Leap Loop. The path winds through dense forest, tops out on a rocky knoll, and descends toward the Cathance River. After crossing a creeklet, pass by a huge old hemlock, then meander down through a hemlock grove and scattered old bull pines.

Reach a wide turn in the Cathance River and turn right to follow along its south bank. After a bench beneath a tall white pine, the path swings around another turn in the placid river. Just beyond, the river begins to drop, the roar of rapids signaling its descent through a short gorge.

At an old bridge site (fenced off for safety) and bench, Barnes Leap Loop departs right, but continue straight ahead along the river on a connector trail that leads to Beaver Loop. Along here the river makes several S turns, flows around an island, and drops over ledges.

Avoid the spur trail on the right leading to Barnes Leap Loop and remain on the river, which flows around a larger island and then falls over a ledge drop into a big pool. Here the trail cuts across the steep bank above. Ahead, where the trail traverses a point of land, a spur leads left to a big turn in the river.

Back on the main path, the river makes another ledge drop and churns into more rapids below. Bear right uphill to connect with Beaver Loop. Here, turn left and follow yellow-blazed Beaver Loop along the river. Pass below a rock outcrop to reach a spur to a viewpoint overlooking a big bend in the river. Beyond, the trail trends away from the river and soon travels along a bluff high above it. At the junction of Beaver Loop and Rapids Loop, turn left onto blue-blazed Rapids Loop to continue along the river.

The path descends to the river's edge at a wide bend. Cross a creeklet on an old footbridge and amble through an understory of young hemlocks along the once again placid river. But here the river turns and enters a gorge to flow over a series of ledge drops and then down a corkscrew falls complete with a big rooster tail. Whitewater paddlers know this spectacular section of river as the Magic Carpet Ride, a Class IV drop.

Rapids Loop circumvents the frothy white falls on a ridge above before winding down and around to a spur trail leading left to a wonderful river-level view of the falls from a semi-open point of land replete with red and white pines.

Ahead, the river drops into one last pool before the trail turns right and leads up a slope away from the Cathance River. Above, it's easy going on a wide trail through a young stand of beech, maple, and birch trees.

Just beyond a large rock outcrop on the right, the path bears left through a semi-open field that is certain to be chock-full of raspberries in late summer.

The trail soon meets the orange-blazed Ravine Loop. Here, turn right to continue on Rapids Loop, which soon crosses a wide wooden footbridge. Fifty feet beyond the bridge at a junction, where Rapids Loop goes right, stay straight on an old woods road. At a T junction not far ahead, go left, pass around a gate, then cross the dirt road (Evergreen Circle). The trailhead parking lot is just 50 feet beyond.

DID YOU KNOW?

Cathance is the American Indian name for the river; it means "crooked," an apt description for a river that follows a sinuous course south, then east, then north, and finally south again.

MORE INFORMATION

Cathance River Education Alliance (creamaine.org; 207-331-3202). A trail map is available on their website.

NEARBY

Brunswick and Topsham have a complete range of civilized amenities. The Peary-MacMillan Arctic Museum, located in Hubbard Hall on the campus of Bowdoin College in downtown Brunswick, features a collection of artifacts and images relating to the arctic exploration and research of Robert E. Peary and Donald B. MacMillan from the early to mid-1900s (bowdoin.edu/arctic-museum; 207-725-3416).

MORE HIKING

Cathance River Trail connects Head of Tide Park on Cathance Road with Ravine Loop in Cathance River Nature Preserve, a distance of about two lovely miles. The Brunswick-Topsham Land Trust is a good source for plenty of other local walking opportunities (btlt.org; 207-729-7694), as are the towns of Topsham (topshammaine.com; 207-725-5821) and Brunswick (brunswickme. org; 207-725-6659). The *Bowdoin College Trail Guide* is an excellent resource for hiking trails in the six-town region of Freeport, Brunswick, Topsham, Bath, West Bath, and Harpswell (bowdoin.edu/it/pdf/trailguide.pdf).

TRIP 17
WHISKEAG TRAIL

Location: Bath, ME
Rating: Moderate
Distance: 5.3 miles, one-way
Elevation Gain: 125 feet
Estimated Time: 3.5 hours
Maps: USGS Bath; *Maine Atlas and Gazetteer*, Map 6 (DeLorme); *Whiskeag Trail* (Bath Trails)

Take a hike on this diverse pathway connecting the wilds of Thorne Head and Sewall Woods along Whiskeag Creek.

DIRECTIONS

Southbound on US 1: Cross the bridge over the Kennebec River into downtown Bath and immediately take the Front Street exit off US 1. Proceed past Front Street and Water Street to Washington Street. Turn right onto Washington Street and go one block. Turn left onto Centre Street and go 0.2 mile to High Street. Turn right onto High Street and follow it 2.1 miles to its end at a trailhead parking lot in the Thorne Head Preserve, where there is space for ten cars and an information kiosk.

Northbound on US 1: Take the exit for High Street and ME 209 in Bath. At the top of the ramp, turn left onto High Street and follow it 2.2 miles to its end. *GPS coordinates: 43° 56.586′ N, 69° 49.116′ W.*

To spot car at the southern end of the hike: From the junction of Centre Street and High Street in Bath (see above), drive 0.4 mile west on Centre Street to the city of Bath YMCA. Park in the paved lot in front of the YMCA; the trailhead kiosk is found to the left of the building. *GPS coordinates: 43° 54.817′ N, 69° 49.680′ W.*

TRAIL DESCRIPTION

Whiskeag Trail traverses three conservation preserves and several municipally owned properties on its 5-mile journey through the wooded outskirts of the city of Bath, much of it along the waters of Whiskeag Creek. The trail is a project of Bath Trails, a collaboration of the Kennebec Estuary Land Trust, the city of Bath, Healthy Maine Partnerships, schools, mountain bikers, land owners, and citizens. Once overseeing a system of unofficial paths, the Bath Trails group worked for four years to establish a formal trail corridor and continuous trail connections with adequate signage. Using 200 acres of Kennebec Estuary Land Trust holdings at Thorne Head, Sewall Woods, and Whiskeag Creek preserves—plus 450 acres of city land at Bath Landfill, Bath Public Works, Oak Grove Cemetery, McMann Fields, Bath Middle School, and Bath YMCA— Whiskeag Trail was finally opened to the public in 2010.

Close to downtown yet with a wild and primitive feel along much of its length, Whiskeag Trail offers fine hiking and opportunities for running, mountain biking, birding, and other low-impact outdoor recreation, while protecting important wetland habitat that is home to several threatened species of plants and fish.

Blue-blazed Whiskeag Trail leaves from the left side of the parking lot and heads north into the 96-acre Thorne Head Preserve, which protects more than a half-mile of shoreline along the Kennebec River and Whiskeag Creek. Cross a creeklet on a footbridge and quickly arrive at a T junction. White-blazed Ridge Runner Trail leaves to the right here, but bear left to follow Whiskeag Trail past boulders and big pines. Trend downslope on the wide track, passing by the Bath Landfill on the left as you go. Cross a shallow ravine, turn sharply right and hike over a low hill through a hemlock wood. Pass through a stone wall and then by a huge, half-dead white pine to arrive at a junction. Here, a white-blazed trail goes right to the top of Thorne Head; stay left, heading west on the undulating trail to reach Narrows Trail, which departs right. Continue southward on the Whiskeag Trail to follow along the edge of Whiskeag Creek. Ahead, a side trail leads 100 feet right to a viewpoint on Whiskeag Creek amid a stand of red and white pines.

Back on Whiskeag Trail, swing around a small cove to cross a wet, rooty area, then pass through a grove of nice 12-inch diameter white pines. After a short footbridge over North Creek, the trail returns to the water's edge. Beyond, Blue Dot Trail leaves to the right; stay straight on Whiskeag Trail to enjoy views of the creek through the hemlocks and old pasture pines. Pass by the corner of a stone wall, then turn sharply right (marked by double blaze on large oak). Soon, a side trail on the right leads 150 feet to an outlook with a fine view up and down Whiskeag Creek.

The stretch of trail ahead goes over a series of bog bridges, walkways, and a short footbridge. Keep an eye out for eagles, ospreys and hawks, herons, egrets and ducks, and other birds while along the creek. The woods and waters en route are also home beavers, deer, coyotes, and wild turkeys.

Bear away from the creek on the raised and hardened trailway. Climb an easy slope to swing behind the landfill. Ahead on the level, take a sharp right

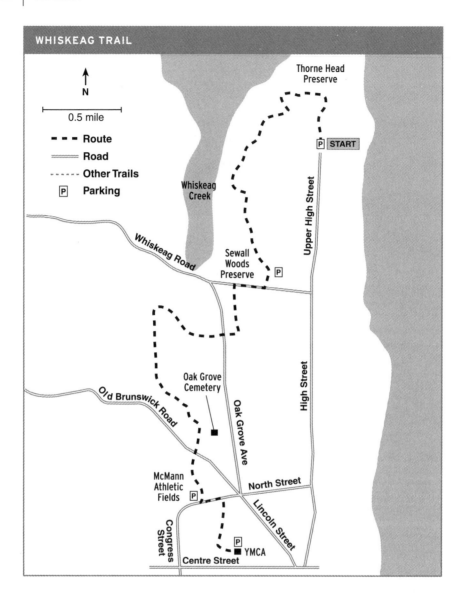

WHISKEAG TRAIL

N

0.5 mile

- - - Route
═══ Road
----- Other Trails
P Parking

Thorne Head Preserve

P START

Whiskeag Creek

Upper High Street

Whiskeag Road

Sewall Woods Preserve P

High Street

Oak Grove Cemetery

Old Brunswick Road

Oak Grove Ave

McMann Athletic Fields P

North Street

Lincoln Street

Congress Street

P YMCA

Centre Street

(left here leads to the landfill) through the thick growth of young pines. The trail now follows a long ledge of rock and soon bears left to make a short climb to a ridge. Bear left along a stone wall, going past a spur to an old foundation. After a stone wall, climb a knob and then saunter easily along a ridge. Pass by a white-blazed trail on the right, then cross several bog bridges.

Where an unmarked but well-worn trail leads left uphill, bear right and down slightly to enter Sewall Woods, a 91-acre preserve that protects 2,300 feet of frontage on Whiskeag Creek and its brackish tidal marshes. Ahead

The fresh water of Whiskeag Creek flows north from its source at Lilly Pond to empty into the brackish estuarine waters of the Kennebec River at Thorne Head.

at a big blue signpost, turn left onto a white-blazed trail to head to the Sewall Woods trailhead parking lot on Whiskeag Road at 2 miles. A sign indicates that Thorne Head is to the right, while McMann Field and the YMCA are to the left.

Turn right onto Whiskeag Road and walk west for 0.2 mile. Cross the road (trail sign in pine tree) just before a white house with a red barn. Hike the lovely footpath along the fence line, fields to the left and homes to the right. Ahead at a stone wall, take a sharp right (west) to follow around behind an apartment complex.

Cross Oak Grove Road, then a small creek on a bog bridge. Pass by a Quonset-shaped building as well as a number of other structures within the fenced enclosure of the Bath Public Works complex. With a powerline and big pine stump on the left, bear right uphill. Beyond a wet area and deep streambed, saunter through thick pines and then hemlocks. The path circles around the city maintenance complex to return to Whiskeag Creek.

There are few signs of civilization outside of one house on this quiet stretch. Kayakers often float on the cove, while mountain bikers frequent this section of trail, but mostly it's a surprisingly wild and tranquil spot. Further ahead, pass a huge boulder and rock amphitheater just left of the trail, then a sitting bench at a powerline crossing. Cross an old woods road, then swing back to the creek to pass an old and gnarled three-stemmed sugar maple on the right.

Continuing south along the water, the creek narrows, and there are several sunny, grassy spots along its banks. Look for an old railroad trestle on the other side of the creek. After a wet ravine bottom, bear sharply left and switchback up a hill. At Cemetery Road, turn left, and at the next trail sign, turn right. Ahead, cross the John C. "Jack" Hart Jr. Memorial Bridge, built in 2008, over the railroad tracks.

After the bridge, bear left at a fork and follow the road around the perimeter of Oak Grove Cemetery and then out to Old Brunswick Road. Cross the road and enter the woods beyond. Pass to the left of the athletic fields, descend an easy slope through the pines, then bear left around behind the baseball fields. Morse Stadium and basketball courts are in view farther off to the right. Bath Middle School is up to the left. Pass to the left of the tennis courts to reach a kiosk and the parking lots for the Edward J. McMann Outdoor Recreation Area. Beyond, cross Congress Avenue, then a cattail swamp on a footbridge.

The wide trail soon narrows and climbs a spine of rock in a cool hemlock forest. Follow the foot trail behind the YMCA. Follow along a stone wall, then climb up a few feet to reach the Born Learning Trail area. A trailhead kiosk marking the southern end of Whiskeag Trail is just ahead, right of the YMCA and just before the parking lot.

DID YOU KNOW?

Whiskeag Creek gets its name from an Abenaki word meaning "a creek that runs dry at low tides." The fresh water of Whiskeag Creek flows north from its source at Lilly Pond not far from downtown Bath, joining the brackish estuarine waters of the Kennebec River at Thorne Head.

MORE INFORMATION

Kennebec Estuary Land Trust (kennebecestuary.org, 207-442-8400). Bath Trails (cityofbath.com/Bath-Trails, 207-443-8360). Whiskeag Trail and Thorne Head and Sewall Woods preserves are open from dawn to dusk year-round. Dogs are welcome on leash.

NEARBY

Stroll the streets of the historic and picturesque city of Bath on the west shore of the Kennebec River, then take in the Maine Maritime Museum for a taste of Maine's rich seafaring history, from watercraft and lobstering to shipbuilding and the sea trade. Take a trolley tour inside the gates of neighboring Bath Iron Works for a fascinating look at how modern U.S. Navy destroyers are built (mainemaritimemuseum.org).

TRIP 18
CENTER POND PRESERVE

Location: Phippsburg, ME
Rating: Moderate
Distance: 4.7 miles
Elevation Gain: 520 feet
Estimated Time: 3.0 hours
Maps: USGS Phippsburg; *Maine Atlas and Gazetteer*, Map 6
(DeLorme); *Center Pond Preserve: Trail Map and Guide* (Phippsburg
Land Trust)

**In historic Phippsburg, explore the natural environs around Center
Pond, from pleasant forests and old stone walls to granite ridge
tops and a beaver bog.**

DIRECTIONS

From the junction of US 1 and ME 209 in Bath, take the exit ramp and proceed to its end at High Street (ME 209). Turn right (south) and follow ME 209
through the outskirts of Bath. At 2.5 miles, ME 209 bears left across a bridge
over Winnegance Creek, which feeds into the Kennebec River, off in the distance to the north. At 6.0 miles, pass Drummore Bay, an arm of the Kennebec
River that passes around the west side of Lee Island. At 6.6 miles, with Bisson's
Center Store on the right, turn left (east) onto Parker Head Road. Enter the
village of Phippsburg and soon cross a narrow causeway, with Center Pond on
the right and the Kennebec River on the left. Just uphill from the causeway, at
7.1 miles, reach a sign for Center Pond Preserve and the trailhead on the right,
where there is parking for six to eight cars. *GPS coordinates: 43° 48.887′ N,
69° 48.584′ W.*

TRAIL DESCRIPTION

Center Pond Preserve is a 253-acre parcel owned and managed by the Phippsburg Land Trust, its first, largest, and most popular conservation property. The
trust owns 450 acres of land outright and holds conservation easements on another 350 acres on eighteen separate properties on the Phippsburg Peninsula.
In the mid-1990s, former summer resident Eleanor Cooley of West Newton,
Massachusetts, put what is now the preserve up for sale. Local townspeople,

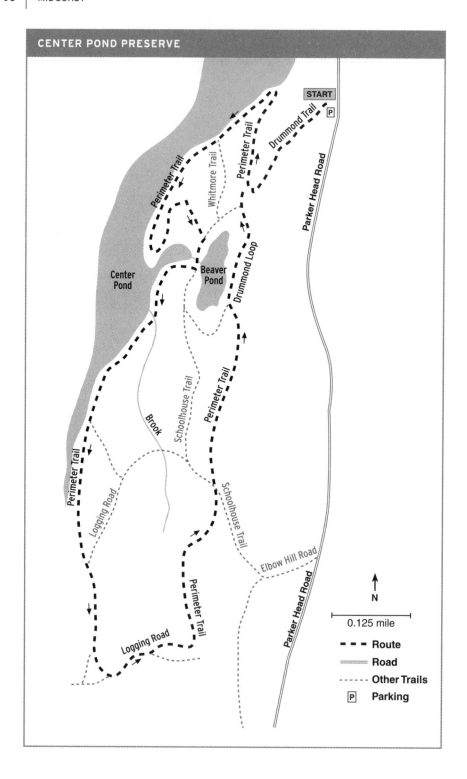

CENTER POND PRESERVE

START

P

Drummond Trail

Perimeter Trail

Whitmore Trail

Perimeter Trail

Parker Head Road

Drummond Loop

Center
Pond

Beaver
Pond

Perimeter Trail

Schoolhouse Trail

Brook

Logging Road

Perimeter Trail

Schoolhouse Trail

Elbow Hill Road

Perimeter Trail

Logging Road

Parker Head Road

N

0.125 mile

- - - Route

Road

- - - - Other Trails

P   Parking

recognizing the tremendous historical, scenic, and recreational value of the Center Pond parcel, raised the necessary funds to buy it.

Five trails crisscross the Center Pond Preserve, providing 10 miles of hiking over two granite ridges and into two ravines, past a number of vernal pools in season, and to an old beaver pond tucked away in the middle of the preserve. The central feature, of course, is Center Pond, an 84-acre shallow-water gem that is popular for ice fishing in winter and paddling in summer. Hikers like it too, and several miles of pleasant foot trails trace a winding route along its scenic eastern shore. To fully explore the natural beauty and abundant wildlife at Center Pond, tackle this nearly 5-mile loop on portions of Patrick Drummond Trail and the entirety of Perimeter Trail.

From the trailhead information kiosk (maps are usually available here), take orange-blazed Patrick Drummond Trail uphill through a stone wall. Climb easily through a forest of pines and oaks to reach the ridge line, pass by a corner post in a stone wall on the left, then trend downhill to the right. A short spur leads to a ledge-top view over the woods below. Continue walking along the ridge, then take one long switchback into a shallow ravine to the junction with Perimeter Trail.

Drummond Trail turns left here, but you'll continue to the right on red-blazed Perimeter Trail. Head up the ravine through young hardwoods, with ledges rising up to the right. Pass between a low wet area and the cliff face and a jumble of boulders covered with a thick growth of ferns, moss, and lettuce lichen. Soon, the wide trail trends downhill through a shallow ravine to the Center Pond. Where Perimeter Trail makes a sharp left, a spur trail leads 75 feet to the shore of the pond and views across it to a white farmhouse and ME 209.

Back on the main trail, follow the shoreline through hemlocks and oaks with views north to the causeway and the white steeple of Phippsburg Congregational Church. Amid cedars and pines, pass an outlook on a ledge, then follow a narrow, undulating trail to another viewpoint at the water's edge.

Hike around a small cove to a point shaded by white pines and a broad view up the pond to Phippsburg village. Continue ahead at pond level, ascend to a ledge, then drop down again. Phippsburg Town Hall comes into view across the water on ME 209.

Swing around to the east on a level point of pines and oaks, with Minott Island off to the right. Anywhere along here would make for a nice lunch or snack stop.

Follow the shore of the cove through semi-open forest, and then bear away from the pond through mixed woods. Swing back toward the pond again, rising over a low knoll. Then take a sharp right past a cellar hole on the left, and the remains of some old apple trees and field pines.

Ahead, cross a stone wall and immediately bear right onto a wide trail, a former road that passes through a wet area. Reach the junction with Patrick Drummond Trail near the old beaver pond and bear right. Follow the wide trail past the beaver bog, with an arm of Center Pond visible to the right, then cross the outlet on bog bridging. From a rock just beyond the outlet, enjoy a nice view down the bog, where there are plenty of cranberries to pick in season.

Shortly after the outlet, follow Perimeter Trail as it diverges right. Track the outlet stream to the edge of Center Pond, with views to the pine point across the cove and Minott Island beyond. The trail hugs the shoreline before reaching an old woods road. Turn right here to cross an inlet stream on a short footbridge. Where the old road continues straight ahead, bear right onto Perimeter Trail. Hike along Center Pond to its narrow southern end, passing through a dense stand of hemlocks en route.

Bear left away from the pond, up a ravine next to a brook. At the junction with Middle Trail, continue to the right on Perimeter Trail to cross a dip on a bog bridge. Continue easily uphill through the hemlocks alongside the brook. Pass a metal boundary post stake. Drop into another ravine with a mossy rock face on the left. Scramble up through these rocks (*Note: this is an easy turn to miss!*) and soon arrive at another old woods road, the continuation of Middle Trail. Turn right here, and in 30 feet, bear left off the road (*Note: no sign; another turn easily missed*).

Quickly come to another old road and turn left. Ahead, leave the old road and pass between a wet area on the right and rock ledges on the left. Meander easily to the ridge top and a rock outcrop with treetop views. Follow the spine of the ridge, then descend, crossing the head of a ravine. Reach a junction with Schoolhouse Trail in an open area. Go straight to stay on Perimeter Trail.

Follow a long, dry ridge of scrub oaks and pitch pines, then cross a beautiful old stone wall. Beyond the wall, continue on the level for a distance, then trend gently downhill to a junction and bear right onto Drummond Trail. Pass around the east side of the old beaver bog on bog bridges, and cross an inlet to reach a junction where Drummond Trail bears left. Continue straight on Perimeter Trail. Close the loop at the original junction, and bear right out of the ravine on Drummond Trail back to the parking area.

DID YOU KNOW?

The English linden tree on the grounds of Phippsburg Congregational Church, just up the road from Center Pond, is well over 200 years old. It was planted sometime around 1774 by James McCobb when he built his house nearby.

MORE INFORMATION

Phippsburg Land Trust (phippsburglandtrust.org; 207-443-5993). Center Pond Preserve is open year-round. A trail map is available on-site and online.

NEARBY

The unfinished, semicircular fortification of Fort Popham is located on Hunnewell Point at the mouth of the Kennebec River, at the very end of ME 209 near the southern tip of the Phippsburg Peninsula. Construction of the fort began in 1861 but ended in 1869 before the work could be completed. The granite blocks for the fort were quarried on nearby Fox and Dix islands. The 30-foot high, crescent-shaped wall facing the river mouth measures nearly 500 feet in circumference. Fort Popham State Historic Site is open Memorial Day through September 30 (parksandlands.com; 207-389-1335).

In sight of the fort is the site of the short-lived Popham Colony. Established in 1607, this first English attempt to establish a permanent settlement in New England was abandoned just a year later. The first ship ever built in North America, the *Virginia of Sagadahoc*, was constructed nearby in 1608.

MORE HIKING

The Phippsburg Peninsula is home to a 31 miles of hiking trails on lands owned by Phippsburg Land Trust, The Nature Conservancy, Maine Coast Heritage Trust, Bates–Morse Mountain Conservation Area, Maine Department of Inland Fisheries & Wildlife, and Maine Department of Agriculture, Conservation, and Forestry, Bureau of Parks and Lands.

Sprague Pond Preserve abuts Basin Preserve and offer miles of great hiking. There is a maze of trails in the Ridgewell Preserve and the adjoining Phippsburg Town Forest. The Bijhouwer Forest is home to Maine's largest stand of mountain laurel, as well as a waterfall and a huge trailside boulder, while the trails at Spirit Pond Preserve wind around a lovely tidal embayment. Some 4 miles of trails wend along oceanfront beach and through quiet woods at Popham Beach State Park.

For a complete overview, get a paper copy of *Walking Phippsburg*, the trail guide published by the Phippsburg Land Trust.

MAINE'S LAND CONSERVATION MOVEMENT

Maine is a recognized as a national leader in conservation, not only in acreage preserved but in the number of land trusts and conservation organizations, which now total about 100 in the Maine Land Trust Network. Over the last 40 years, millions of acres in the state have been preserved.

Until the early 1970s, conservation lands in Maine were few and far between. Baxter State Park, Acadia National Park, the Allagash Wilderness Waterway, national wildlife refuges at Moosehorn and Rachel Carson, the White Mountain National Forest, and two dozen state parks accounted for just 1 percent of the Maine's landscape. When increasing development pressures and a burgeoning population began to alter the traditional character of the Maine coast, concerned citizens in communities from Kittery to Eastport began to take notice. Fearing the loss of critical wildlife habitat, scenic natural landscapes, and precious public access, a grassroots movement to protect and preserve the coastal islands, salt marshes, and headlands began.

The conservation easement became the tool of choice, followed later by outright land acquisition, with the state of Maine, The Nature Conservancy, and the Maine Coast Heritage Trust playing active roles early on. Soon, a growing number of citizens groups forming land trusts entered the conservation arena. The first Land for Maine's Future bond passed in 1987, making $35 million available to conservation groups statewide, one of eight such initiatives providing critical funding needed to protect many of special places threatened with development and loss of access.

Changes were also afoot in Maine's north woods. For more than a century, the paper companies that owned not only the mills but vast tracts of forest began to monetize their land assets by selling off large swaths of timberland, thereby threatening traditional uses such as forestry and recreation. But this period of uncertainty in the paper industry also created new and unforeseen opportunities for conservation, and over the next two decades many conservation projects of notable size and scale were secured. AMC's Maine Woods Initiative is part of this movement, protecting 66,500 acres of forestland.

Today, an estimated 20 percent of Maine's land area—3.97 million acres—is under some form of conservation protection, either owned outright or in conservation easement. This includes 1.73 million acres owned by conservation organizations, the state of Maine, or the federal government, and another 2.24 million acres in conservation easements.

TRIP 19
REID STATE PARK

Location: Georgetown, ME
Rating: Moderate
Distance: 4.7 miles
Elevation Gain: 345 feet
Estimated Time: 2.5 hours
Maps: USGS Boothbay Harbor; *Maine Atlas and Gazetteer*, Map 7 (DeLorme); mainetrailfinder.com

Explore a long stretch of sand beach, quiet coastal forests, and wildlife-rich wetlands on this pleasant walk through one of Maine's most popular state parks.

DIRECTIONS

From the junction of US 1 and ME 127 in Woolwich just east across the Kennebec River from Bath, turn south onto ME 127. Travel 10.4 miles through Arrowsic and Georgetown to the end of ME 127 at the junction of Five Islands Road and Seguinland Road. Bear right onto Seguinland Road and follow it 2.1 miles farther to the entrance station of Reid State Park. Just past the gatehouse at a Y junction, bear left onto Griffith Head Road. Ahead, pass the lower parking lot on the left before reaching the upper parking lot at the end of the road. Here you'll find picnic tables, a snack bar, and a bathhouse with flush toilets. A broad salt marsh and tidal lagoon with a small sandy beach is found to the right of the lot down the grassy slope. Mile Beach is reached by several paths emanating from the bathhouse at the south end of the lot. *GPS coordinates: 43° 46.536′ N, 69° 43.950′ W.*

TRAIL DESCRIPTION

Reid State Park, at the mouth of Sheepscot Bay on the southeastern tip of Georgetown Island, holds the honor as Maine's first state-owned saltwater beach. Local resident and businessman Walter E. Reid donated the land in 1946 for preservation. The 766-acre park is home to Mile Beach and Half Mile Beach, two of Maine's most beautiful sand beaches and rare natural gems on this rocky stretch of Maine's Midcoast. The beaches and the barrier dunes protecting them are home to endangered least terns and piping plovers and serve as resting and feeding areas for many other shorebirds. Two rocky headlands

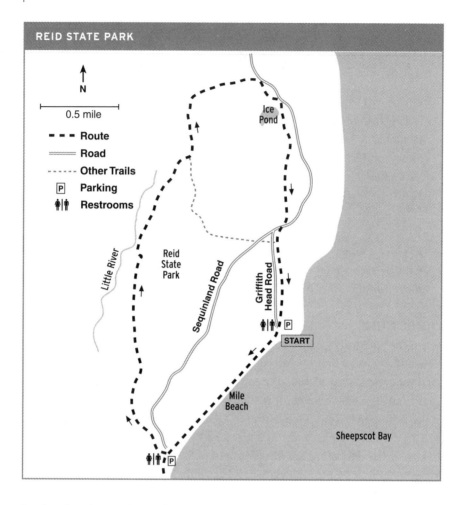

REID STATE PARK

N

0.5 mile

- - - Route
═══ Road
----- Other Trails
P Parking
Restrooms

Ice Pond

Little River

Reid State Park

Sequinland Road

Griffith Head Road

START

P

Mile Beach

Sheepscot Bay

bookend Mile Beach: Griffith Head to the east and Todd's Point to the west. From these rugged vantage points, sweeping ocean views stretch to the lighthouses on Seguin Island, the Cuckolds, and Hendricks Head, as well as Southport and Damariscove islands. The west side of the park is bounded by Little River and its extensive salt marshes. The interior of the park is home to mixed woodlands, wetlands, and a freshwater pond. For a good walking tour of the park's diverse landscapes, combine a stroll along the length of Mile Beach with a hike along Little River and Ski Loop trails to complete a pleasant loop.

Begin your hike at the park sign to the right of the bathhouse. Proceed toward the beach on the paved path, which quickly turns to gravel. Pass a bench and path to the beach on the right. Continue straight ahead to a junction. The short path to the left scrambles up through a thick growth of wild roses, beach peas, and poison ivy to the rocks of Griffith Head, a highly rewarding detour.

Mile Beach, bounded by the rocks of Griffith Head and Todd's Point, became Maine's first state-owned saltwater beach in 1946, donated for preservation by local resident and businessman Walter E. Reid.

To the right, the path leads down the steps and over the rocks to reach Mile Beach, the main route. For nearly a mile the trail treads the coarse sands of the beach, much of it pinkish-orange in color from its high feldspar mineral composition. To your right, the continuous high bank of the barrier dune stabilized with beach grass helps protect the salt marsh environment beyond. The rhythm of the breaking waves is constant and mesmerizing as you stroll along. Driftwood, seaweed, shells, and various other interesting items washed ashore offer the occasional diversion.

Nearing the trees of Todd's Point, angle right across the beach to the obvious path. Take this up and left to a parking lot and Todd's Point Bathhouse, where there are picnic tables, toilets, and a snack bar in season.

Half Mile Beach is just beyond and worth a short side trip. To reach Half Mile Beach from the bathhouse, continue left along the edge of the parking lot. Look for a low post that reads, "Do Not Block Road." The gravel-and-grass road beyond winds ahead through a corridor of beach rose and winterberry, first right then left to the beach, which extends southwest to Little River.

To continue the hike, retrace your steps to the parking lot. Turn left and follow the edge of the lot to its far end. There, angle right to the woods and a low post marked, "Do Not Block Road." Follow the grassy track beyond to a picnic area with a kiosk in a small field. Bear left and angle across the field into woods to find a footpath, the start of Little River Trail. A small brown-and-white sign just ahead on the right marks the trail.

Hike through the forest along the edge of the salt marsh, navigating the rocks and roots of the trail. Reach a grove of tall white pines and spruce, then a recently harvested area on the right. Pass around the cut area on the left to cross a mossy stone wall.

Continue along the often narrow wooded ridge bordering the marsh and river, a lovely meandering path on a soft carpet of needles. Ahead, the route undulates somewhat, up and down easily through gullies and along wet areas. After several boardwalks the terrain flattens out. Step across a short rock culvert, then ascend through huckleberries to an opening at a pair of green water tanks, a round concrete pad, and a power line, the conclusion of Little River Trail. Continue straight ahead and downhill on the old road to an unsigned junction. Ski Loop Trail, marked by blue paint blazes, is the woods road that goes left and right from this point.

Bear left onto the road to follow Ski Loop Trail clockwise. Ahead, pass through a small opening in the forest. Beyond, the trail narrows to a footpath with stone walls to either side. Pass an old apple orchard and foundation hole on the left. The wide path continues along the outer edge of the park boundary, often marked by "No Hunting" signs, to a large wetland on the right. Ahead, the trail bears sharply right just before the Seguinland Road. An old stone schoolhouse is visible across the road.

Continue through the cattails around the margin of the wetland to a stone causeway at the head of a pond. Cross and continue to circle the unnamed pond. Easy walking on a the level pathway leads past a cluster of maintenance buildings on the left. Beyond, the park gatehouse and a privy are visible through the woods up to the left.

Pass under a power line to reach the paved Todd's Point Road. Bear left across the road, then make an immediate right to quickly reach Griffith Head Road (the same road you drove in on). Follow this road back to your car, crossing a bridge over the tidal lagoon outlet en route.

DID YOU KNOW?

Before the park was established, World War II Navy fighter pilots from nearby Brunswick Naval Air Station trained by firing on floating targets moored just offshore from Mile Beach.

MORE INFORMATION

Reid State Park (parksandlands.com; 207-371-2303). The park is open year-round. There is a daily entrance fee. Dogs are allowed on-leash, but not on the beaches from April through September.

NEARBY

Enjoy a meal of fresh Maine lobsters on the wharf in the tiny fishing village of Five Islands, just off ME 127 on the Sheepscot River. In the picturesque city of Bath on the west shore of the Kennebec River, take in the Maine Maritime Museum for a taste of Maine's rich seafaring history, from watercraft and lobstering to shipbuilding and the sea trade. Include a trolley tour inside the gates of neighboring Bath Iron Works for a fascinating look at how modern U.S. Navy destroyers are built (mainemaritimemuseum.org).

MORE HIKING

The adjacent 119-acre Josephine Newman Audubon Sanctuary has 2.5 miles of trails featuring woods and meadows, rocky ridges and beaver ponds, and coastal walking along the saltwater Robinhood Cove (maineaudubon.org). Several preserves of the Kennebec Estuary Land Trust also offer several additional miles of hiking possibilities in Georgetown, including the Weber-Kelley and Higgins Mountain preserves (kennebecestuary.org).

TRIP 20
OVENS MOUTH PRESERVE

Location: Boothbay, ME
Rating: Moderate
Distance: 3.5 miles
Elevation Gain: 525 feet
Estimated Time: 2.5 hours
Maps: USGS Westport; *Maine Atlas and Gazetteer,* Map 7 (DeLorme), Ovens Mouth Preserve brochure and map

Three miles of moderate hiking lead through pleasant woodlands and along the salt marshes, tidal rivers, and basins of the secretive Ovens Mouth.

DIRECTIONS

From the junction of US 1 and ME 27 in Edgecomb, just east of the Sheepscot River and 1.5 miles from downtown Wiscasset, turn right (south) onto ME 27 and drive 8.0 miles. Turn right (west) onto Adams Pond Road and follow this for 0.2 mile to Dover Road. Turn right (north) onto Dover Road and drive 1.9 miles to Dover Cross Road. The preserve's eastern trailhead is straight ahead on Dover Road, another 0.5 mile past the intersection. To reach the western trailhead and the start of the described hike, drive left (west) on Dover Cross Road for an additional 0.2 mile, where a small parking area (sign) for three cars is found. *GPS coordinates: 43° 55.400′ N, 69° 38.553′ W.*

TRAIL DESCRIPTION

The Boothbay Region Land Trust purchased 146 acres encompassing the eastern and middle peninsulas on Ovens Mouth in 1994. Settled by Europeans in the mid-1700s, this narrow and deep passage connects the Sheepscot and Back rivers to Cross River, a large tidal basin. One of the area's first shipyards was located here, and American and British ships often hid in its coves during the Revolutionary War. After the Civil War, the Tibbetts and Welsh families acquired the land and owned it for more than a century. Today, Ovens Mouth is home to a variety of wildlife, including bald eagles, osprey, ducks, wading birds, otters, and harbor seals. Once almost entirely cleared for farm and pasture land, a large portion of the forest canopy on the heavily wooded property is now composed of eastern white pine. Five miles of trails wend through

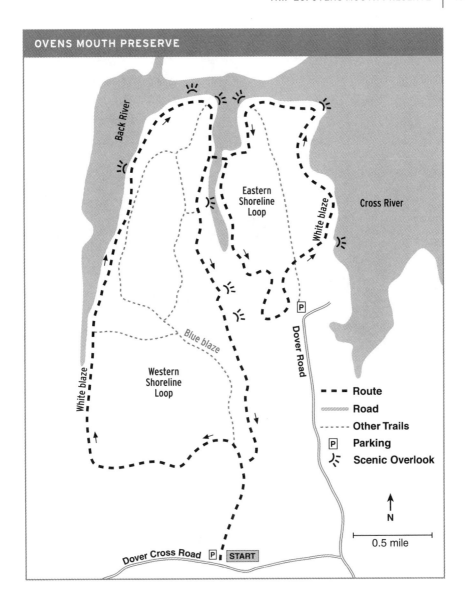

Ovens Mouth Preserve, tracing a route around the shoreline of both peninsulas and crisscrossing the interior, allowing for extensive exploration of its woodlands, coves, and salt marshes.

From the information kiosk at the western trailhead, take the wide trail easily uphill through the oak-and-pine forest, following white and blue blazes. Just beyond the crest of the hill, reach a junction, where a trail leaves to the right. Stay on the main path and quickly arrive at a second junction. Turn left (west) here and trend easily downhill on a pleasant path marked by red and

The secretive Ovens Mouth is a deep and narrow passage connecting the Sheepscot and Back rivers to the Cross River, an extensive tidal basin.

white blazes. Enter a dark forest of hemlocks in a ravine. Slab the steep hillside before descending to the head of a tidal inlet. Pass a trail on the right, and then climb briefly. Contour along to a viewpoint amid the pines and a split log bench overlooking a cove.

Just ahead, reach the Ovens Mouth and another viewpoint. A home and camp are visible across the passage, as are several landings. Look for sailboats and lobster boats plying the quick waters here. Turn east and hike through dense forest to another bench. Beyond, a short, steep climb leads to a junction with a spur trail on the left to a lookout and views of Ice House Cove and the footbridge connecting the two peninsulas. After moderate rise, reach a junction with a blue-blazed trail. Pass another bench before reaching another trail junction. Turn left (east) here and cross the bridge over Ice House Cove.

In 1880, Ice House Cove was dammed to form a freshwater pond, and an ice house was built. Ice was shipped from here as far south as Boston and New York to satisfy a growing demand. The remains of the old dam can be seen from the bridge at low tide.

Bear left after the bridge and meander along the eastern edge of the cove to a park bench on a scenic point amid a nice stand of red and white pines.

Ahead, the path reaches a bench on a point with sweeping views over Cross River basin. No development can be seen, only trees, shoreline, and water. Continuing on, hug the shoreline, then swing around another point, rising about 100 feet above the water. Pass a viewpoint on the left, cross a stone wall, and soon leave the cove.

The trail skirts a house and barn on the left before crossing a wide, grassy road. After a lovely stand of white pines, reach the eastern trailhead and its parking area and kiosk. Beyond, continue west to a salt marsh. Turn north and circle around the marsh to reach a bench at its far end, then follow the west shore of the inlet to the footbridge.

Cross the bridge again, then turn left and climb the hillside to a viewpoint high over the inlet. Continue to ascend, passing in and around mossy boulders to a trail junction. Ahead, wind along the rim several hundred feet above the salt marsh, passing a few outlook ledges. Finally, bear away from the rim and climb to meet the original trail junction. Turn left (south) here to return to the western trailhead.

DID YOU KNOW?

The Ovens Mouth was so named by early English explorers, who are thought to have seen in this natural feature—two coves projecting south from the water passage between the Back River and Cross River— a resemblance to a Dutch oven.

MORE INFORMATION

Boothbay Region Land Trust (bbrlt.org; 207-633-4818). The preserve is open year-round. Dogs are allowed, but must be kept in sight and under control. If the western trailhead parking area is full, try the eastern trailhead, a larger lot with space for four to five cars. The same loop hike can be done from there, with just a slight variation from the description. A trail map is available online.

NEARBY

The pretty village of Boothbay Harbor is situated near the southern end of the Boothbay Peninsula. A classic maritime New England fishing port, Boothbay Harbor is also a busy summer tourist attraction, its narrow waterfront streets chock-full of shops and galleries, restaurants and pubs. A walk across the harbor on the famous footbridge is recommended for a nice salty air stroll, especially around sunset. Learn more about marine life on the Maine coast at the Maine State Aquarium, operated by the Maine Department of Marine Resources, on the west shore of the harbor.

TRIP 21
SALT BAY HERITAGE TRAIL

Location: Newcastle, ME
Rating: Easy
Distance: 3.0 miles
Elevation Gain: 105 feet
Estimated Time: 2.0 hours
Maps: USGS Damariscotta; *Maine Atlas and Gazetteer*, Map 7 (DeLorme); mainetrailfinder.com

Follow the shoreline of Great Salt Bay, a tidal estuary rich with marine, bird, and animal life, to the Glidden Midden, an ancient oyster shell heap on the Damariscotta River.

DIRECTIONS
From the intersection of US 1B and ME 215 in Newcastle, drive north on ME 215. In 0.4 mile, pass underneath US 1. In another 0.2 mile, pass the Newcastle Post Office on the left, and immediately beyond, the Lincoln County Publishing Company. Trailhead parking is in the gravel lot behind the business, next to ME 215 (Mills Road) at the far end away from the office. Directly across the road is a green sign that reads, "Great Salt Bay Preserve—Hart Family Heritage Trail." *GPS coordinates: 44° 2.514′ N, 69° 31.969′ W.*

TRAIL DESCRIPTION
The watershed of the Upper Damariscotta River is one of immense natural beauty, a scenic landscape of bays and islands, salt marshes and mud flats, and rivers and streams. Bordered by hills, fields, and forests, the nutrient-rich tidal estuary is home to a diverse array of marine life, birds, and animal life. The Damariscotta River Association (DRA), established in 1973, has worked to protect more than 2,900 acres of land and 23 miles of shoreline here. The majority of the area around shallow, warm, and brackish Great Salt Bay was designated the state's first Marine Shellfish Preserve by the Maine legislature in 2002 "because of its undisturbed nature, its support of common and uncommon biodiversity, and its rich prehistoric and historic record," according to the DRA. Take advantage of numerous opportunities to explore this special area, starting with Salt Bay Heritage Trail.

Cross Mill Road, enter the woods, and quickly reach an information kiosk with trail maps. Immediately beyond, the trail turns sharply right. It soon leaves the woods and arrives at two interpretive signs. Ahead, the path makes a wide arc around the southwest cove through a salt marsh on plank bridges (may be submerged at high tide; plan accordingly). Amid the eelgrass, look for the skeletons of horseshoe crabs, which are shed as they grow, much the same as lobsters. Horseshoe crabs are neither crabs nor crustaceans but members of the arachnid family and related to spiders and ticks. Great Salt Bay is an important breeding ground for these ancient creatures, which have survived nearly unchanged for 200 million years.

Poison ivy is prevalent along the trail through the salt marsh, but can be avoided with care. After paralleling US 1 for a distance, the trail leaves the marsh and enters a wood of oaks and pines. Proceeding on the soft, needle-covered trail with occasional sections of roots, swing around a point on the far side of the cove and turn east, hugging the shore of the bay. Along Great Salt Bay from Grandfather Point to Lookout Point there are numerous spots where you can scramble out among the rocks and seaweed at low tide to enjoy broad views over the bay and look for clam, mussel, and horseshoe crab shells. Bald eagles, ospreys, herons, kingfishers, cormorants, and gulls are commonly seen.

Beyond the wooden benches at Grandfather Point, turn inland and cross a tidal cove on an aluminum footbridge. Return to the shore of the bay and soon reach the park-like Picnic Point in a lovely grove of white pines. A spur trail to the left leads 50 feet to the water's edge amid junipers and a lone white pine.

Beyond, follow the grassy trail through the pines, then swing inland through a stand of old field pines. On the far side of a shallow cove, pass through a thick growth of young balsam fir, then large hemlocks beyond. Pass a painted rock in a small clearing and soon reach Lookout Point. A spur trail here leads left to a bench and views across the bay to Salt Bay Farm and the headquarters of the DRA. The US 1 bridge over the Damariscotta River is visible to the south.

The trail continues on around Glidden Point, first passing through a stand of spruce trees bearded with moss, then some large red and white oaks and hemlocks. Beyond a large boulder, the trail swings inland slightly to follow the ridge of an esker. Soon after a large, green, lichen-covered rock, the path parallels US 1 along a fence line.

Cross beneath US 1 using an old sheep culvert. Occasionally the culvert may fill with water and you will have to carefully cross over the highway above. Emerging on the other side of the road, the trail soon reaches a junction. A small sign points left to "middens."

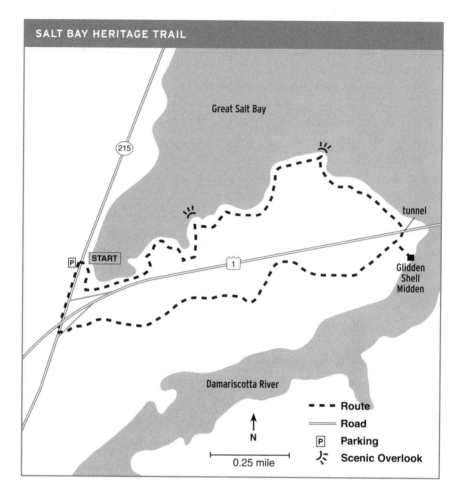

SALT BAY HERITAGE TRAIL

Great Salt Bay

215

tunnel

START

Glidden Shell Midden

Damariscotta River

- - - Route
===== Road
P Parking
Scenic Overlook

N

0.25 mile

Follow the spur 100 yards to the shore of the Damariscotta River. To the left along the river is a high bank of bright-white oyster shells known as the Glidden Midden. This impressive ancient shell heap—30 feet deep, 150 feet long, and 75 feet wide—is estimated to be 2,400 years old and represents the refuse accumulated by American Indians over the course of 1,500 years of feasting on this spot.

Directly across the river are the remains of the once equally prominent Whaleback Midden, now a state historic site. The archaeological treasures on both sides are recorded in the National Register of Historic Places, and federal law prohibits disturbing them in any way.

Back at the main trail junction, head south amid the tall pines and hemlocks on a low ridge between the road and the river. Stay straight at a junction with an old woods road entering from the left. Ahead, reach a side trail leading

The oyster shell midden on the Damariscotta River at Glidden Point is estimated to be 2,400 years old and represents the refuse accumulated by American Indians over the course of 1,500 years of eating on this spot.

left to a large field and then another 100 yards down to the river. The main trail follows the wood line along the edge of the field. Avoid a spur to US 1 on the right. Beyond, the trail narrows briefly, then passes left of a tidal marsh, thick and wet with barberry and alder.

Just ahead, take a sharp right off the wide path and wend through a mixed forest of white oaks, aspens, red maples, and some gnarly trunks of white pine. A private home is visible up to the left as the trail passes close to and then crosses a rock wall. The highway and a cove of Great Salt Bay are visible off to the right.

After a power line, cross a creeklet on a bog bridge, then swing right around a marsh. At a junction, bear left onto the wet trail to the cattail-lined pond and a beaver dam. Follow the edge of the pond to a pine tree with an arrow indicating the route out to the road on the right. Pass a sign post ("Shell Trail") on the left, then climb a bank up to the road and scramble over the guardrail.

Turn left and follow the highway ramp 100 feet to a junction. Turn right onto Mills Road and walk underneath the overpass of US 1 back to the trailhead parking lot just ahead on the left.

DID YOU KNOW?

The Damariscotta River was formed 10,000 years ago when rising sea water from melting glaciers flooded an ancient river valley. About 5,000 years ago, American Indians made use of the Damariscotta River, the "river of many fish," for its abundance of food and as a travel route between the ocean and inland hunting grounds.

MORE INFORMATION

Damariscotta River Association (damariscottariver.org; 207-563-1393). The Great Salt Bay Preserve, as all DRA lands, is open to the public year-round from dawn to dusk. A trail map is available on-site.

NEARBY

The historical Fish Ladder at Damariscotta Mills (damariscottamills.org) was built in 1807. The ladder provides passage for spawning alewives, also known as river herring, on their annual migration from the ocean to Damariscotta Lake. The fish ladder, composed of 1,500 linear feet of stone walls, rises 42 feet from the bay to the lake. Some 300,000 alewives make the journey each year. Restoration of the ladder began in 2007, and a short pathway gives visitors a close-up look at this amazing spot and the work in progress to protect this important fishery.

MORE HIKING

The Great Salt Bay Farm in Damariscotta is a 100-acre preserve of rolling fields, salt and freshwater marshes, woods, and a mile of water frontage. Here also is the Salt Bay Farm Heritage Center, an eighteenth-century farmhouse that is home to the DRA. The center is busy year-round with environmental education programs and cultural events open to the public. Four trails wind through the farmstead; combine Bayside, Fox Run, and Blackstone trails for a pleasant loop walk. Additional Newcastle hiking trails include the 165-acre Baker Forest, a DRA preserve, and Dodge Point Public Reserved Land, a state-owned 521-acre preserve with more than 8,000 feet of frontage on the Damariscotta River (parkslandlands.com).

WHALEBACK SHELL MIDDEN

The Upper Damariscotta River region is renowned for its enormous oyster shell heaps, also known as middens. These refuse dumps were left behind by the native peoples who camped, fished, and hunted here several thousand years ago. Accumulated in deep, layered piles along the riverbank over many centuries, the middens contained not only oyster shells but pottery fragments, pieces of stone tools, and bones. Because oyster shells are high in calcium carbonate, they are alkaline, reducing the normal soil acidity and thus helping to preserve the contents of the midden.

The Glidden Midden, along the Salt Bay Trail on Glidden Point in Newcastle (Trip 21), is the largest remaining midden not only in Maine but on the East Coast of the US north of Georgia. The largest midden of all, however, was once the Whaleback Midden directly across the Damariscotta River in Damariscotta, which measured 30 feet deep, 1,650 feet long, and 1,500 feet wide.

Archaeologists have studied the contents of the Whaleback Midden and determined that the midden builders were skilled hunters and fishers who ate a balanced diet of game, birds, and fish. Analysis of the oyster shells have indicated that the bivalve was harvested in winter and early spring. After the bountiful alewife run in mid-May, these native peoples moved inland to other hunting grounds.

Beginning in 1886, the Whaleback Midden was mined for its bounty of oyster shells, which were used for the manufacture of a fertilizer additive that was fed to chickens to strengthen their egg shells. The Damariscotta Shell and Fertilizer Company of Massachusetts built a factory, mill, dryer, well, and storehouse for its operation on-site. More than 200 tons of shells were mined, processed, and shipped, much of this in the first year, quickly decimating the midden. The buildings burned in 1891 and the operation was abandoned.

Only a fraction of the original midden remains. Protected as a Maine state historic site, a 0.5-mile interpretive trail leads visitors through the property (parksandlands.com; 207-287-3200).

TRIP 22
LA VERNA NATURE PRESERVE

Location: Bristol, ME
Rating: Easy
Distance: 3.6 miles
Elevation Gain: 340 feet
Estimated Time: 2.0 hours
Maps: USGS Louds Island; *Maine Atlas and Gazetteer,* Map 7
(DeLorme); La Verna Nature Preserve brochure and map

Enjoy a pleasant loop hike that winds through old growth forests and along 3,600 feet of spectacular oceanfront on Muscongus Bay.

DIRECTIONS

From the junction of US 1B and ME 129 at the east end of downtown Damariscotta, turn right (south) onto ME 129/ME 130 and drive south along the Damariscotta River. In 2.9 miles, ME 129 bears right, while ME 130 bears left past Hanley's Market. Remain on ME 130 and continue south. In another 2.8 miles, reach the village of Bristol and Lower Round Pond Road on the left. Turn left (east) here, cross over the Pemaquid River, and follow Lower Round Pond Road for 2.7 miles to a T intersection with ME 32. Turn right (south) onto ME 32 and drive an additional 3.1 miles to the trailhead parking area on the right (sign), just past Ocean Hill Cemetery. Parking is available for six to eight vehicles. *GPS coordinates: 43° 54.152′ N, 69° 28.786′ W.*

TRAIL DESCRIPTION

The 120-acre La Verna Nature Preserve is owned and managed by the Pemaquid Watershed Association, which has been working to conserve the natural resources of the Pemaquid Peninsula since 1973. The preserve features 3.6 miles of trails that meander through a mix of forest types, including mature stands of white and red spruce, and along a spectacular 3,600-foot stretch of shoreline on Muscongus Bay. The preserve was acquired in three separate transactions between 1965 and 1973. Dr. Elizabeth Hoyt and her sister, Anna Mavor, donated a 30-acre parcel, and their family trust, the La Verna Foundation, donated an additional 55 acres. The Nature Conservancy (TNC) purchased the remaining 34 acres to bring the preserve to its present size and configuration. TNC donated the preserve to PWA in 2009. Masters Machine

Company in Bristol has adopted the trails at La Verna, and generously supports their ongoing maintenance.

Immediately across ME 32 from the parking area and information kiosk, Hoyt Trail enters the woods beside an old stone wall. A small white sign and blue diamond markers denote the trail. This first portion of the hike passes through private property on a right-of-way; please stay on the trail.

The path wends downhill, at first going along a stone wall, then crossing several more. Bog bridges span a few wet areas. After jogging to the left, then back to the right, the trail crosses Meadow Brook on a footbridge. Rising easily, the preserve boundary and then a trail junction are soon reached. Here, Ellis Trail leads left (north) while La Verna Trail leads right (south). Bear left onto Ellis Trail, marked by yellow diamonds, to begin the loop.

Ahead, cross a stone wall and wind up a knoll topped by large-diameter white pines and spruces. Impressive red oaks line the trail ahead. At a clump of four oaks on the right, descend the slope to cliff-top views of Muscongus Bay. From this point, the trail swings southwest to follow the shore, where numerous lookout points afford far-reaching views across the bay to Louds Island, tiny Bar Island, Ross Island, Haddock Island, and several others. Look farther out to sea to glimpse Monhegan Island, 10 miles offshore.

Continue at an easy grade about 30 feet above the water, peeking in and out of the trees. Circle around a shallow cove to a boulder-top viewpoint, and beyond, reach the folded and layered metamorphic rocks and igneous intrusions formed eons ago at Leighton Head. Scramble out to the rocks for an undeniable feeling of wildness amid the crashing waves and wind-whipped ocean vistas. *Please note signs here and ahead on the trail that warn of poison ivy.* At the trail junction at Leighton Head, Ellis Trail ends. La Verna Trail departs right (west), a shortcut back to the car. Tibbitts Trail, your route marked by green diamonds, continues on, leading quickly to a junction with Lookout Trail, a short spur to a long ledge with unobstructed views up and down the coastline. Continuing on, pass through a jumble of trees uprooted and blown over by powerful coastal storms. After a grassy stretch, reach a boulder and a gnarled spruce, and turn inland away from the ocean. Walk uphill to a junction, where a side trail goes to one last viewpoint.

Pass through a stand of mature spruce, then more windthrow. Follow the wide trail, an old woods road, for a short distance. Leave the road to the right at a stone wall, hike over a mossy forest carpet, and cross a stone wall, then a footbridge. Ahead, the trail merges with La Verna Trail (blue diamond markers). Follow this quickly to the junction with Ellis and Hoyt trails. Turn left (west) onto Hoyt Trail to return to the trailhead parking area.

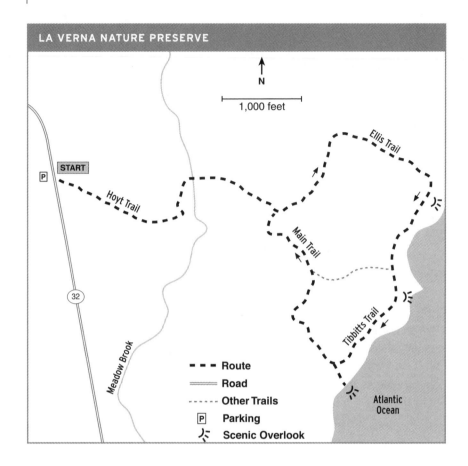

DID YOU KNOW?

Muscongus Bay derives its name from the American Indian word for "fishing place." Fed by the warm waters of the Medomak and Saint George rivers, the relatively shallow but extensive bay is a fertile habitat for Maine lobsters.

MORE INFORMATION

Pemaquid Watershed Association (pemaquidwatershed.org; 207-563-2196). The La Verna Nature Preserve is open to the public year-round during daylight hours. There is no fee, but hikers may leave a donation in the iron ranger at the trailhead kiosk. Dogs are permitted on-leash. A trail map is available on-site and online.

NEARBY

The Pemaquid Lighthouse has been standing watch on Pemaquid Point since 1827. The original lighthouse was short-lived, but the existing stone structure

The trails at La Verna Nature Preserve lead out to Muscongus Bay and more than a half-mile of bold oceanfront shoreline on the eastern shore of the Pemaquid Peninsula.

dates to 1835. The wood-framed keeper's house was built in 1857. A 7-acre park owned by the town of Bristol (bristolparks.org) now surrounds it. The iconic lighthouse, one of Maine's most recognizable human-made features, is depicted on the official state quarter. Tour the lighthouse, which is operated by the American Lighthouse Foundation, then the adjacent Fisherman's Museum, which chronicles the local maritime history.

MORE HIKING

Of its seven other properties on the peninsula, three of the Pemaquid Watershed Association (PWA) holdings have significant hiking trails. At the Crooked Farm Preserve, a nice loop hike leads along the Pemaquid River to Boyd Pond. Doyle and Bearce-Allen preserves both feature a mile of walking. The Bristol Recreational Trail affords lovely views along a tidal stretch of the Pemaquid River. At Osborn Finch Wildlife Sanctuary on Dutch Neck in Waldoboro, a small rustic cabin may be rented for overnight stays. The PWA produces the *Hike and Paddle Pocket Guide* (available for purchase), a handy reference to all of its preserves, plus paddling opportunities on the Pemaquid River.

TRIP 23
MONHEGAN ISLAND

Location: Monhegan Island Plantation, ME
Rating: Moderate
Distance: 5.5 miles
Elevation Gain: 705 feet
Estimated Time: 3.5 hours
Maps: USGS Monhegan; *Maine Atlas and Gazetteer*, Map 8
(DeLorme); *Monhegan Associates Trail Map*

**Explore the rugged cliffs and spruce forests of the extensive trail
system on this remote island 10 miles off the Maine coast.**

DIRECTIONS

Monhegan Island, located in the Atlantic Ocean 10 miles from the nearest
mainland, is reached by privately operated ferry services from the ports of
Port Clyde, New Harbor, and Boothbay Harbor. Sailing times are about an
hour each way, and provide for a 3-to-5-hour stay on the island, depending
on the ferry. No cars are allowed on the island. The departure point for hiking on Monhegan Island is the wharf where the ferry docks. *GPS coordinates:
43° 45.906′ N, 69° 19.284′ W.*

Contact the following ferry companies for current schedules, fares, and
parking rates: Monhegan Boat Line in Port Clyde (monheganboat.com; 207-
372-8848); Hardy Boat Cruises in New Harbor (hardyboat.com; 800-278-
3346); and Balmy Day Cruises in Boothbay Harbor (monhegandaytrip.com;
800-298-2284).

TRAIL DESCRIPTION

Monhegan Island, roughly 1.75 miles long and 0.75 miles across, is heavily forested with spruce and fir trees, except along its rugged ocean margins, which
are dominated by cliffs of dark-colored gabbro, an igneous rock of volcanic
origin. On the west, Manana and Smutty Nose islands hem in the island's snug
harbor and wharf. The rocky hump of Nigh Duck guards the initial entrance.
A compact village of 75 year-round residents—more during the summer season—rises on the slope above the harbor, crowned by a granite lighthouse
constructed in 1824. Lobster fishing dominates the Monhegan economy, and

each year from October through June, island workers harvest lobsters from the only such official conservation area in the state.

Outside the village, the balance of the island's 480 acres of forests, cliffs, wetland, and headlands is preserved in an undeveloped state. In the first half of the twentieth century, Monhegan summer resident Ted Edison, son of the inventor Thomas Edison, wished to preserve the headlands and woods he loved and began buying land to thwart further subdivision and development of the island. In 1954, Edison helped organize these purchased lands into a trust and formed Monhegan Associates to manage them. Well-known as an artist colony for more than 100 years, the island, with its incredible natural beauty, preserved through the foresight and dedication of many, inspires thousands of visitors each year.

Nine miles of trails crisscross the island, creating extensive opportunities for exploration, limited only by your available time and energy. This hike utilizes a portion of four different trails and several village byways to reach into the dense interior forests and the dramatic rocky headlands along the eastern edge of the island. Monhegan trails are numbered 1 through 18 and marked by small green blocks of wood with painted white numbers.

From the wharf, with the Barnacle Café on your left and an anglers' shack with a message board on its wall on your right, stroll uphill on the gravel road past the charming Island Inn. Quickly reach a T junction, with the Lupine Gallery straight ahead across the road. Turn right here to amble through the village and its collection of shops and cottages. Ahead, go right or left around the church to arrive at an intersection next to the Monhegan House. The only public restrooms on the island are 250 feet uphill to the left (50 cents donation).

The hike continues straight through the intersection on Lobster Cove Road. Just after a red house with a white picket fence is the junction with Underhill Trail, which leaves to the left. Continue walking south on the lane, soon bearing left at a Y junction and sign for Lobster Cove. Just past the Monhegan Brewing Co., turn left at a junction and proceed downhill. In 50 feet, bear right onto a narrow foot trail (sign) that leads out into the open at Lobster Cove.

The route is now Cliff Trail, which is designated as 1. It leads all the way around the outer edge of the island to Calf Cove on its northwest side. Occasionally Cliff Trail splits, and an alternative trail, designated as 1A, takes the more wooded and easier interior route away from the open shoreline rocks.

From Lobster Cove, hike down the path and through the meadow, then cross the head of the beach to reach the rocks above the cove proper and a life preserver ring hanging on a post. Pass down to the left and around the

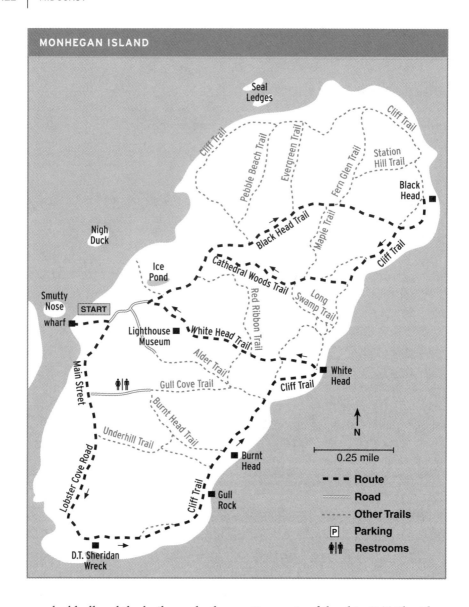

MONHEGAN ISLAND

Seal Ledges

Cliff Trail

Station Hill Trail

Black Head

Cliff Trail

Pebble Beach Trail

Evergreen Trail

Fern Glen Trail

Nigh Duck

Black Head Trail

Maple Trail

Ice Pond

Cathedral Woods Trail

Long Swamp Trail

Cliff Trail

Smutty Nose

START

Lighthouse Museum

White Head Trail

Red Ribbon Trail

Alder Trail

wharf

Main Street

Gull Cove Trail

Cliff Trail

White Head

Burnt Head Trail

N

0.25 mile

Underhill Trail

Burnt Head

Lobster Cove Road

Cliff Trail

Gull Rock

D.T. Sheridan Wreck

- - - Route
——— Road
- - - - - Other Trails
P Parking
Restrooms

wrecked hull and the boiler and other rusting parts of the ship *D.T. Sheridan*, a 110-foot tug that ran aground here in dense fog in November 1948. Ahead, cross a meadow of beach rose, wildflowers, and spruce clumps to arrive at Christmas Cove, where visitors often build interesting cairns of rocks, also known as inukshuks.

Proceed northward past Norton's Ledges to a huge slab of rock known as Gull Rock. A spur trail leads right to the top of Gull Rock, a fun scramble.

The rugged eastern shoreline of Monhegan Island, located 10 miles off the mainland, features a series of rocky headlands that rise as high as 160 feet above the pounding ocean waves.

Burnt Head is visible to the north, and soon enough you are climbing to its top, passing Underhill Trail (3) just below. Burnt Head Trail (4) enters from the left atop Burnt Head, which provides fine views from its grassy ledges. Beyond, descend to the water's edge, where White Head looms in the distance. Cross a grown-up meadow with skeletons of dead spruce. Gull Cove Trail (5) soon joins from the left.

Circle around Gull Cove, then climb to the top of White Head and enjoy its huge, grassy ledges 160 feet above the ocean. Gull Rock and Burnt Head are visible to the south, the rooftops of the village and its cell tower can be seen to the west, and Black Head is in full view up the coast to the north. A variety of shore- and seabirds, plus porpoises and seals, may be seen from this and other such vantage points on the island.

From White Head, follow White Head Trail (7) west or inland toward the village, passing the alternate Cliff Trail (1A), Red Ribbon Trail (9), and Alder Trail (6) en route. Soon, pass through an open lot and a cell tower, storage containers, water tanks, and a generator house. The trail, now a road, passes to the right of the lighthouse and soon reaches the entrance to the Monhegan Museum on the left, situated atop Lighthouse Hill. See "Nearby" below for more information on the museum. Settle down on one of the benches to enjoy the terrific panoramic view over the village.

To continue the hike, head downhill on the road toward the village. At the first junction, turn sharply right and follow the main road northward. Pass a road on the left leading to the old ice pond. Stroll out of the village on the main road, passing Red Ribbon Trail (9) and then Cathedral Woods Trail (11) on the right in a spruce grove. Just ahead at a fork, bear right, and in another 100 feet, the road ends. Continue into the woods on Black Head Trail (10), and in 25 feet, reach a junction with Pebble Beach Trail (14). Bear right to stay on wide and rocky Black Head Trail, which soon narrows in the park-like woods. Black Head Trail soon trends gradually downward with occasional rough footing to reach its end at the junction with Cliff Trail (1). Turn left onto Cliff Trail and drop into a gully. Beyond, climb a short, steep pitch to reach the open rocks atop the windswept grassy ledges of 160-foot Black Head. To continue, retrace your steps on Cliff Trail to the Black Head Trail junction.

Stay left to remain on Cliff Trail, and soon descend again on a rough footway. Pass several more viewpoints north and south before making your way down to the rocks and surf at Squeaker Cove. Duck into the woods here and soon reach the Cathedral Woods Trail (11), which departs to the right. Take the Cathedral Woods Trail and follow it along a moss-fringed streamlet through a thick forest of tall spruce trees. Pass Maple Trail (16) on the right, then Long Swamp Trail (12) on the left. Just beyond is a favorite area to build fairy houses on the forest floor. Look closely for small structures constructed of sticks and twigs, cones and shells, rocks and pebbles, and other natural materials. *Note: Prospective fairy house builders should not pick any living plants.*

Cross a streamlet on a footbridge and soon reach the main road. Turn left here to return to the village, a half-mile distant. Just beyond the library and schoolhouse, close the loop and turn right for the Island Inn and then the wharf and ferry.

DID YOU KNOW?

Monhegan Island—its name is derived from *Monchiggon*, Algonquin for "out-to-sea island"—was first settled by the British in the early 1600s prior to the settlement of the Plymouth Colony, and operated as an important fishing and trading outpost under both British and French control. Monhegan was incorporated as an island plantation in 1839.

MORE INFORMATION

Monhegan Associates (monheganassociates.org). Ferry passengers receive *A Visitor's Guide to Monhegan Island Maine*, a helpful twelve-page booklet on island sights. A trail map is available online or may be also purchased from any of the boat ticket offices or at shops on the island; the proceeds support trail maintenance efforts.

NEARBY

The Monhegan Museum (open 11:30 A.M. to 3:30 P.M. in summer) preserves, documents, and exhibits the natural and human history of the island in the thirteen rooms on two floors of the old lightkeeper's house, plus numerous outbuildings, including replicas of an ice house and a fish house, an art gallery, and, of course, the lighthouse. The large bell on the lawn is the old signal bell from the nearby Manana Fog Signal Station. A small entrance fee supports the museum. More details on exploring the island are available at monheganwelcome.com.

MORE HIKING

Eighteen trails crisscross Monhegan Island, from Lobster Cove to Green Point, the wharf to White Head, providing 9 miles and many hours and even days of walking exploration for everyone from the casual to the intrepid visitor.

TRIP 24
NORTHERN HEADWATERS TRAIL

Location: Montville, ME
Rating: Moderate
Distance: 3.8 miles (loop)
Elevation Gain: 480 feet
Estimated Time: 2.5 hours
Maps: USGS Liberty; *Maine Atlas and Gazetteer*, Map 14 (DeLorme); *Sheepscot Headwaters Trail Network* (Sheepscot Wellspring Land Alliance)

Hike along old stone walls amid a pleasant mix of forestlands to the headwaters of the Sheepscot River and the start of its 58-mile journey to the sea.

DIRECTIONS
From the junction of ME 3 and ME 220 in Liberty (opposite the Corner Restaurant and near Peaslee's General Store), turn north onto ME 220. In 3.2 miles, turn left onto Halldale Road. At 3.7 miles, bear right at a fork. Halldale Road becomes a dirt road at 4.7 miles. Reach the gravel Whitten Hill Trailhead parking lot on the left at 4.8 miles. There is parking for ten to twelve cars. An information kiosk marks the start of the trail. *GPS coordinates: 44° 27.864′ N, 69° 18.354′ W.*

TRAIL DESCRIPTION
Since 1991, Sheepscot Wellspring Land Alliance (SWLA) has been working to preserve ecologically significant lands in the watershed of the Upper Sheepscot River. To date, more than 1,500 acres have been protected through outright purchase and conservation easements. These conserved lands include pleasant forests and open fields, winding streams and scenic marshes, and the high points of Whitten Hill and Goose Ridge. The alliance also developed and maintains the Sheepscot Headwaters Trail Network, an 18-mile trail system in Montville, Liberty, and Knox that includes a total of fifteen interconnected trails.

This walk combines a short section of Whitten Hill Trail with Northern Headwaters Trail for a fine loop through the hill country of northwest Montville, where the headwaters of the Sheepscot River is located.

Orange-blazed Whitten Hill Trail leaves to the right of the kiosk. Pass by a stone wall to reach a junction in 75 feet, where Whitten Hill Trail spits. To the left, the trail leads back across Halldale Road to Bog Brook Trail. To the right, the trail leads a short distance to Northern Headwaters Trail. Note the large cellar hole just behind the trail sign. Go right (west) on Whitten Hill Trail. Follow a stone wall gradually uphill, then cross a stone wall to reach the junction with Northern Headwaters Trail. Turn right (north) here to walk counterclockwise on this blue-blazed loop.

Ascend very gradually along the ridgeline of Whitten Hill. A magnificent old stone wall follows on the left for the better part of a half-mile through a forest of mixed woods. Ahead, pass a number of gnarled white ash trees, which perhaps once marked a property line along with the stone wall. Pass over the unmarked and wooded high point on Whitten Hill (865 feet). Beyond, notice the blue paint blazes along the stone wall. After a pleasant grove of old field pines and spruce, pass through a gap in the wall. Immediately beyond, at a small opening to the right with apple trees, the trail takes a sharp left (arrow).

Continue along another beautiful section of the stone wall, which at times is 4 feet high and is in excellent condition. Where several walls join to form a double L, pass through a gap in the wall. Ahead, the trail now follows the opposite, or west side, of the stone wall.

Pass through a stone wall at the junction of Hemlock Hollow Trail, which leaves to the right. Wind downhill from this point, bearing left around a big bull pine. After a stretch thick with bright-green ferns, reach an old foundation on the left. A handful of rusting farm tools and stove parts mark the site. Hike through the cherry and apple trees to a spur leading right to the Northern Headwaters Trailhead. Turn left here to continue on Northern Headwaters Trail.

Pass an old orchard field on the left, then trend gradually downhill. After a low, wide stone wall, the footway becomes rough with roots and mud. Pass the huge double trunk of an ancient white ash on the left at the junction of several stone walls. Ahead, more sizable ash and oak trees line the wide path, which proceeds between two stone walls. Rock-hop over several wet areas to reach Goose Ridge Trail, which departs to the right in an extensive hillside grove of hemlocks. Pass through a stand of diseased beech trees to arrive at a hemlock stand at the base of the slope. Here, Mink Run Trail leaves to the right. Bear left to continue on Northern Headwaters Trail.

Weave between the impressive hemlock trunks, then descend a short pitch to a bend in the Sheepscot River, not far from its headwaters. The river is about 10 feet wide here. Nearly 58 miles from this point, the Sheepscot

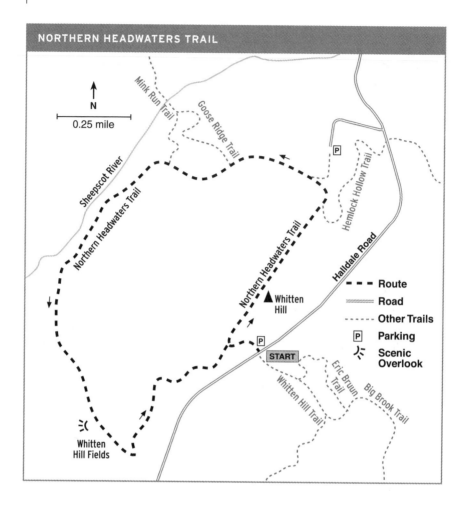

NORTHERN HEADWATERS TRAIL

River empties into the Gulf of Maine at Sheepscot Bay between George-town and Southport islands. The watershed is prized for its habitat diversity, which supports and abundance of wildlife, including bald eagles, ospreys, deer, moose, otters, bobcats, a variety songbirds, alewives, trout, sturgeon, Atlantic salmon, and lobsters.

Continue south along the gurgling river through a park-like forest of hem-locks. After crossing a brook, the river corridor is choked with shrubby growth and is difficult to see or reach. Angle up the slope above the river, follow a contour for a while, then drop down to the bottomlands along the river. Cross two small brooks, then pass the sharp corner of stone wall.

Soon, bear left away from the river, up the hillside to a stone wall. Follow along the wall, then bear sharply left through it. Go left of a squarish rock, then right of a huge, decaying white pine stump. Follow a wide track, barely

Beautiful old stone walls, some 4 feet high and still in excellent condition, line the route of Northern Headwaters Trail on Whitten Hill.

discernible as an old woods road. Bear left onto a narrow footpath and hike through a classic northern hardwood forest of beech, maple, and birch. Go right along a stone wall to its end. Soon after, look to the left of the trail for a huge sugar maple that is 5 to 6 feet in diameter.

After a stretch of rough footing, uneven with roots and wet ground, cross a brook at a stone wall. Then bear left and hike up through a lovely pine grove to a large field. Enter the field and follow along its northern edge. Look for strawberries as you go and enjoy the sweeping views of the rolling hills to the west in Freedom. The beautiful vista underscores the long-term vision of the SWLA: to establish a contiguous protected area of 10,000 acres in Waldo County in the towns of Freedom, Liberty, Montville, and Palermo. Connecting these working woodlands, forever wildlands, wetlands, and fields in and around the Sheepscot headwaters with the 5,240-acre Frye Mountain Wildlife Management Area and other protected lands would effectively create the largest area of conservation land in Midcoast Maine.

At the top of the field, reach a junction. Whitten Fields Trail leaves right to cross the field; instead, turn left into the woods. The path rises gradually to a stone wall, then bears left along it. Roots make the wet trailway uneven. Pass through several more stone walls, then bear left on the ridge top to the original junction. Turn right to descend to the trailhead.

DID YOU KNOW?

The little town of Montville was incorporated on February 18, 1807. Its name means "mountain town" in French.

MORE INFORMATION

Sheepscot Wellspring Land Alliance (swlamaine.org; 207-589-3230). Dogs are allowed under control. Pick up a Sheepscot Headwaters Trail Network map at the trailhead or download a copy online.

NEARBY

Lake Saint George State Park in Liberty occupies a lovely spot on the north shore of the island-dotted, 1,017-acre Lake Saint George, much of which is undeveloped. Visitors can enjoy swimming in the lake and relaxing and picnicking in the sun on the grassy promenade. Canoe, paddleboat, and rowboat rentals are available. The park also features overnight camping at 38 sites (parksandlands.com; 207-589-4255).

MORE HIKING

As outlined above, the Sheepscot Headwaters Trail Network includes 18 miles of hiking on fifteen interconnected trails. A variety of access points are possible. Nearby Hogback Mountain and Frye Mountain boast an additional 11 miles of hiking on trails maintained by the Georges River Land Trust; a spur from the Sheepscot Headwaters Trail Network connects both systems (also depicted and described on the aforementioned map).

TRIP 25
HIDDEN VALLEY
NATURE CENTER

Location: Jefferson, ME
Rating: Moderate
Distance: 5.1 miles, round-trip
Elevation Gain: 390 feet
Estimated Time: 3.0 hours
Maps: USGS North Whitefield; *Maine Atlas and Gazetteer*, Map 13 (DeLorme); HVNC Trail Map

Explore the privately owned Hidden Valley Nature Center and one of the most ecologically diverse tracts of undeveloped and roadless forestland in the Midcoast region.

DIRECTIONS

From the junction of ME 17 and ME 32 in Jefferson, just east of Peaslee's Quick Stop, turn right (south) onto ME 32. In 1.0 mile, turn right onto ME 215. At 3.5 miles from ME 17, at the intersection of ME 215 and ME 126, turn right onto the combined ME 126/215. Turn left just ahead to continue south on ME 215. In another 4.5 miles, turn right onto Egypt Road and drive an additional 0.5 mile to the trailhead parking lots for Hidden Valley Nature Center on the right. The gravel lot has parking for at least 20 cars. Several smaller overflow lots on the other side of the entrance road provide additional space. *GPS coordinates: 44° 8.766' N, 69° 34.145' W.*

TRAIL DESCRIPTION

Tucked into the rural countryside east of Randolph and the Kennebec River, the Hidden Valley Nature Center (HVNC) in Jefferson surely lives up to its name. This woodland jewel encompasses 1,000 remote acres of forests, ponds, wetlands, streams, rocky ridges, and old woods roads and trails, all told one of the most ecologically diverse tracts of undeveloped and roadless forestland in this part of the Midcoast, right in the heart of the 320-square-mile Sheepscot River watershed.

Landowners Bambi Jones and Tracy Moscovitz purchased the property in 2005 to both protect the land and use it as a place for friends and family to recreate. After a yurt erected in 2006 proved popular, the couple decided to

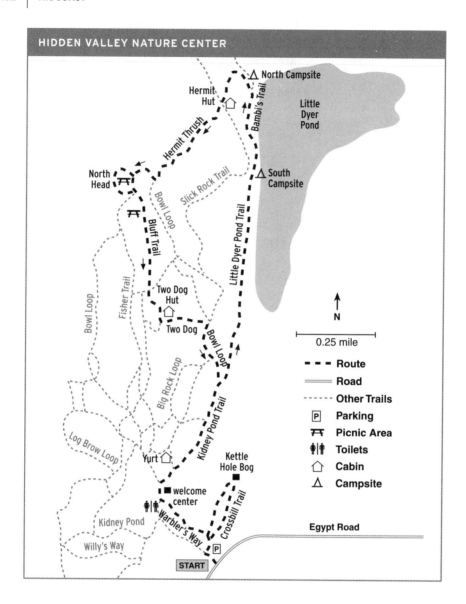

HIDDEN VALLEY NATURE CENTER

North Campsite

Hermit Hut

Little Dyer Pond

Bambi's Trail

Hermit Thrush

North Head

Slick Rock Trail

South Campsite

Bowl Loop

Bluff Trail

Little Dyer Pond Trail

Fisher Trail

Bowl Loop

Two Dog Hut

Two Dog

Bowl Loop

N

0.25 mile

Big Rock Loop

Kidney Pond Trail

Log Brow Loop

Yurt

Kettle Hole Bog

welcome center

Warbler's Way

Crossbill Trail

Kidney Pond

Willy's Way

Egypt Road

P

START

- - - Route
═══ Road
----- Other Trails
P Parking
🗴 Picnic Area
♦♦ Toilets
⌂ Cabin
△ Campsite

officially open up the property for public use, and that's how Hidden Valley Nature Center came to be in 2007.

The HVNC is dedicated to providing nature-based education, nonmotorized outdoor recreation, and sustainable forestry for the outdoor community. Users can enjoy hiking, trail running, mountain biking, horseback riding, canoeing and kayaking, fishing, swimming, wildlife watching, and in winter, cross-country skiing and snowshoeing. There's also a robust series of ongoing educational programs on ecology, conservation, sustainable forestry, botany,

Few signs of civilization can be seen around lovely 109-acre Little Dyer Pond, which supports a good population of smallmouth bass.

outdoor recreation, and many other such topics. Some 30 miles of multiuse trails at HVNC allow plenty of opportunity for exploration. This hike combines nine trails for a nice introductory loop hike that takes in a good chunk of the property.

To reach the HVNC trail system proper, walk around the entrance gate and follow the service road west into the nature preserve. Quickly reach a gatehouse information kiosk on the right. There's also a donation box; a small fee is requested of non-members.

Leave the road and hike into the woods on Warbler's Way. In 150 feet, pass an outhouse on the right. The trail goes left another 50 feet to the Crossbill Loop junction. Take the wide track of Crossbill Loop through mixed woods, noting the tree identification placards as you walk. Reach a bench and Bog Boardwalk, a short spur leading to Kettle Hole Bog; six interpretive panels describing life in the bog—including the carnivorous horned bladderwort, roundleaf sundew and pitcher plant—make this an interesting side trip.

Resume your circuit on Crossbill Loop, which makes its way around the forested finger of land that extends into the boggy areas around it. At Warbler Way, turn right and soon cross a bridge over a swampy area. Note the colorful gnome-like trail creatures mounted to trailside trees in this stretch. These

"Trail Guys" were created by Aaron Weissblum, a renowned game maker. Each of the numbered "trail guys" contain a clue to be decoded, and after decoding them all, the secret message spells out the location of the final prize, a great exercise for kids and adults alike.

Ahead, a feint trail goes straight; follow the wide trail left to reach a woods road and an outhouse. Turn right onto the dirt road, which is Kidney Pond Trail, and proceed through this central area of activity, which includes a large dome tent, various and sundry woods equipment, and Hi Hut, an education facility and welcoming center. Trail maps, a table and chairs, and a woodstove make up the cozy interior.

Beyond Hi Hut, pass a fire pit and picnic tables to arrive at an information kiosk. Just beyond the road forks. Bowl Loop goes both left and right; bear right (counterclockwise). The woods road crosses a culvert bridge over a pond outlet, then passes a steep shortcut trail on the left which leads to the Yurt, one of three remote overnight structures (as well as two tent sites) in the preserve. Continuing on the road, pass a red maple swamp on the right to reach the crest of a hill and the junction with Yurt Trail, which leads left to the Yurt. Stay straight here, following the road easily downhill. (For reference, the Yurt is 20 feet in diameter, sleeps six, and features a large deck, outside grill, and gas stove inside.). Ahead, just after a small gravel pit, Little Dyer Pond Trail diverges right, while Bowl Loop proceeds straight. Turn right to follow Little Dyer Pond Trail, which offers easy going along the base of the hillside.

Little Dyer Pond soon comes into view through the trees. Pass a private campsite on the right, and just beyond, a boat launch. Then bear left at a sign indicating that the HVNC campsites are ahead. Cross a brook on a wide footbridge, then follow a nice path along the pond, reaching Campsite #1 and a picnic table at about the 2-mile mark of the hike. Here also Little Dyer Pond Trail goes left, but continue straight ahead on Bambi's Trail. Just beyond, a spur leads right 50 feet to a small point amid the pines, where there are nice views up and down Little Dyer Pond. Note the nearly complete lack of development along the shore of this lovely 109-acre pond. Its shallow depths support a good population of smallmouth bass.

Ahead on Bambi's Trail, reach Campsite #2 and a tent platform, fire pit, and picnic table. Cut left here to pass through the campsite. Just beyond the platform, reach unsigned Hermit Thrush Trail. Pass by the outhouse to continue away from the pond on a narrow trail, which is occasionally marked by orange flagging tape. After a wet area the trail becomes a grassy track, which leads up an incline to a meadow. The Hermit Hut is 100 feet left at the far edge of the meadow, a worthwhile side trip. The fully outfitted frame cabin was built is 2008 and sleeps six. Returning to Hermit Thrush Trail, the hike continues straight ahead through the meadow and quickly reaches the wood line and Little Dyer Pond Trail, which goes both left and right. From this junction, go straight into the woods on Hermit Thrush Trail.

The wide track soon reaches a small clearing, where the route bears left and proceeds gently uphill to arrive at a junction with Bowl Loop. Turn left onto Bowl Loop and soon reach North Head Loop. Turn right onto North Head Loop to climb around and up the wooded knob of North Head. On top, a spur leads right to a picnic table at North Head Lookout, which is mostly obscured in high summer but may provide views when the leaves are gone.

Beyond the spur trail, hike along the rocky ridge, then bear right and descend to Bowl Loop. Turn left onto Bowl Loop and head uphill. Just ahead on the right is the escarpment of Bluff Wall and a picnic table. One hundred yards after Bluff Wall, leave Bowl Loop and turn sharply right on Bluff Trail. (*Note: This unsigned and somewhat obscure junction is easy to miss.*) Climb the short pitch up the bluff. On the ridge above, bear right to hike an undulating route through the pleasant semi-open forest of oaks and red and white pines. Reach Western Mountain Overlook and a bench on the right. Treetop views extend to the northwest from this point.

From the overlook, continue along the rolling ridgetop, climbing over several high points. At the four-way junction with Mountain Cut-Off, continue straight through on Bluff Trail to reach Two Dog Hut. This rather unique cabin was built from pine logs harvested from the surrounding woods. A sleeping loft can comfortably accommodate two people.

Below the hut, bear left on Two Dog Trail and immediately pass a large vernal pool on the left. Ahead, bear sharply right onto a woods road and proceed downhill to a large, open old wood yard and the junction with Bowl Loop. Turn right to follow Bowl Loop downslope, passing two trails on the right en route. The first is marked "to Yurt" while the second is signed "Big Rock Trail." At the base of the hill, Little Dyer Pond Trail merges from the left.

From this point you are on familiar ground. Follow Bowl Loop back to the Hi Hut area, then just after it, bear left off the dirt road at the outhouse to follow Warbler's Way back to the gatehouse information kiosk on the entrance road. Go left on the entrance road to reach the gate and the trailhead parking lots on Egypt Road.

DID YOU KNOW?

In 2014, HVNC and its founders Tracy Moscovitz and Bambi Jones were named the state of Maine and Northeast Regional Outstanding Tree Farmer of the Year for their sustainable forestry operations and related outreach and education efforts.

MORE INFORMATION

Hidden Valley Nature Center (hvnc.org, 207-200-8840). The center is open year-round from dawn to dusk. Overnight visitors must make advance reservations to stay at the two primitive cabins, the yurt or the two pond-side tentsites. Canoes are available for rent. Download a trail map online.

NEARBY

Damariscotta Lake State Park (maine.gov/dacf/parks, 207-549-7600 [park season]) is a popular day-use park featuring a nice swath of sandy beach and picnicking facilities situated at the north end of the 12-mile long, 4,381-acre freshwater lake.

MORE HIKING

With 30 miles of trails HVNC visitors could spend many hours and even days exploring the preserve on foot. The Sheepscot Valley Conservation Association (sheepscot.org, 207-586-5616) maintains a nice system of trails of its seven public preserves in the region.

TRIP 26
GEORGES HIGHLAND PATH
/ RAGGED MOUNTAIN

Location: Rockport, ME
Rating: Moderate
Distance: 5.0 miles, one-way
Elevation Gain: 1,270 feet
Estimated Time: 3 hours
Maps: USGS West Rockport; *Maine Atlas and Gazetteer*, Map 14 (DeLorme); *Ragged Mountain Area/Georges Highland Path* (Georges River Land Trust)

Grand views from open ledges atop Ragged Mountain range from the Georges River Watershed east across Penobscot Bay to Acadia and northwest to the White Mountains.

DIRECTIONS

To reach the starting trailhead: From the junction of ME 17 and ME 90 in West Rockport, proceed northwest on ME 17. In 4.5 miles, turn right onto Hope Street and follow this for another 0.4 miles to the Thorndike Brook trailhead amid the apple trees on the right. There is an information kiosk and space for eight cars. *GPS coordinates: 44° 13.026′ N, 69° 10.242′ W.*

   To reach the ending trailhead: From the junction of ME 17 and ME 90 in West Rockport, proceed northwest on ME 17. In 1.8 miles, arrive at the ME 17 trailhead parking lot for Georges Highland Path. Spot a car here to avoid a 1.5-mile road walk back to the starting trailhead. *GPS coordinates: 44° 12.127′ N, 69° 9.540′ W.*

TRAIL DESCRIPTION

Georges Highland Path is a low-impact conservation trail system offering 50 miles of hiking on six distinct trail sections between Montville and Thomaston. From craggy mountain peaks to leafy woodlands to interesting bogs, the path provides some of the most scenic and least traveled hiking to be found on the Midcoast. The Georges River Land Trust has been conserving land in the 225-square mile St. George River watershed since 1987, having protected some 3,500 acres in the region to date. The nonprofit group began building trails in 1996 and was instrumental in establishing Georges Highland Path. Other land

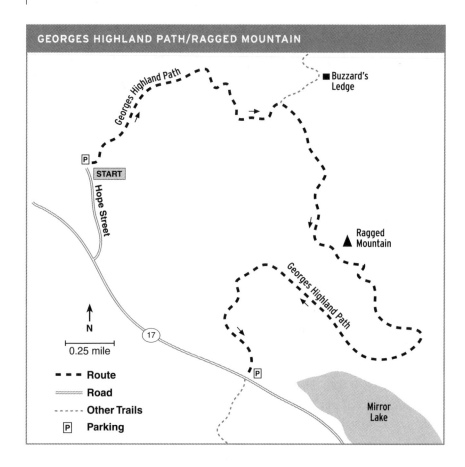

GEORGES HIGHLAND PATH/RAGGED MOUNTAIN

trusts active in the watershed include the Coastal Mountains Land Trust and the Sheepscot Wellspring Land Alliance.

Most of Georges Highland Path crosses private land. No easements exist: rather more than 60 landowners along the route have kindly given permission for hikers to access the land and use the trail through informal handshake agreements, a rather unique arrangement. On Ragged Mountain, the destination for this hike, the Coastal Mountains Land Trust has established the Ragged Mountain Preserve, a 459-acre conservation property assembled from eleven different tracts of land. All told since 1986, the trust has protected 9,503 acres of land in 25 preserves totaling 4,612 acres; 56 conservation easements totaling 3,323 acres; and 1,568 acres through projects facilitated by trust. This route over Ragged Mountain features extensive open ledges with views ranging from the Atlantic Ocean at Penobscot Bay north and west to Maine's high interior mountains, even as far as Mount Washington in New Hampshire's Presidential Range on a clear day.

Georges Highland Path traces a route over the rocky crest of Ragged Mountain for three very scenic miles. Pictured below is Mirror Lake, a public water supply for nearby towns.

Blue-blazed Georges Highland Path leaves from the corner of the lot and proceeds through an aspen stand along the edge of a field. Look for blueberries in season as you pass through a gap in a stone wall. Cross a wet area on bog bridges, then Thorndike Brook on a footbridge. Soon after, the trail begins to rise up the northwest side of the mountain, passing through a forest of sizeable oaks, ash, beech, and hemlock. Ahead, the trail swings right and up the hillside in earnest, crossing over two old stone walls in close succession. After alternating stretches of switchbacks and contouring, the trail climbs more steeply through a stand of spruce to reach an outlook on the right.

Continue to zigzag upward, then drop down to a ledge with a nice view west to Grassy Pond. Just ahead the view opens up to include the slopes of Spruce Mountain and Mount Pleasant, both traversed by Georges Highland Path west of ME 17. The trail bears left and up to leave the west face of the mountain, following more switchbacks to reach the ridgeline above. After a patch of semi-open forest, Georges Highland Path arrives at a junction.

Here, a spur departs left to Buzzard's Ledge before descending to a trail-head parking lot on Barnestown Road. (From the parking lot, Bald Mountain Trail climbs to the neighboring summit of 1,280-foot Bald Mountain, the focal point of the 583-acre Bald Mountain Preserve.) Bear right at the junction to resume the hike over Ragged Mountain on a wide path along the ridge. Descend to a sag and then climb gradually beyond through a semi-open forest canopy of oak and spruce, with juniper, mosses, and grasses (as well as blueberries) beneath. After a grove of oak copses and some old red blazes, ascend again, staying right (small sign) to avoid an old trail on the left. Contour across the mountainside, passing some mature spruce trees en route.

Where Ledge Loop leaves left, continue right to climb up through rocks. Where Ledge Loop reenters ahead, scamper up the rocky knob beyond. Views open up to the north and west as you climb a second knob. At a cairn on the open ledges ahead, enjoy wide open vistas ranging east to the ocean at Penobscot Bay, west over Spruce Mountain and Mount Pleasant, and north along the ridgeline of Ragged Mountain.

With the summit communication tower atop Ragged Mountain in view up and left, descend along the edge of the cliff face on the airy path and soon turn a corner of the mountain to see Mirror Lake ahead and below. Continue in the open toward the tower and its outbuildings before bearing left and up over rocks to enter a deep ravine. Descend a short, steep pitch, cross a streamlet, then pass to the right of a lichen-covered boulder. Climb up through the rocks on the far side of the ravine to emerge at the base of the open slabs below the 1,300-foot summit.

Continue through blueberry bushes and juniper to another fine view of Mirror Lake and beyond to the Atlantic Ocean at Rockport. Follow rock cairns and blazes up the open slope of rocks and ledges toward the tower above. The trail reaches its highpoint just below the tower. Here, the path veers right to enter a grove of scrub oak. Ahead, leave the oaks and enjoy another fine view of Mirror Lake and the south ridge of Ragged and beyond to Mount Hosmer. Past the pretty harbor and village of Camden is Penobscot Bay and the big islands of North Haven and Vinalhaven. Deer Isle and Isle au Haut are visible beyond.

After another stretch of oak woods, reach the next viewpoint marked by a cairn, where the mountainous profile of Mount Desert Island and Acadia National Park more than 30 miles slightly north of east is revealed. Bear right and down into the woods, passing one last viewpoint before beginning the long descent of the southeast ridge of Ragged Mountain. The foot trail merges with an old carriage road of sorts, which it follows on a long, straight descent of the mountainside.

In a forest of large diameter oaks, the path bears sharply right through a gap in the ridge and continues to wind downslope toward Mirror Lake. Note: The trail ultimately avoids Mirror Lake as it is the public water supply for Camden, Rockport, Rockland, Thomaston and several other towns. Mirror Lake, also known as Oyster River Pond, is the headwaters of the Oyster River. Interestingly, *The History of Camden and Rockport, Maine*, published in 1907, described Mirror Lake as having "water of extraordinary purity" in the late 1800s.

At the base of the descent, the trail bears north along the west side of Ragged Mountain, threading a route between the talus slopes up on the right and a brook down to the left. The trail along the western base of Ragged Mountain will one day be part of Round-the-Mountain Trail, a 10-mile multiuse loop trail that will encircle the mountain and provide year-round recreational opportunities. The trail is a cooperative effort of the Camden Snow Bowl, Coastal Mountains Land Trust, and the Midcoast Chapter of the New England Mountain Bike Association.

Soon after a sweeping view right up the west face of the mountain, the trail bears right to cross the inlet brook of Mirror Lake. From this point it's a pleasant, undulating ramble through mixed woods out to ME 17, passing by and through a series of old stone walls along the way. Finally, cross a creek on a footbridge, then climb the steps to the information kiosk at the trailhead parking lot on the east side of the highway.

If you've spotted a vehicle here, you're all set. If not, walk back to the Thorndike Brook trailhead via ME 17 and Hope Street, a distance of 1.5 miles.

DID YOU KNOW?

Ragged Mountain and neighboring Bald Mountain are the fourth and fifth highest mountains respectively on the East Coast of the US.

MORE INFORMATION

Georges River Land Trust (georgesriver.org, 207-594-5166). Coastal Mountains Land Trust, (coastalmountains.org, 207-236-7091). Trails in the Ragged Mountain Preserve are open during daylight hours. Dogs must be under voice control or on a leash at all times; in winter, pets are not allowed on any skiing terrain. Refer to the winter guidelines in-season (posted online).

NEARBY

The little harbor village of Rockport is home to the Center for Maine Contemporary Art, which exhibits the work of living artists across a spectrum of styles and genres. Marine Park on the waterfront features the statue of Andre the Seal, a local Maine coast legend. The bustling town of Rockland, steeped in maritime heritage, has a host of shops, eateries, lodging and entertainment options, including the renowned Farnsworth Art Museum and Wyeth Center, the Maine Lighthouse Museum and the annual Maine Lobster Festival (rocklandmainstreet.com).

TRIP 27
FERNALD'S NECK PRESERVE

Location: Lincolnville and Camden, ME
Rating: Easy
Distance: 3.6 miles
Elevation Gain: 265 feet
Estimated Time: 2.5 hours
Maps: USGS Lincolnville, Camden; *Maine Atlas and Gazetteer*, Map 14
(DeLorme); *Fernald's Neck Preserve* (Coastal Mountains Land Trust)

**Circumnavigate Fernald's Neck while enjoying impressive
old growth forests of pine and hemlock and miles of scenic
Megunticook Lake shorefront.**

DIRECTIONS
From the junction of US 1 and ME 52 in Camden, turn left onto ME 52 and
drive west. In 4.6 miles, ME 52 bears sharply left past the Youngtown Inn. In
another 0.2 mile, turn left onto Fernald's Neck Road. The pavement ends at 0.4
mile; about 500 feet farther, bear left at a junction. Pass through a farmstead
after 0.4 mile, and turn right and then quickly left to pass around a clapboard
house. In 500 feet, proceed through a gate to reach the trailhead parking lot.
There is parking for twelve cars in the grassy lot. An information kiosk marks
the start of the trail system. *GPS coordinates: 44° 15.630′ N, 69° 6.594′ W.*

TRAIL DESCRIPTION
The 328-acre Fernald's Neck Preserve occupies a sizeable portion of a large
peninsula that juts out into the center of Megunticook Lake. Five color-coded
trails combine for a wonderful tour of the property, with its 4 miles of pretty
lakefront and great stands of mature forests.

Owned and managed by the Coastal Mountains Land Trust, Fernald's
Neck was protected for conservation in 1969, after the threat of development
motivated local citizens to take serious action to preserve the natural beauty
of this scenic gem as well as the water quality of the lake. The Nature Conservancy, which assisted with the conservation deal, became the owner of
the initial 285 acres upon completion of the purchase. In 1979, an additional
36 acres known as the Hattie Lamb Fernald Section was donated by Mar-
garet Thurlow in memory of her mother. Between 1991 and 1992, several

small inholdings, 3 acres at Balance Rock and the 2-acre Narrows Lot, were purchased from the Ethel Harkness Trust. In 2007, The Nature Conservancy transferred ownership of Fernald's Neck Preserve to the Coastal Mountains Land Trust, while holding the conservation easement. Two more acres were donated to the trust by Douglas Warren in 2008, bringing the preserve to its present size.

From the kiosk, walk 100 feet to a junction. Bear left onto White Trail, which leads 0.1 mile across the field, an important habitat for butterflies, insects, snakes, rodents, and nesting bobolinks. After a stone wall, continue through the piney woods to an outcrop on Megunticook Lake, which stretches 1,305 acres with a maximum depth of 65 feet. The lake is drained by the Megunticook River, which flows 3.5 miles east to empty into Penobscot Bay at Camden. Enjoy nice views of the escarpment known as Maiden's Cliff and the 3-mile-long ridge of Mount Megunticook.

Return to the junction to continue on Blue Trail across the field and through a stone wall—evidence of the land's agricultural past—to the lovely woods of pine, hemlock, and spruce. Pad over the soft trail to a junction where Blue Trail splits. To the left, Blue Trail leads a short distance to Yellow Trail, which continues to Balance Rock. You'll return via this route. Instead, bear right to continue through the big pines along Blue Trail. Bog bridges keep your feet dry as you cross several wet areas. Reach a group of mossy boulders; one on the left has a plaque dedicated to Charles Chatfield, a supporter of the conservation of Fernald's Neck who raised funds and formed a corporation that worked to buy the Fernald's Neck property.

Not far ahead, Red Trail diverges to the left, a shortcut across the peninsula that joins Blue Trail again. Remain on Blue Trail to pass a mossy green erratic. Ahead, amble through a forest of old growth white pines and hemlocks. One of the pines measures at least 3 feet in diameter, and there are many other impressive examples of big trees nearby.

With the lake in view down to the right through the foliage, traverse an area of downed trees, likely uprooted by strong storm winds that sweep across the Fernald's Neck peninsula. Soon, Red Trail enters from the left. Continuing on Blue Trail, cross a shallow ravine and proceed through the woods of big oaks and hemlocks, red and white pines. Top out on a knoll and emerge on an open ledge overlooking an arm of Megunticook Lake, 60 feet below. Several cottages are in view along the lakeshore, and the profile of Bald Mountain can be seen farther south.

Wind down from the viewpoint on the soft path through a thick understory and canopy dominated by red pines. Beyond a vernal pool and a wet

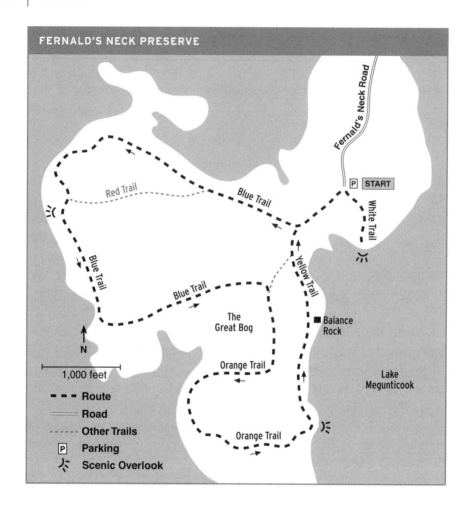

FERNALD'S NECK PRESERVE

Red Trail

Blue Trail

START

P

White Trail

Blue Trail

Blue Trail

Yellow Trail

The
Great Bog

■ Balance
Rock

N

1,000 feet

Orange Trail

Lake
Megunticook

- - - Route
——— Road
------ Other Trails
P Parking
)ξ Scenic Overlook

Orange Trail

area, reach an unmarked spur leading right to a view overlooking a 14-acre heath known as the Great Bog.

Ahead, where Blue Trail goes straight, turn right (south) onto Orange Trail. Trend mildly down to the level of the heath, then bear left to cross a creeklet on a footbridge. Follow around the margin of the bog with frequent views over it. The bog—which acts as a natural water purifier and helps to prevent flooding—is home to a variety of plants, including mountain holly, sweet gale, highbush blueberry, leather leaf, and rhodora.

Orange Trail soon splits into a loop; turn right here to walk the loop counterclockwise. Cross a creeklet and continue to hug close to the heath before finally bearing away south to reach the lakeshore in an area of wind-thrown pines. The path follows along the lake just above it in the woods. Pass a huge boulder, then a flat rock perfect for sitting. Contour on sloping trail over mossy

The trails of the Fernald's Neck Preserve meander through great stands of mature white pine and hemlock trees, some more than 3 feet in diameter.

rocks. After a dip, bear away from the lake to cut across the peninsula through mixed woods.

A short pitch leads to the lake level again and very soon to a wonderful and aptly named outlook on Megunticook Lake known as Mountain View. Here, enjoy broad views up and down Fernald's Neck and east to the white cross atop Maiden's Cliff and the lengthy mass of Mount Megunticook. Continue around the shallow cove, then leave the lake to head inland. At the junction of an old trail, turn right to continue through the woods not far from the east shore of the peninsula.

Note: Due to heavy blowdowns in this area in 2013, the trail was being re-routed by trail crews in 2014. Its exact future location may be somewhat different than described when the route is finalized and officially marked.

After a stretch through a grove of white pines reaching 100 feet or more in height, reach Balance Rock—a glacial erratic dislodged by ancient glaciers and deposited here eons ago—and a junction with Yellow Trail. A plaque nearby is dedicated to Vinton and Elizabeth Harkness, who generously donated the 3 acres around the rock. Continue past the huge rock to Megunticook Lake and a beautiful park-like spot on the water set amid the pines.

To complete the hike, saunter back past Balance Rock and take wide Yellow Trail to its junction with Blue Trail. Turn right onto Blue Trail to return to the trailhead.

MORE INFORMATION

Coastal Mountains Land Trust (coastalmountains.org; 207-236-7091). The preserve gate is locked each evening at 7:30 P.M. Dogs are not permitted.

NEARBY

Lincolnville Beach is a popular visitor attraction, with its variety of shops, galleries, and eateries as well as a nice stretch of sandy beach offering views across Penobscot Bay to Grindel Light on Islesboro. The light is open to visitors via the state-operated Islesboro Ferry (lincolnvillemaine.com; maine.gov/mdot/msfs/Islesboro).

MORE HIKING

Camden Hills State Park features more than 30 miles of hiking on 21 trails across 6,000 acres of parkland (parksandlands.com; 207-236-3109). Coastal Mountain Land Trust preserves at Beech Hill (295 acres) and Bald Mountain (600 acres) offer several miles of pleasant hiking with stunning coastal vistas. Get the helpful CMLT brochure, *Take a Hike: Your Local Guide to Our Favorite Hikes*, which is available online. On Ragged Mountain, the Georges Highland Path makes a traverse of the peak, continuing on Spruce Mountain and Mount Pleasant (georgesriver.org; 207-594-5166).

TRIP 28
CAMDEN HILLS STATE PARK

Location: Camden, ME
Rating: Strenuous
Distance: 6.0 miles, one-way
Elevation Gain: 2,780 feet
Estimated Time: 4.0 hours
Maps: USGS Camden and Lincolnville; *Maine Atlas and Gazetteer,*
Map 14 (DeLorme); *AMC Maine Mountains Trail Map*, Map 4;
Camden Hills State Park Map

**Combine six trails for a grand traverse over the long ridgeline of
Mount Megunticook from Maiden Cliff to Mount Battie.**

DIRECTIONS
From the junction of US 1 and ME 52 in Camden, drive north on ME 52 for
2.8 miles to the signed trailhead parking lot on the right. Parking space is
available for ten to twelve cars. *GPS coordinates: 44° 14.843′ N, 69° 5.282′ W.*

The end point for the hike is the Carriage Trail trailhead on ME 52, 1.3
miles north of its junction with US 1 in Camden. Parking is along the road.
GPS coordinates: 44° 13.591′ N, 69° 4.711′ W.

TRAIL DESCRIPTION
The mountainous terrain of Camden Hills State Park lies along the west shore
of Penobscot Bay in the towns of Camden and Lincolnville. The Camden Hills
share many characteristics with the mountains of Acadia on Mount Desert
Island 30 miles to the east: fine softwood forests; bold cliffs and ledges; and far-
reaching vistas of ocean, lakes, and mountains. At 1,385 feet, Mount Megunticook is not only the highest summit in the park, but the highest mainland
mountain on the Atlantic Coast of the United States.

Camden Hills State Park dates to the Great Depression of the 1930s, when
the National Park Service and Maine State Parks Commission developed the
park from what was once unproductive farmland. The federal government
purchased 1,500 acres of this poor land as part of a nationwide effort to create
accessible and affordable outdoor recreational opportunities for Americans.
The Civilian Conservation Corps cleared brush and leveled terrain, then built
roads, trails, parking lots, footbridges, and campground amenities. Continued

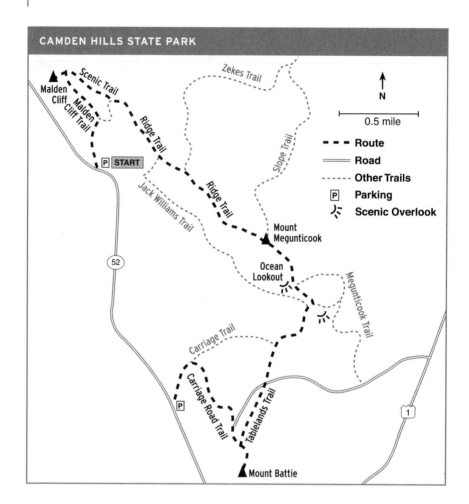

land acquisitions over time have brought the park to its present size of nearly 6,200 acres.

The Megunticook Traverse covers a good chunk of the park with its fine ridge walk that combines six different trails over 6.0 miles, taking in the peaks of Mount Megunticook and Mount Battie and the airy viewpoints atop Maiden Cliff and Ocean Lookout. Spot a car or bike at the Carriage Trail trailhead for a point-to-point hike or plan a not-unpleasant 1.5-mile road walk.

Wide, blue-blazed Maiden Cliff Trail starts from the far end of the lot and climbs a ravine next to a stream, soon crossing it on a footbridge. Ascend rock steps and a stony trail to the junction with Ridge Trail on the right. Continue on Maiden Cliff Trail as it rises steeply on switchbacks before making a mostly level run west through oaks and pines, then beech and maples, to the junction with Scenic Trail, reached in just under a mile.

The many ledge outlooks high on the long ridgeline of Mount Megunticook provide frequent views over Megunticook Lake in the scenic Camden Hills.

Follow a short spur left to the top of Maiden Cliff. Scramble down a few feet for an outstanding view over Megunticook Lake to Ragged Mountain and the ski slopes of Camden Snow Bowl, as well as Bald Mountain just next door. The great arm of Fernald's Neck extends far into the lake, and the Camden town beach at Barrett's Cove is visible as well. Just below the clifftop are the famous cross and a granite marker dedicated to Elenora French, the young woman who fell to her death near this spot in 1864 trying to catch her windblown hat.

Next, continue the hike on Scenic Trail, following an undulating route over several knobs with extensive open ledges and more bucolic views of the surrounding hills and farmlands as well as the ocean. Occasional cairns mark the route. The dark forests capping the heights of Mount Megunticook are soon visible ahead.

Join Ridge Trail and cross a couple of small brooks before trending gradually upward past several outlooks. On a sometimes-rough trail of roots and rocks amid the hemlocks, spruce, and pines, pass Jack Williams Trail on the right. Soon, after detouring up a shallow ravine, pass Zeke's Trail coming in from the left in a thick grove of spruce. A level stretch ahead leads to a nice lunch ledge and a fine window to Mount Battie and its winding auto road, and to the homes and farms in the Megunticook River valley.

Traverse a narrow ledge and pass several cairns to arrive at the wooded summit of Mount Megunticook, marked by a big rock pile. Just beyond, Slope Trail enters from the left. Continue ahead on Ridge Trail, traversing easily over bog bridges and through spruce woods along the ridgeline before dropping slightly to Ocean Lookout, a huge system of ledges and cliffs and a popular spot that rivals Maiden Cliff for views. If any place on the mountain is going to be crowded on a nice day, this will be. Fortunately there's plenty of room for all to find a place to relax and enjoy.

Camden village and its harbor are in focus below, and offshore are the islands of Vinalhaven and North Haven. Farther out is Deer Isle, and Isle au Haut, part of Acadia National Park. On a clear day you can even see all the way to Casco Bay some 60 miles south.

From Ocean Lookout, pass Megunticook Trail on the left, then descend steeply down the east side of the ledges via Tablelands Trail. The exposed cliff edge here offers more great views. Continue steeply downward to pass Adams Lookout Trail on the left, and then, after a series of rock steps, pass Jack Williams Trail. A wide and easy trail through a beech, oak, and maple forest turns into a steady descent on rocky trail past numerous large red oaks. Finally, level off at the junction with Carriage Trail, which enters from the right.

Ahead, cross several gullies and pass Nature Trail on the left before emerging on the Mount Battie Auto Road. There is a trailhead parking lot along the road to the left. Cross the road at an angle, and then continue on Tableland Trail, ascending easily over slabs and ledges. The trail parallels the road, which is visible at times down to the right. There are good views back to the north and Mount Megunticook.

After 0.5 mile, leave the woods and cross the auto road and summit parking lot and amble up to the stone observation tower and World War I memorial on top. Pit toilets are in the woods just behind the tower.

The 26-foot tower, designed by Camden summer resident Parker Morse Hooper, was erected in 1921 by the Mount Battie Association. The bronze plaque on the front of the tower reads, "In grateful recognition of the men and women of Camden in the World War, 1914-1918."

The extensive view of Camden Harbor and the myriad islands of Penobscot Bay from both the grassy lawn and the tower is a Maine coast classic, and ranges from the mountains of Acadia to Vinalhaven and North Haven.

To descend, follow the auto road downhill for 0.25 mile to Carriage Road Trail on the left. Now a simple footpath, this old carriage road was built by

Columbus Bushwell of Camden in 1897 and was the original route to the top of Battie and the Summit House Hotel, which operated until it was torn down in 1920. The existing 1.6-mile auto road to the summit of Mount Battie was constructed by the Maine State Park Commission in 1965, allowing easy access for thousands of visitors each year.

At the base of the mountain, the path joins Carriage Trail and follows this out to ME 52, 1.5 miles south of the original starting point.

DID YOU KNOW?

The Abenaki named the Camden Hills *Megunticook*, meaning "great swells of the sea."

MORE INFORMATION

Camden Hills State Park (parksandlands.com; 207-236-3109 during summer). The park is open for hiking year-round. Dogs are allowed, but must be leashed at all times. There is a daily entrance fee. Camping is available in the park at 106 campsites, complete with hot showers, restrooms, and other amenities.

NEARBY

Barrett's Cove Beach on Megunticook Lake is a nice spot for a swim after your hike. Adjacent to the beach is a grassy area with picnic tables and grills, and a nearby toilet. Afterward, meander through the picturesque harbor town of Camden and its bounty of shops and boutiques, galleries and restaurants, and colorful array of sailboats, lobster boats, and windjammers.

MORE HIKING

Camden Hills State Park features more than 30 miles of hiking on 21 trails. At least nine trails coming from all compass directions reach the high point of Mount Megunticook. Multi-Use Trail reaches into the interior of the park from both the US 1 side in the east and the Youngtown Road side in the north. This same trail also provides access to the blueberry fields atop Cameron Mountain, the craggy summit of Bald Rock Mountain, and Derry and Frohock mountains. Two primitive shelters on Bald Rock Mountain are available for backcountry camping.

POETS, ARTISTS, AND WRITERS ALONG THE MAINE COAST

The Maine coast has been the home and workplace of many poets, artists, and writers over time, its rugged natural beauty and remote character providing inspiration for a wealth of enduring works of art and literature.

Rockland-born poet Edna St. Vincent Millay (1892–1950) is best known for her 1912 work *Renascence*, which lyricized about the Camden Hills and Penobscot Bay. Henry Wadsworth Longfellow (1807–1882) was born in Portland and educated at Bowdoin College in Brunswick; his works of poetry include "Paul Revere's Ride," *The Song of Hiawatha*, and *Evangeline*.

Winslow Homer (1836–1910) is considered one of the foremost nineteenth-century American painters. *Breezing Up,* his 1876 painting of a father and three boys out for a sail, is thought to be his most famous work. N.C. Wyeth (1882–1945) summered in Port Clyde and is best known for his illustrations for Robert Louis Stevenson's *Treasure Island*. His son, Andrew Wyeth (1917–2009), spent summers up the coast in Cushing; his 1948 painting *Christina's World* is one of the best known images in twentieth-century American art. The landscape paintings of Mount Desert Island by Thomas Cole (1801–1848), founder of the Hudson River School, and his pupil Frederic Church (1826–1900), brought the beauty of what would eventually become Acadia National Park to East Coast city dwellers.

Abolitionist Harriet Beecher Stowe (1811–1896) published her internationally acclaimed anti-slavery novel *Uncle Tom's Cabin* in 1852 while living in Brunswick. Elwyn Brooks White, better known as E.B. White (1899–1985), lived on a Brooklin farm; he authored the enduring writing reference text *The Elements of Style* and beloved children's novels including *Charlotte's Web, Stuart Little,* and *The Trumpet of the Swan*. Sarah Orne Jewett (1849–1909), best known for her novella *The Country of the Pointed Firs*, lived her entire life in South Berwick. Rachel Carson (1907–1964) was the world-renowned marine biologist, environmentalist, and author of five books, including the groundbreaking *Silent Spring* in 1962.

Linda Greenlaw (1960–) of Isle au Haut is a best-selling author of a number of books about life as a commercial swordfishing boat captain, including *The Hungry Ocean*. Maine's most famous full-time resident is Stephen King (1947–) of Bangor, the prolific author having achieved worldwide fame with an incredible collection of novels, short stories, and nonfiction books, most of them in the horror genre and many set in Maine.

TRIP 29
LITTLE RIVER COMMUNITY TRAIL

Location: Belfast, ME
Rating: Moderate
Distance: 4.2 miles, one-way
Elevation Gain: 400 feet
Estimated Time: 2.5 hours
Maps: USGS Belfast, Searsport; *Maine Atlas and Gazetteer*, Map 14 (DeLorme); Belfast Bay Watershed Coalition trail map

Enjoy a wooded ramble along the undeveloped shoreline of two reservoirs and a scenic stretch of the Little River.

DIRECTIONS

To the starting trailhead: From the junction of US 1 and ME 3 on the western outskirts of Belfast, turn south onto US 1 and drive 2.8 miles to the entrance of the Belfast Water District facility (marked by a blue-and-gold sign) on the right. Follow the drive past the garage buildings to a dirt parking lot beyond, where a red-and-white sign reads, "Hikers, please park here." There is space for four to six cars next to the white fence. An information kiosk and the start of the trail are to the left of the lot, just above the reservoir. *GPS coordinates: 44° 23.736′ N, 68° 59.412′ W.*

To the ending trailhead: From the junction of US 1 and ME 52 (traffic light) on the western outskirts of Belfast, turn south onto ME 52 and drive 0.1 mile to the Walsh Ballfields. Trailhead parking is in the lower lot near the information kiosk. *GPS coordinates: 44° 24.918′ N, 69° 1.242′ W.*

TRAIL DESCRIPTION

Little River Community Trail was built by the Belfast Bay Watershed Coalition and opened to the public in 2007. After devastating fires swept through downtown Belfast in 1865 and 1871, its citizens voted in 1887 to accept a proposal by a Boston civil engineering firm to create the Belfast Water Company, which constructed a 175-foot dam near the mouth of the Little River to create a large reservoir. Belfast Reservoir No. 1 is the body of water visible beyond the information kiosk. A short distance away is the red-brick building of the old water works, now a local landmark and the offices of the Belfast Water District. The water district discontinued using its reservoirs in 1980, and now relies entirely

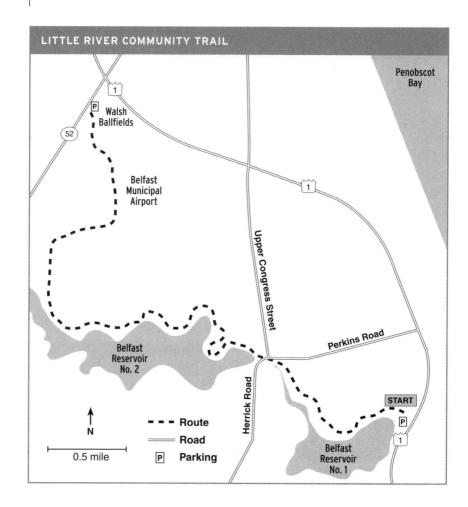

LITTLE RIVER COMMUNITY TRAIL

Penobscot Bay

Walsh Ballfields

Belfast Municipal Airport

Belfast Reservoir No. 2

Upper Congress Street

Perkins Road

Herrick Road

START

Belfast Reservoir No. 1

N

0.5 mile

- - - Route
=== Road
P Parking

on two wells in a sand-and-gravel aquifer on the east side of the city. Today, the brick pump house is a popular landmark and serves as the offices of the Belfast Water District. Water from the reservoirs empty into Penobscot Bay on the other side of US 1.

The trail is a point-to-point hike: spot a car or bicycle at the hike terminus on ME 52. Another option is to phone for a taxi cab to return you to your car at the end of the hike (Bay Taxi, 207-338-1993).

To begin the walk, follow the wide, blue-blazed trail above the lake, where there is a nice view east back to the US 1 bridge over the outlet and beyond to the bay. Ahead, enjoy another lake view at a small pebbly beach. Cross a trickle of an inlet on rocks, and then proceed along the lake through a beautiful park-like stand of tall white pines. Soon, turn uphill away from the water and begin

An old red-brick pump house and 175-foot dam that impounds Belfast Reservoir No. 1 mark the start of Little River Community Trail.

the first of several short and easy up-and-downs as the trail makes its way over the washboard terrain along the lake.

After weaving through a lovely stand of big pines, reach a grassy lawn on the edge of the lake. Ahead is a junction; here the "high water" bypass leaves to the right. Continue left to follow along a narrow arm of the lake. The high water trail enters from the right a short distance ahead. After a rope swing and swimming hole, negotiate several bog bridges at the head of the inlet, then meander through a semi-open grove of big pines. Cross a creek bed, then turn sharply left (a field is visible ahead through the trees). Stay left at an arrow and double blaze to reach a rocky ledge above the rushing Little River.

Continuing on, the trail proceeds through the woods along the edge of a large field. Several small waterfalls can be seen in the gorge below to the left. The trail soon emerges from the woods at the paved Perkins Road. Turn left onto Perkins Road to reach its junction with Herrick Road and Upper Congress Street a short distance ahead. Continue on Herrick Road to a dam and waterfall at Reservoir No. 2, built in 1913. Cross the road and proceed into the woods right of the dam on a dirt driveway marked by two yellow poles and a sign for Little River Trail.

Pass a fenced-in enclosure at the top of the dam, hiking easily along on the wide old woods road. In 100 feet, bear left off the old road onto a foot trail. A sign on a tree is marked, "Hiking Trail." There are also a map and text description of the trail route.

Walk along the top of a steep bank leading down to reservoir, which, like the first reservoir, has no development along its shores. Enjoy beautiful views across the water from the shoreline lookout. Carry on through young woods of cherry and dogwoods, maple, ash, beech, and oak. It's easy striding on the level as the trail swings around a point revealing a view back to the dam on Herrick Road.

This area was once the domain of the Abenaki Penobscot, who summered here to feast on the abundant fish, shellfish, and waterfowl. The land became part of the Muscongus Patent in 1630, which allowed English settlers to establish trading posts for furs. General Samuel Waldo of Boston owned the patent and the land, then known as the Passagassawakeag Plantation, from around 1720 to his death in 1759. Waldo's heirs sold the tract to a group of Irish and Scot proprietors from Londonderry, New Hampshire, who renamed it after Belfast in Northern Ireland. The seaport of Belfast was finally settled in 1770 and incorporated as a town three years later.

The reservoir opens up to the left as the wide path follows around a cove. Reach a junction with a grassy woods road and turn left (arrow). Ahead, a short spur leads to a viewpoint on the water. Where the wide path bears away to the right, continue straight ahead on a footpath. The narrow trail leads through thick woods away from the reservoir. Cross a ravine on a footbridge, then wind downslope to cross a wet area on rock steps and corduroy trail (logs laid side by side). Ascend the far slope, then pass by a large stump of pine. A spur leads left to the water. Beyond, swing around a point of land beneath a shady canopy of hemlocks and pines, hugging the shoreline. Drop into a ravine, cross a creeklet, then swing around the head of the reservoir.

Negotiate the washboard terrain ahead, crossing several inlets and wet areas on log bridges. After a concrete post marking a property boundary, reach another short spur to the water. Follow a low ridge with wet areas to either side. Beyond, bear sharply left into a patch of fragrant balsam fir. A house and barn can now be seen across the reservoir.

With the Little River just ahead, turn uphill and climb high above the river, then drop down to cross the bottomland on a rock walkway. Cross several tributary streams, one by a log bridge and another by fording, then a wet area as the trail passes through some big old growth hemlocks. Follow along the beautiful, bubbling Little River, which is about 20 feet wide at this point. The

Little River is one of four small watersheds, including the Passagassawakeag and Goose rivers and Wescott Stream, that compose the 69,657-acre Belfast Bay Watershed that drains all or part of nine coastal communities in this area of Waldo County.

Pass a large streamside boulder before taking a sharp right away from the river. Ahead, bear left onto a narrow path, then cross a dip on corduroy. A nice footbridge spans a ravine. Beyond, cross an old, wet woods road. Swing right into a long, wide corridor through the woods. Cross several old woods roads in cutover woods. Several winding sections of nice rock work lead through wet areas. Roots and bog bridges mark the route as it heads for ME 52. Follow the woodline around the edge of a swamp, which is on the property of the Belfast Municipal Airport. Cross a creek, then pass through a gap in a stone wall to emerge into a large open field. Make your way straight ahead to the Walsh Ballfields, bearing left along the outfield fence to reach the large paved parking lot and trail terminus.

DID YOU KNOW?

The name of the nearby Passagassawakeag River in Belfast is American Indian in origin and is believed to mean "a sturgeon's place" or "a place for spearing sturgeon by torchlight."

MORE INFORMATION

Belfast Bay Watershed Coalition (belfastbaywatershed.org). The Little River Community Trail is open year-round from dawn to dusk. Dogs are allowed on-leash.

NEARBY

Stroll through the historical streets of Belfast, a thriving port city of more than 6,000 residents, and enjoy an eclectic mix of shops, galleries, and restaurants (belfastmaine.org; 207-338-5900). The exhibits and collections of the Penobscot Marine Museum, an extensive campus in the heart of Searsport, celebrate the rich maritime history and culture of the Penobscot Bay region (penobscotmarinemuseum.org; 207-548-2529).

MORE HIKING

In-Town Nature Trail in Belfast is a 5.0-mile walk linking the green spaces of the city that can be tackled in four segments, while Hutchinson Center Trail is a pleasant 1.3-mile extension of Little River Community Trail connecting ME 52 with ME 3 (belfastbaywatershed.org). Coastal Mountains Land Trust also has several preserves in Belfast that are part of the Passagassawakeag Greenway (coastalmountains.org, 207-236-7091). Just north in Searsport, a conservation easement protects two-thirds of 936-acre Sears Island, the largest uninhabited island on the East Coast of the US, where a handful of trails and byways allow for several miles of exploration (friendsofsearsisland.org; 207-548-0142).

4

ACADIA NATIONAL PARK

This section describes four hikes that offer a good introduction to the beauty of Acadia National Park. The main portion of the 49,000-acre park is located on lobster claw-shaped Mount Desert Island, an 80,000-acre island connected to the mainland by a short bridge and causeways. Scoured and reformed by the powerful action of glaciers, the island is divided into distinct east and west sections by Somes Sound; Frenchman Bay is to the east, with Blue Hill Bay to the west. The remaining 8,000 acres of the park are on Schoodic Peninsula, Isle au Haut, and a number of scattered islands.

A range of coarse-grained pink-granite mountains—26 in all, with eight over 1,000 feet in elevation—extend across the island from east to west. Cadillac Mountain rises to 1,528 feet, the highest point on the entire eastern seaboard of the US. In the U-shaped valleys between these lovely mountains are quiet forests of coniferous and deciduous trees, and a multitude of streams, meadows, and peatlands that support more than 1,200 plant species. Twenty-six pristine glacial lakes and ponds hold thriving fish populations. The island's 41 miles of coastal shoreline comprises cliffs and tidepools; sand, pebble, and cobble beaches; mud flats and tidal marshes; and many islands large and small. Wildlife is abundant in Acadia, where 40 species of mammals, 11 species of amphibians, 7 species of reptiles, and 230 bird species make their home.

Twelve species of marine mammals are found in the ocean waters surrounding the island, including whales, seals, dolphins, and porpoises.

The earliest evidence of human habitation dates to 3,000 years ago at Fernald Point near the entrance to Somes Sound, which provided access to game, berries, and water. At low tide, abundant clams and mussels could be gathered on the mudflats. More recently, in the 1500s, written records from European explorers describe encounters with the Wabanaki, or "People of the Dawnland," who made their home on the island. In 1604, Sieur de Monts and his navigator Samuel de Champlain claimed all of the land between the 40th and 46th parallels for King Henry IV of France. The expedition mapped the coast of Maine, including "Isle des Monts Desert," the name Champlain gave the island for its barren mountaintops. Acadia is often thought to be from the French *la cadie*, meaning "the place." In the late 1800s, the island attracted summering "rusticators," well-to-do people from the eastern cities who came in search of a quieter, simpler way of life and built their summer "cottages" on the island, which remains a popular resort area.

Permanent protection for the lands that now compose Acadia National Park was sought by citizens concerned about overdevelopment in the early part of the twentieth century, most notably Charles Eliot, George Dorr, and John D. Rockefeller. (Read on through the section for more on the history of the protection of Acadia.) Today, more than 2 million visitors come to the park each year to recreate, reflect, relax, and refresh amid the stunning natural landscape of mountains and ocean, islands and cliffs, lakes and trees, blue skies and pink granite. More than 120 miles of hiking trails, 57 miles of historical carriage roads (45 inside the park, 12 outside), and the 27-mile paved Park Loop Road crisscross the land, offering myriad ways to visit all of the must-see points of interest in the park.

Acadia National Park is open year-round. An entrance fee is charged from May 1 through October 31 regardless of how or where visitors enter the park. Pay entrance fees at the entrance station on Park Loop Road near Sand Beach, Hulls Cove Visitor Center, park headquarters, Blackwoods and Seawall campgrounds, Thompson Island Visitor Center, and Bar Harbor Village Green.

Park and island roads can be very congested during the busy summer months; to beat the traffic and decrease your impact, ride the Island Explorer bus, a free shuttle that operates from late June through Columbus Day. The buses offer service on eight routes linking park destinations, local towns and villages, and the regional airport in Trenton. Regularly scheduled buses stop at points throughout the park, including campgrounds, carriage road entrances, and many trailheads. Hikers can also flag buses along their route.

TRIP 30
BEECH CLIFF/BEECH MOUNTAIN LOOPS

Location: Southwest Harbor, ME
Rating: Moderate
Distance: 3.2 miles
Elevation Gain: 780 feet
Estimated Time: 2.5 hours
Maps: USGS Southwest Harbor; *Maine Atlas and Gazetteer*, Map 16
(DeLorme); *AMC Acadia National Park Discovery Map*

**Walk atop cliffs and trek to a firetower for far-reaching ocean and
mountain views over Mount Desert Island.**

DIRECTIONS
From the junction of ME 102/ME 198 and ME 3/ME 198 in Somesville, proceed south on ME 102 for 0.9 mile. Turn right onto Pretty Marsh Road and
drive west for 0.3 mile. Turn left onto Beech Hill Road and follow it south for
2.8 miles to a gate marking the entrance to Acadia National Park. Continue
an additional 0.3 mile to the end of the road and the paved trailhead parking
lot for Beech Mountain and Beech Cliffs, where there is space for 30 cars. *GPS
coordinates: 44° 19.170′ N, 68° 20.604′ W.*

TRAIL DESCRIPTION
This hike combines all or a portion of four trails—Beech Cliff Loop, Canada Cliff, Valley, and Beech Mountain—en route to cliff-top panoramas of
mountains and the ocean. *Note: Beech Cliff Loop may be closed from March 15
through August 15 in order to protect nesting peregrine falcons and their young
chicks. Contact the park in advance of your hike to be sure.*

Beech Cliff Loop Trail begins from the east side of the road at the base of
the parking lot. Take the wide gravel path into the woods and soon reach a trail
junction. Canada Cliff Trail departs right, while Beech Cliff Loop forks to the
left. Take the right-hand fork—the outer loop—to walk the Beech Cliff Loop
in a counterclockwise direction. The trail leads out to the edge of Beech Cliff
and a striking vista overlooking Echo Lake and its sand beach below. Look east
over Acadia Mountain to Norumbega Mountain and the complex of Sargent
and Penobscot mountains beyond, including Gilmore Peak, and Parkman and

Cedar Swamp mountains. To the southwest you can see the fire tower atop Beech Mountain.

Continue north on the airy cliff walk with extensive views up and down Echo Lake, with the dock and float of AMCs Echo Lake Camp visible on the east shore of the lake. The camp offers comfortable week-long tent camping stays complete with meals and recreational amenities for individuals, couples, and families from late June through early September (amcecholakecamp.org).

Over the north shoulder of Acadia Mountain, the waters of Somes Sound slice into the heart of the island. All too soon the trail bears left away from the cliff and loops back to the junction with Canada Cliff Trail. Continue south on Canada Cliff Trail to arrive at the junction with Beech Cliff Trail, which leaves to the left and descends steeply via a series of iron ladders to Echo Lake.

Ahead, hike through the woods along the top of the cliffs, with occasional views to the beach directly below at the south end of Echo Lake. Descend past an erratic boulder at head height. The fire tower on Beech Mountain comes into view straight ahead in the distance, perched on the open ledges to the west. Continue downward and then contour along, with occasional views east over Saint Sauveur Mountain all the way to Cadillac Mountain, the highest point on the island. Wind down through the pines and cedars, spruce and fir to a trail junction in a deep ravine. Here, a spur leads left to the beach parking lot at Echo Lake. Stay right and head for Valley Trail, which is reached after climbing out of the ravine and up the slope beyond. Turn right onto Valley Trail, an old logging road, and follow it up and over the height-of-land known as Canada Hollow to return to the trailhead parking lot in the notch between Beech Mountain and Beech Cliff.

Cut diagonally across the parking lot to its far left corner to Beech Mountain Trail, which forks a short distance into the woods. Turn left up the mountain on the wide path, at first on log steps then on rock steps. Ahead, the angle of the winding trail eases and the trees of the summit come into view. After a view on the right to Long Pond, climb up the last slabs, then cross the top of the mountain to reach the base of the fire tower and the junction of Beech Mountain South Ridge Trail. Scamper up this trail 10 yards to the tower.

Except for occasional weekends in summer and fall, the Beech Mountain fire tower is closed to the public. No matter: scramble up the steps as high as you can go to enjoy far reaching ocean and mountain views in every direction across the island, which range east to Cadillac Mountain, south to Northeast and Southwest harbors and the Cranberry Islands beyond, and west to Western Mountain and its twin peaks of Mansell and Bernard mountains. The tower is on the National Register of Historic Fire Towers. The original wooden

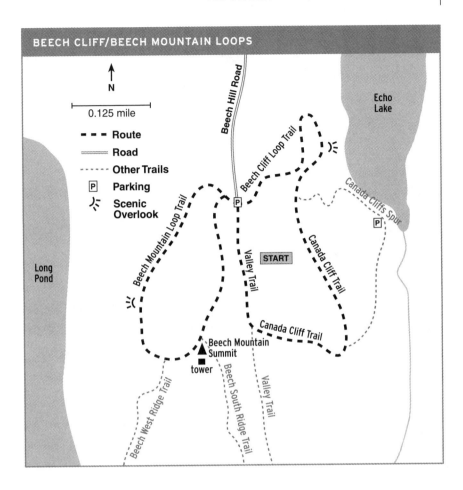

tower constructed by the Civilian Conservation Corps (CCC) was used from 1941 to the mid-1950s; it was replaced by a steel tower in 1962. The tower was last staffed by a park ranger for forest fire spotting in 1976.

From the tower, return to Beech Mountain Trail just below and turn left (west) to continue. Soon, pass Beech Mountain West Ridge Trail on the left. Beyond are the spectacular cliff-top ledges overlooking Long Pond—at 4.0 miles long, it is the largest body of fresh water on the island. The steep cliffs of Mansell Mountain rise more than 800 feet above the water. Early evening along this airy stretch of trail is particularly scenic, when the disappearing sun casts a golden glow across the pink-granite rocks before dipping beyond Blue Hill, the pyramidal bump visible a little north of west.

Continue easily along over the open ledges and then descend into the woods, winding down to reach the final section of wide trail that leads back around the mountain to close the loop and return to the trailhead parking lot.

The Beech Mountain Firetower, on the National Register of Historic Fire Towers, is sometimes open to the public on weekends in summer and fall.

DID YOU KNOW?

In the 1800s, Southwest Harbor and the Cranberry Isles played important roles in the commerce between Europe and Canada and New York, Boston, and Philadelphia. To safely guide shipping vessels around dangerous rocks, four lighthouses were built along the southern coast of Mount Desert Island. Bass Harbor, Bear Island, Baker Island and Egg Rock lights remain today.

MORE INFORMATION

Acadia National Park (nps.gov/acad; 207-288-3338).

NEARBY

At the base of towering Beech Cliff at the south end of freshwater Echo Lake lies a beautiful sandy beach, the most popular swimming spot on the island and a great place to cool off on a warm summer day. South on ME 102, the pretty village of Southwest Harbor has a variety of shops, eateries, and services. The Wendell Gilley Museum in Southwest Harbor features the pioneering decorative bird carvings of Wendell Gilley, while the Seal Cove Auto Museum in Seal Cove houses a unique collection of antique electric, steam-powered, and gasoline automobiles.

TRIP 31
SIX PEAKS CIRCUIT

Location: Mount Desert, ME
Rating: Strenuous
Distance: 6.8 miles
Elevation Gain: 2,110 feet
Estimated Time: 5.0 hours
Maps: USGS Southwest Harbor; *Maine Atlas and Gazetteer*, Map 16 (DeLorme); *AMC Acadia National Park Discovery Map; AMC Maine Mountain Guide*, Map 5: Eastern Mount Desert Island

Tackle six summits and enjoy extraordinary ocean views on this rugged loop over the high peaks between Jordan Pond and Somes Sound.

DIRECTIONS

From the junction of ME 102/ME 198 and ME 3/ME 198 in Somesville, proceed east and then south on ME 3/ME 198 for 4.8 miles to the paved trailhead parking lot (no sign) on the right, a paved turnout with space for fifteen cars. In season, the free Island Explorer shuttle bus (Route 6) makes regular trips between Bar Harbor and Northeast Harbor, with stops at this trailhead. *GPS coordinates: 44° 22.691′ N, 68° 13.777′ W.*

TRAIL DESCRIPTION

This outstanding circuit hike combines all or a portion of eight trails and a section of the historical carriage roads on its rambling route over six mountain peaks in nearly 7 miles. From Bald Peak and Parkman Mountain to Gilmore Peak and Sargent Mountain to Penobscot and Cedar Swamp mountains, the route will treat you to alpine-like terrain and far-reaching ocean and mountain vistas.

Begin across the road from the north end of the parking lot, where a logpost trail sign marks the start of Hadlock Brook Trail. Follow this trail east into the woods. In 100 yards, pass by Parkman Mountain Trail on the left (you'll return on this trail at the end of the hike). A few minutes ahead, reach the junction with Bald Peak Trail.

Turn left onto Bald Peak Trail, and in 50 yards, cross one of the historical crushed-gravel carriage roads that wind through the mountains and valleys in

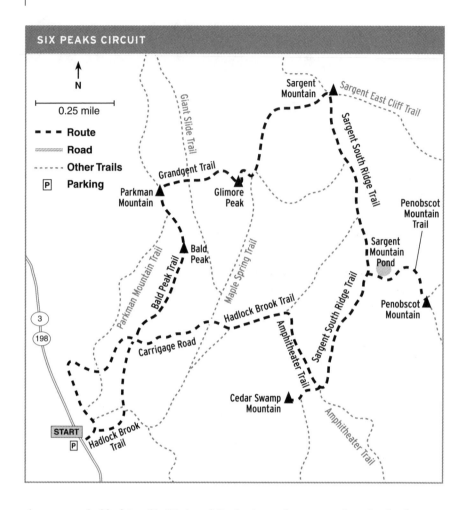

SIX PEAKS CIRCUIT

N

0.25 mile

- - - Route
=== Road
---- Other Trails
P Parking

Giant Slide Trail

Grandgent Trail

Sargent Mountain

Sargent East Cliff Trail

Parkman Mountain

Glimore Peak

Sargent South Ridge Trail

Penobscot Mountain Trail

Bald Peak

Parkman Mountain Trail

Bald Peak Trail

Maple Spring Trail

Sargent Mountain Pond

Hadlock Brook Trail

Penobscot Mountain

Carrigage Road

Sargent South Ridge Trail

Amphitheater Trail

3

198

Cedar Swamp Mountain

Amphitheater Trail

START
P
Hadlock Brook Trail

the eastern half of Acadia National Park. Ascend next to a brook, climbing at a moderate then steep grade over rocks and roots. Cross Around-Mountain Carriage Road and head straight up the slope beyond. Views to the southwest over the spruce- and fir-clad slopes of Norumbega Mountain to the mouth of Somes Sound and the village of Southwest Harbor begin to open up. Beyond are the Cranberry Islands, and close below is Upper Hadlock Pond. The long pink-granite ridgeline to the east is Cedar Swamp Mountain.

Top out on a crag, and then descend briefly into a ravine. Ahead, climb out of the ravine on rocks, ledges, and outcrops before breaking into the open. The monadnock of Blue Hill is now visible to the northwest, while Bald Peak is in sight ahead on the trail.

After a wooded patch, take a sharp left up slabs following cairns. Bernard and Mansell mountains appear over the humped ridge of Norumbega, while to

The Bates cairn, a common trail marker in Acadia National Park, generally consists of two base stones and a mantle topped with a pointer rock.

the east, Penobscot Mountain now rises over Cedar Swamp Mountain. Wind along through the rocks, huckleberry bushes, juniper, pines, and birch. A final easy climb over the barren ridge leads to the summit of Bald Peak (971 feet) and wonderful views north to Parkman Mountain, Gilmore Peak, and Sargent Mountain.

Cross the open ridge, and with a view across Somes Sound to the marina at Mount Desert Yacht Yard on the west shore, drop into the trees and descend steeply into a notch. Traverse the level floor then climb a short pitch. Turn right onto Parkman Mountain Trail and quickly reach the summit of Parkman Mountain (950 feet) and grand views west to the bulk of Western Mountain (includes Bernard and Mansell mountains); Acadia, Saint Sauveur, and Beech mountains; and Blue Hill Bay at the far western edge of the island.

Continue east on Grandgent Trail, bear right along the ridge, and then drop down into the woods. Proceed easily at first, then on rough trail into a deep ravine. Follow the streamlet lined with mossy boulders and thick spruce woods. Giant Slide Trail enters from the left; continue straight ahead on Grandgent Trail up over rocks and roots, passing some impressive ancient spruce.

Ahead, the trail angles off to the southeast, climbing more steeply over ledges before emerging onto the open rocks leading to the broad and bald top of Gilmore Peak (1,030 feet). The forested lower slopes of Sargent Mountain are just ahead across a ravine. Turning clockwise you can see Penobscot and Cedar Swamp mountains, Bald Peak, and Parkman Mountain. West are Somes Sound, Western Mountain, Blue Hill Bay, and Blue Hill. Farther west, the peaks of the Camden Hills can be seen. Northward are the mountains around Bangor.

Somes Sound was long referred to as the only natural fjord on the East Coast of the US, but it is now considered a fjard, a glacial embayment that is shorter, shallower, and broader than the typical Norwegian fjord. Somes Sound is impressive nonetheless at 100 feet deep, 1 mile wide at its mouth, and 6 miles long. The sound is named after Abraham Somes (1732–1819), the primary founder of English settlements on Mount Desert Island.

Drop down into the ravine on steep and rough trail. Cross a stream on a footbridge to arrive at the junction with Maple Spring Trail on the right in a forest of spruce and cedars. Turn left onto Grandgent Trail and proceed north up the valley, crossing and recrossing a stream several times during the climb. After a stretch of very rocky trail, break out of the trees and follow cairns up the broad and barren upper dome of Sargent Mountain (1,379 feet).

Panoramic views are the reward for the effort to reach this beautiful point, the second highest on the island. Four trails converge on the peak: Continue southward on wide-open Sargent South Ridge Trail. Views east look to Pemetic Mountain and, beyond, the long ridge of Cadillac Mountain. Southward are the Cranberry Islands and the Atlantic Ocean. The town of Cranberry Isles archipelago consists of five islands: Great and Little Cranberry, and Sutton, Bear, and Baker islands. Named for the profusion of cranberries that grow there, Great and Little Cranberry are home to a small population of hardy year-round residents.

Pass by Maple Spring Trail. Ahead, Sargent South Ridge Trail makes a wide arc to the right. Hadlock Brook Trail enters from the right, and not far ahead, Sargent South Ridge Trail descends into the trees for a brief stretch. Out in the open once again, Cadillac and Pemetic mountains appear prominently to the east, with Penobscot Mountain more defined to the south.

Reach the junction of Penobscot Mountain Trail and turn left onto it, quickly reaching the pretty tarn of Sargent Mountain Pond. The pond is thought to be Maine's oldest lake, the first to appear after the glaciers retreated some 12,000 years ago. Two benches invite you to relax, and on a warm day, the pond is great for a refreshing swim.

Leaving the pond, Penobscot Mountain Trail climbs a short pitch up to a shelf, and then turns sharply left. Ahead, make a steep descent into a rocky ravine to meet Deer Brook Trail, which enters from the left. Continue straight ahead on Penobscot Mountain Trail and quickly gain open ground again. Reach the summit of Penobscot Mountain (1,196 feet) and panoramic views. To the east and northeast you can now see all the way to Lead Mountain and Tunk, Black, and Schoodic mountains of the Donnell Pond Public Reserved Land in Downeast Maine.

The long ridge of Penobscot Mountain extends to the south. Looking back toward Sargent Mountain, the backsides of The Bubbles are in view just to the right. Amble across the rocks to the east for a short distance to get a look out over lovely Jordan Pond, one of the most popular sights in the park. Ringed by mountains, miles of trails trace its shores, and its scenic waters attract canoeists and kayakers. The south end of the pond is home to the historical Jordan Pond House, a bucolic spot where looking out over the pond to The Bubbles while enjoying tea and fresh-baked popovers on the grand lawn is an age-old tradition.

To continue the hike, retrace your steps to the junction of Sargent South Ridge Trail via Penobscot Mountain Trail. From the junction, turn left to hike south on Sargent South Ridge Trail, crossing a semi-open ridge. Ahead, the trail alternates in and out of the trees as it winds down the slope at a moderate grade, offering a variety of views to the south and west. Walk high above the valley that separates you from the long summit ridge of Penobscot Mountain before dropping down into a dark ravine. Below, but just above Birch Spring, reach the junction with Amphitheater Trail.

Proceed down to Birch Spring (water on the left) on Sargent South Ridge Trail, and then climb steeply out of the rocky defile. A short distance ahead, the trail levels off to reach a spur trail on the right leading to the summit of Cedar Swamp Mountain (950 feet). From here you can get a good look at the entire circuit and all the peaks you've climbed this day.

Return to Birch Spring and just beyond, turn left onto Amphitheater Trail. Follow bog bridges around the margin of a wet area, and then contour easily along. Descend briefly, contour again, then drop down to intersect Hadlock Brook Trail. Turn left onto Hadlock Brook Trail to Around-Mountain Carriage Road. Turn right to follow the carriage road to Waterfall Bridge, one of seventeen fine stone bridges in the park. Hemlock Bridge and the junction of Maple Spring Trail are just ahead.

The wide carriage road winds along the base of Bald Peak and Parkman Mountain. Intersect Bald Peak Trail, and soon reach a junction of carriage roads at signpost 12. Bear left here, and quickly intersect Parkman Mountain Trail. Stay on the carriage road and wind around on a hairpin turn to a junction at signpost 13; proceed straight ahead. Beyond, where the carriage road bends back to the east, turn right off the road onto Parkman Mountain Trail. Follow this downhill to Hadlock Brook Trail. Turn right here and soon emerge from the woods on ME 3/ME 198, just across from the trailhead parking lot.

DID YOU KNOW?

In the early 1900s, Waldron Bates developed the first trail handbook for Acadia, establishing construction and maintenance standards to guide early trail building efforts. Bates pioneered the style of cairn, or trail marker, that appears on trails throughout the park and now bears his name—two base stones and a mantle rock are topped with pointer rock, the Bates cairn.

MORE INFORMATION

Acadia National Park (nps.gov/acad; 207-288-3338).

NEARBY

In Northeast Harbor, located high on the western slope of Eliot Mountain overlooking the water, is Thuya Garden, a private 140-acre preserve that features a lovely mix of semiformal English border gardens and native Maine woodlands (gardenpreserve.org/thuya-garden). Just west of Thuya is the Asticou Azalea Garden, a wonderfully inspirational private preserve with rhododendrons and azaleas from mountainous regions around the world (gardenpreserve.org/asticou-azalea-garden). The Cranberry Islands, accessible by ferry from Northeast Harbor, Southwest Harbor, and Manset, are home to two historical societies, shops, and galleries, and quiet lanes and trails for walking and biking.

MORE HIKING

The park maintains an extensive network of trails on this western edge of the eastern side of Mount Desert Island, with plenty of hiking nearby on Norumbega Mountain and Lower Hadlock Pond to the west and Jordan Pond and The Bubbles to the east. Just outside the park boundary near Northeast Harbor is Eliot Mountain, home to some of the oldest trails on the island. Named for Charles W. Eliot, one of the founders of Acadia National Park, the peak and its environs are worth a visit.

ACADIA'S CARRIAGE ROADS

An elaborate system of carriage roads winds through the scenic mountains and valleys on the eastern side of Mount Desert Island. Closed to motorized traffic, the carriage roads are wide open for use by walkers and hikers, road bicyclists and mountain bikers, joggers and runners, horseback riders and horse-drawn carriages, and, in winter, cross-country skiers and snowshoers. Within Acadia National Park, 45 miles of carriage roads extend from the visitor center at Hull's Cove to Day Mountain and from Upper Hadlock Pond to Bubble Pond, connecting many of the park's most popular attractions. An additional 12 miles of private carriage roads outside the park in the Seal Harbor area are also accessible to the public, with the exception of bicycle use.

The carriage roads are the brainchild of millionaire philanthropist, natural resource steward, and island summer resident John D. Rockefeller, who financed and closely supervised their construction from 1913 to 1940. Rockefeller later gifted the carriage roads and his considerable land holdings to the park, increasing its acreage by one-third.

The 16-foot-wide, fine-gravel-surfaced carriage roads are good examples of the broken-stone roads common in the United States at the turn of the twentieth century. Given the enormous amount of hand labor involved in creating them, the roads are considered to be somewhat of an engineering marvel. Large blocks of local granite or coping stones line the roads and serve as guardrails. Elaborate cedar signposts at intersections provide directions. Two impressive gate lodges, near Jordan Pond and in Northeast Harbor, welcome users. Seventeen stone bridges span the many streams, waterfalls, roads, and cliffsides along the carriage roads. Each unique in style and design, the bridges are constructed of steel-reinforced concrete faced with native granite.

Rockefeller paid to maintain the carriage roads until his death in 1960, but over the next two decades, the roads fell into disrepair due to a lack of funding. In 1989, Rockefeller's son David and the nonprofit Friends of Acadia created an endowment matched by federal funds in order to rehabilitate the carriage roads and bridges. The $8 million construction project was completed in the early 2000s. Through the endowment, Friends of Acadia continues to contribute $200,000 annually for carriage road maintenance (friendsofacadia.org).

A free *Carriage Road User's Map* is available at park facilities and at nps.gov/acad/planyourvisit/brochures.htm.

TRIP 32
CADILLAC MOUNTAIN TRAVERSE

Location: Bar Harbor, ME
Rating: Strenuous
Distance: 6.0 miles
Elevation Gain: 1,320 feet
Estimated Time: 4.5 hours
Maps: USGS Southwest Harbor; *Maine Atlas and Gazetteer*, Map 16 (DeLorme); *AMC Acadia National Park Discovery Map; AMC Maine Mountain Guide*, Map 5: Eastern Mount Desert Island

Make a spectacular north–south traverse of Acadia National Park's highest summit with nearly continuous ocean and mountain views in all directions.

DIRECTIONS

During the busy summer season: Hikers must use the Island Explorer shuttle bus to reach Cadillac North Ridge Trail, as the extremely limited parking available at the overlook on Park Loop Road must be shared with throngs of sightseers. Park your vehicle at the Hulls Cove Visitor Center, in downtown Bar Harbor, or at Jordan Pond. Ride the shuttle bus to the start of Kebo Brook Trail on Paradise Hill Road, 0.3 mile south of the ME 233 overpass. This new approach trail was developed by the park to provide access to popular Cadillac North Ridge Trail, Gorge Path, and Kebo Mountain Trail. There is no parking at this trailhead. *GPS coordinates: 44° 22.767′ N, 68° 13.917′ W.*

During the less crowded spring and fall seasons: From the junction of ME 3 and ME 233 in Bar Harbor, turn west onto ME 233 and drive 1.1 miles to the entrance of Acadia National Park on the right. Turn right here and, just ahead, bear left to reach the Paradise Hill Road in just 0.1 mile. Turn left (south) onto Paradise Hill Road and travel 0.5 mile to the junction of the Park Loop Road and Jordan Pond Road. Turn left onto the one-way Park Loop Road and drive 0.3 mile to the trailhead on the right, marked by a log-post trail sign. Parking spaces for fifteen cars are available on the opposite side of the road at the overlook. *GPS coordinates: 44° 19.559′ N, 68° 17.474′ W.*

TRAIL DESCRIPTION

At 1,528 feet in elevation, Cadillac Mountain is the highest point not only in Acadia National Park, but on the entire Atlantic seaboard between Labrador and Brazil. Its summit is the first place in the United States to see the morning sun in autumn and winter, when the sun rises south of due east (in spring and summer the sun first touches the summit of Mars Hill, 150 miles to the north; for a short time around the spring and fall equinox, West Quoddy Head in Lubec holds the honor). Though its first English name was Green Mountain, Cadillac was renamed in 1918 by park superintendent George Dorr to honor the French explorer and adventurer Antoine Laumet de la Mothe, Sieur de Cadillac. In 1688, the governor of New France granted Laumet a parcel of land that included what is now Mount Desert Island and much of mainland Downeast Maine. This traverse combines North Ridge and South Ridge trails for a magnificent mountain walk over the alpine-like terrain of this windswept peak.

From the trail post on the east side of Paradise Hill Road, take Kebo Brook Trail away from the power line and uphill into the woods. Contour along to reach a junction. Here, Kebo Brook Trail continues left to Gorge Path; climb the steps on the right to reach Park Loop Road. Turn left and walk along the road for 100 feet, then cross the road at the crosswalk to reach the start of Cadillac North Ridge Trail proper.

Climb the granite steps and hike south through thin tree cover to an outlook eastward over Bar Harbor to Bar Island, the Porcupine islands, Frenchman Bay, the Schoodic Peninsula, and beyond to the mountains of Donnell Pond Public Reserved Land. Wind up over a big slab, level off, then climb again to a view west over Eagle Lake to the bulk of Sargent Mountain. The summit of Cadillac is just visible ahead over the treetops.

It's easy walking through the woods of spruce, fir, and birch on this lower portion of the mountain's north ridge. The narrow trail passes through a corridor of pitch pines and proceeds on the level for a good stretch. Ahead, the upper part of the north ridge comes into view, including the gorge separating Cadillac and Dorr mountains. Beyond Dorr, a portion of Champlain Mountain can now be seen.

At just under a mile into the walk the trail passes just below Cadillac Mountain Road, and soon a broad view opens up over the Great Heath and all the way east to Schoodic Peninsula. The obvious large complex just outside of Bar Harbor is the Jackson Laboratory, the world-renowned genetics research facility. A long rock staircase leads through a dwarf birch forest to more views,

CADILLAC MOUNTAIN TRAVERSE

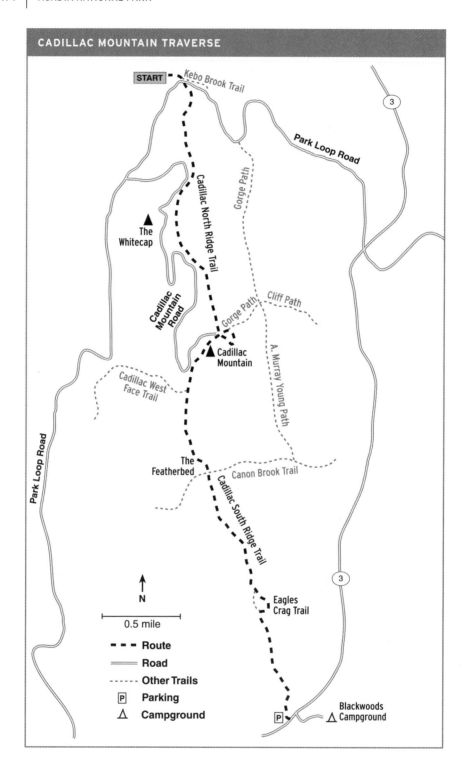

START

Kebo Brook Trail

Park Loop Road

3

Gorge Path

Cadillac North Ridge Trail

▲ The Whitecap

Cadillac Mountain Road

Gorge Path

Cliff Path

▲ Cadillac Mountain

A. Murray Young Path

Cadillac West Face Trail

The Featherbed

Canon Brook Trail

Cadillac South Ridge Trail

Park Loop Road

3

Eagles Crag Trail

N

0.5 mile

- - - **Route**
═══ **Road**
- - - **Other Trails**
P **Parking**
△ **Campground**

P

Blackwoods
△ Campground

Hikers on the alpine-like Cadillac Mountain Traverse are treated to panoramic ocean and mountain views for much of the 6-mile distance.

east to Bar Harbor and west to the summit road. Just ahead, the trail leaves the forest and remains in the open to the summit of Cadillac Mountain and well down its south ridge, an amazing stretch of about 4 miles.

The path leads along the base of the granite retaining wall of the summit road before meeting the road and descending a short distance to the left. A long moderate slope of exposed bedrock leads into a grove of low trees near the summit. Pass a hawk-watching area to the left, then bear right. The summit's communications towers soon come into view. Not far beyond, the trail ends at the summit road, with a parking lot and kiosk on the left. The paved Cadillac Mountain Road that snakes 3.5 miles up the mountain was opened to the public in 1931, replacing the old buckboard road. Many decades before, however, the Green Mountain Cog Railway carried visitors to the Green Mountain Hotel on top from 1883 to 1893. The hotel burned in 1895 and the railway was sold to the Mount Washington Cog Railway in New Hampshire.

Bear left to walk around the edge of the long, curving lot. Along the way, pass two entrances on the left for Cadillac Summit Path, a short walk around the top of the peak that features far-reaching 270-degree views to the north, east, and south. Four waysides with interpretive signs line the route, describing the many fine views and some of the natural and human history of the park. To the south, look for the Cranberry Islands, Otter Point, Otter Creek, and Gorham Mountain. Now looking east, there are The Beehive and Champlain Mountain, and closer in, Dorr Mountain. Swinging toward the north are the islands of Frenchman Bay, and out across the bay forming its far shore, the Schoodic Peninsula. The hills east of Bangor are visible due north.

From Cadillac Summit Path, continue around the edge of the parking lot. Just before reaching the Cadillac Summit Center and its gift shop, snack bar, and toilets, wide Cadillac South Ridge Trail departs to the left. Perhaps 100 yards from this intersection, the true summit lies 50 feet to the right of the trail, atop a flat rock with a USGS marker.

Ahead, Cadillac South Ridge Trail descends the mountain. Cross an old service road, climb the rock steps on the other side, and soon reach a ledge overlooking Cadillac Mountain Road. Step down the rock on one iron rung. Here, the Blue Hill Overlook is just across the road on the right, a popular spot to watch the sunset. The trail proceeds through a scraggly growth of cedar, birch, spruce, fir, and pine before breaking out onto the long and open south ridge. A cairn and sign mark the junction of Cadillac West Face Trail, which enters from the right. Here catch a nice view west to the forested hump of Pemetic Mountain, with Sargent and Penobscot mountains beyond it. Jordan Cliffs form the precipitous east face of Penobscot Mountain, while far to the right are the cliffs of Conners Nubble overlooking Eagle Lake.

Amble along the wide-open, rock-strewn ridge with long views south toward Eagle Crag. As you walk it's easy to see why, in 1604, French explorer Samuel de Champlain first described the island's mountains as "destitute of trees, as there are only rocks on them," and subsequently named it *Isle des Monts Desert,* or "Island of Barren Mountains." Ahead, the trail gradually descends with views east to The Bowl on the backside of The Beehive. Descend more steeply to The Featherbed, a lovely tarn set amid the rocks. On the shore of the shallow pond is the junction with Canon Brook Trail, which departs to the left. Circle around The Featherbed, passing several benches, then climb out of the depression.

With nice views north back to Cadillac, climb to the top of the rocky ridge and continue along it, eventually reaching an extensive forest of pitch pines with a carpet of juniper below. After a fair stretch, traverse an almost pure stand of jack pines with their classic gnarled trunks. Enjoy expansive ocean views from a ledge just beyond.

Bear left ahead onto Eagle Crag Trail, which loops down and around to a large ledge looking out over Otter Creek village to Otter Point, and east to

The Beehive and Gorham Mountain. Pass another ledge view, and then swing around to the west to rejoin Cadillac South Ridge Trail. Turn left and descend, soon reaching an improved path with stone steps. After a series of bog bridges, pass a kiosk to arrive at ME 3 and the end of the hike, just west of the entrance to Blackwoods Campground.

DID YOU KNOW?

Wealthy Bostonian, gentleman scholar, and nature lover George B. Dorr (1855–1944) worked tirelessly for more than four decades to acquire land on Mount Desert Island for protection. Now considered to be the father of Acadia National Park, Dorr established the Sieur de Monts National Monument in 1916 and served as its first superintendent. Designation as Lafayette National Park followed in 1919; the name was changed to Acadia National Park in 1929.

MORE INFORMATION

Acadia National Park (nps.gov/acad; 207-288-3338).

NEARBY

Just east of Cadillac and Dorr mountains is Sieur de Monts Spring, home to three wonderful visitor attractions. The Wild Gardens of Acadia features 400 species of flowers, shrubs, trees, and other plant life native to Mount Desert Island. The Sieur de Monts Nature Center has a park information desk, books, maps, and interesting interpretive displays on the park's natural history. The Mediterranean-style building housing the Abbe Museum displays Wabanaki stone tools, weapons, pottery, and carved bone flutes. There's also a monument to George Dorr as well as a pretty arched dome enclosing Sieur de Monts Spring, the "Sweet Waters of Acadia" (nps.gov/acad).

MORE HIKING

The park maintains an extensive network of trails on the eastern side of Mount Desert Island, with a wide variety of hikes in the vicinity of Cadillac Mountain, including Pemetic Mountain, The Triad, and Day Mountain to the west, and Dorr, Champlain, and Gorham mountains and The Beehive to the east.

TRIP 33
OCEAN PATH

Location: Bar Harbor, ME

Rating: Easy

Distance: 2.2 miles, one-way

Elevation Gain: 340 feet

Estimated Time: 2.0 hours

Maps: USGS Seal Harbor; *Maine Atlas and Gazetteer,* Map 16 (DeLorme); *AMC Maine Mountains Trail Guide,* Map 5, Eastern Mount Desert Island

Enjoy boundless ocean and mountain views on this spectacular shoreline walk, which ranges from Sand Beach and Thunder Hole to Monument Cove and Otter Cliffs.

DIRECTIONS

From the junction of ME 3 and ME 233 in Bar Harbor, turn left and drive into town (ME 3 is Mount Desert Street along here). At 0.4 mile, with the Village Green immediately on the left, turn right onto Main Street (ME 3) and drive south out of town. At 2.5 miles, turn right off ME 3 at the Sieur de Monts Spring Entrance to Acadia National Park. At the next junction at 2.7 miles (just after passing Sieur de Monts Spring on the left), turn right to reach Park Loop Road. This section is one-way, so you must turn right. Drive south on Park Loop Road, and at 5.3 miles reach the Sand Beach Entrance Station (pay fee in season). Ahead at 5.9 miles, turn left into the Sand Beach parking lot and park in one of the three tiers of lots (parking for 100 cars). In season, the free Island Explorer shuttle bus (Route 3) makes regular stops at Sand Beach. The trailhead is located to the left of the bus kiosk. *GPS coordinates: 44° 19.782′ N, 68° 11.010′ W.*

TRAIL DESCRIPTION

Ocean Path meanders along the eastern shore of Mount Desert Island from Sand Beach to Otter Point through the most popular section of Acadia National Park, taking in the famous Thunder Hole and dramatic Otter Cliffs en route. With pink-granite cliffs and ledges, pounding ocean surf and far-reaching mountain and island vistas, deep-green forests of spruce and pitch pine, cobble beaches and tide pools, and an abundance of sea birds and marine mammals, Ocean Path offers a steady stream of spectacular scenery. This easy and mostly level hike closely parallels Park Loop Road (also referred to as Ocean Drive from Sieur de Monts Spring to Hunters Brook), so to avoid the traffic and crowds along the route in high summer and experience a reasonable amount of solitude, tackle this walk early in the morning or later in the evening. Ocean Path is especially delightful and not nearly as busy in the spring and autumn months, and you'll see next to no one in winter.

A paved path starts a few feet to the left of the bus kiosk and heads toward Sand Beach. Follow this path for 50 feet, where a sign on the right marks the connector trail leading to Ocean Path proper. Before you make this right turn, however, scamper down the granite stairs just ahead for a pleasant oceanfront stroll along Sand Beach. A close look at the pinkish-white sand reveals its composition, tiny fragments of seashells that have been ground into a fine, soft sand over the course of the millennia. The ocean waters here are rarely warmer than 55 degrees Fahrenheit, even on the hottest days of summer, so swimming can be a rather bracing experience.

Returning to the path at the top of the stairs, turn left onto it and walk ahead, going behind the restrooms and changing rooms. Climb the wide path through the woods beyond on log steps to an overflow parking lot. Turn left to find the official start of Ocean Path in the far corner of the lot. The path rises to meet Park Loop Road, which remains close to the trail until the path breaks away for Otter Cliffs more than a mile ahead.

As you make your way south, Sand Beach comes into view just below, tucked into Newport Cove. The barren rock island just beyond the cove is Old Soaker, a favorite of seagulls, terns, cormorants, and other local seabirds. Great Head rises east of the beach, capped by a dark forest. Looking southward you can now see as far as Otter Cliffs. Pass several parking areas across the road, and the view eastward extends all the way across Frenchman Bay to Schoodic Peninsula and the islands just off Schoodic Point. Broad rock shelves just below you invite a lingering look.

A third of the way along, Ocean Path arrives at Thunder Hole, a narrow cleft in the oceanside rocks that is rightfully one of the most popular attractions in the park. When the weather and tides are just right, the pounding surf rushes from the open ocean into the chasm in the rocks below, forcing the air out from the concave space of the hole. This powerful action causes a thundering boom like no other sound in nature, and the resulting waves can send splash and spray dozens of feet into the air. Generally, the best chance of catching Thunder Hole in action is two hours before high tide, when the seas are about 3 to 6 feet high, although it can be uncooperative. Across the park

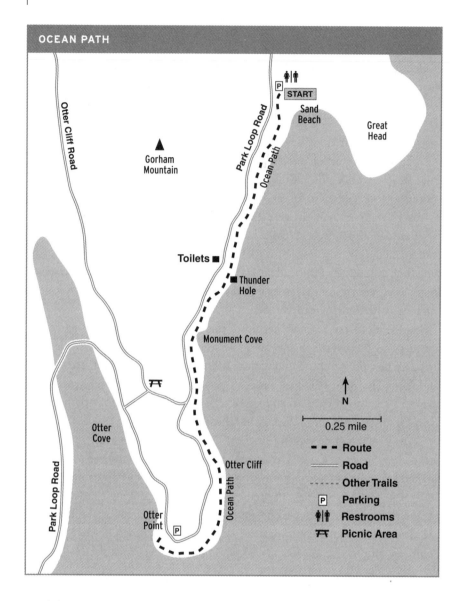

OCEAN PATH

road from Thunder Hole are a parking area and the former Thunder Hole Ranger Station, which houses a park information desk and gift shop. Vault toilets are nearby.

The next natural attraction reached by Ocean Path is the compact beach of polished cobblestones at Monument Cove, which features its very own sea stack detached from the shoreline, a monument to the forces of nature. From the cove you can now glimpse more clearly the sheer 50- to 80-foot walls of Otter Cliffs not far ahead. Directly across the park road from the cove is the

Ocean Path leads hikers past some of the most popular sights in Acadia National Park, including Sand Beach, Thunder Hole, and Otter Cliffs.

trailhead parking for Gorham Mountain Trail. Take a look back from here to see the bumps of Gorham Mountain and The Beehive.

Beyond Monument Cove, the trail passes another parking area, and then bears away from Park Loop Road for the first time. The path takes on a wilder feel as it threads through the dark corridor of spruce forest. Several side trails reach down to the top of Otter Cliffs below to the left, but the one to look for is the somewhat obscure climber's path: look closely for the registration kiosk in the woods below. Scramble down this informal path past the kiosk to emerge on the wide-open level shelf atop Otter Cliffs. *Take care to avoid any climbing anchors or stepping ropes.*

On any given sunny and warm day in spring, summer, or fall you're very likely to find a cadre of technical rock climbers here, with their brightly colored ropes, specialized shoes, and clanking climbing gear, scaling the vertical walls. This spot also provides what is perhaps the best viewpoint of the hike. To the north along the route you've just walked, the vista ranges from Gorham Mountain all the way to Great Head. In-between is the steep face of The Beehive, the margin of pink-granite cliffs along the shore, and Sand Beach. Cadillac and Dorr mountains rise prominently beyond the ridgeline of

Gorham Mountain, separated by the obvious notch at the top of The Gorge. Even Champlain Mountain makes an appearance just over the shoulder of The Beehive.

Continuing on, Ocean Path reaches another clifftop view, and then turns right to climb stone steps up to the park road high on Otter Point. Follow the walled path along the road, and at the far end, descend down and to the left away from the road on a winding series of steps. Many open spots offer views of the islands offshore to the southwest, including Great and Little Cranberry islands and Baker Island.

Eventually the path drops down to the lower shoreline rocks, providing numerous opportunities to explore the many tide pools for barnacles, anemones, whelks, starfish, and other colorful and tiny marine life. After a side trail on the right leading across the road to the Otter Point parking lot, the path passes several official shore access points. At a grassy shelf, the trail turns northward, revealing views along Otter Cove to the peaks of Cadillac and Dorr mountains.

Ocean Path ends just ahead at Park Loop Road, opposite the exit for the Otter Point parking lot.

DID YOU KNOW?

The 27-mile Park Loop Road is the primary route through Acadia National Park, leading millions of visitors each year to many of its most popular natural attractions. The brainchild of John D. Rockefeller Jr., construction of the road began in 1922 and proceeded under the guidance of the renowned landscape architect Frederick Law Olmsted Jr. Completed in 1952, Park Loop Road is considered one of the most beautiful drives in the National Park System.

MORE INFORMATION

Acadia National Park (nps.gov/acad; 207-288-3338).

NEARBY

Bar Harbor is the largest community on Mount Desert Island and considered to be the visitor gateway to Acadia National Park. The bustling village features a wealth of shops, restaurants, and accommodations as well as galleries, museums, theaters, and many other attractions, events and festivals (barharborinfo. com; 800-345-4617).

5

DOWNEAST

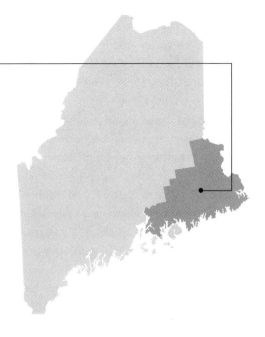

The entirety of Hancock County (except Mount Desert Island and Acadia National Park) and Washington County encompasses 4,049 square miles, together comprising Downeast Maine. The term "Downeast" broadly refers to Maine's coast from Penobscot Bay to the St. Croix River on the Canadian border. It originated in New England's early sailing days, when ships from Boston sailed east to ports on the Maine coast, downwind of prevailing winds at their stern. These ships were said to be heading "down east," while returning ships were heading upwind. Many Mainers still refer today to going "up to Boston."

Hancock County has the longest coastline of any county in Maine. Washington County is the easternmost county in the US. Thanks to its geography, the county has the honor of seeing first sunrise in the country at West Quoddy Head for a few weeks around the autumn and spring equinoxes. Nearly 85 percent of the world's wild blueberries come from the vast blueberry barrens of Washington County. Both Hancock and Washington counties were incorporated in 1789. Fishing, agriculture, and forestry are their primary industries.

Along the coast between Penobscot Bay and Campobello Island, wide forested headlands or peninsulas are interspersed with a series of large bays and a handful of large spruce-studded islands. East from Penobscot Bay are Blue Hill, Deer Isle, and Blue Hill and Frenchman bays. Beyond the Schoodic Peninsula are Gouldsboro Bay and Dyer Neck, then Dyer Bay and Petit Manan Point, followed by Pigeon Hill Bay. Narraguagus and Pleasant bays are south of Milbridge, Harrington, and Addison. Jonesport and Beals separate Whoa and Chandler bays. Englishman Bay is south of Roque Bluffs. Machias Bay is the last great bay before the Bold Coast, a rugged stretch of precipitous headlands leading to West Quoddy Head at Lubec.

Local land trusts working along or near the coast include the Maine Coast Heritage Trust (Trip 35), the Blue Hill Heritage Trust (Trip 36), the Island Heritage Trust (Trip 37), the Frenchman Bay Conservancy (Trip 42), and the Downeast Coastal Conservancy (Trip 45). The Nature Conservancy protects the pleasant forests and wild shores of Great Wass Island (Trip 44). The state-owned Donnell Pond Public Reserved Land protects more than 15,000 acres, including the Schoodic and Black mountains and Tunk Mountain (Trip 40). The 12,500-acre Cutler Coast Public Reserved Land is home to 4.5 miles of bold oceanfront wilderness (Trip 47). Quoddy Head State Park protects West Quoddy Head (Trip 49), the easternmost point in the US. State parks also conserve Roque Bluffs' sublime woods and a fine crescent of sandy beach (Trip 46), and Shackford Head's scenic peninsula on Cobscook Bay (Trip 50). Among federal conservation lands here are the 29,000-arcre Moosehorn National Wildlife Refuge (Trip 48) and the many dispersed units of the Maine Coastal Islands National Wildlife Refuge (Trip 43).

The first swath of the Downeast interior runs between US 1 in the south and ME 9 to the north. East of Verona Island in Bucksport to ME 193, there are several substantial freshwater lakes and ponds, as well as a jumble of low hills and mountains that reach to just over 1,200 feet in elevation. In and around ME 193 east to ME 191 and beyond, the land is composed mostly of commercial timberlands in unorganized townships. South and east of Meddybemps Lake is the St. Croix River. East of Garden and Rocky lakes are the coastal waters and islands of Dennys, Whiting, South, Cobscook, and Passamaquoddy bays; their massive tides range from 12 to 26 feet, some of the greatest in the world. The Great Pond Mountain Conservation Trust owns 4,500 acres of wildlands in Orland, including the great granite cliffs of Great Pond Mountain (Trip 34).The city of Ellsworth protects a pretty parcel bordering on the clear, clean waters of Branch Lake (Trip 38).

Further inland—from ME 9, north to ME 6, east to US 1—vast swaths of commercial timberland and large lakes with prime game fishing dominate the area. Four major waterways—the Machias, Union, Narraguagus and Pleasant—slice through the Downeast woods. The state has protected a significant percentage of the Machias River corridor. The Amherst Mountains Community Forest (Trip 39), a combined local, state, and private conservation project, encompasses deep woods, bumpy hills, and a system of remote ponds. Centered in the region around West Grand Lake is the incredible 34,000-acre Farm Cove Community Forest (Trip 41), managed by the Downeast Lakes Land Trust.

TRIP 34
GREAT POND MOUNTAIN

Location: Orland, ME
Rating: Easy
Distance: 2.6 miles, round-trip
Elevation Gain: 840 feet
Estimated Time: 2.0 hours
Maps: **USGS Orland;** *Maine Atlas and Gazetteer,* Map 23 (DeLorme); *Great Pond Mountain Wildlands* (Great Pond Mountain Conservation Trust)

A granite bedrock trail leads to extraordinary mountaintop cliffs and far-reaching views to Acadia, Blue Hill, and Penobscot Bay.

DIRECTIONS
From the junction of US 1/ME 3 and ME 15 at the Verona Bridge over the Eastern Channel of the Penobscot River in Bucksport, turn east onto US 1/ME 3/ME 15 and drive 4.2 miles. Here, ME 15 departs right (south). Continue east on US 1/ME 3 for an additional 1.6 miles. Turn left onto Hatchery Road. Just ahead, Toddy Dam Road merges from the right. Continue another 1.2 miles to the headquarters and visitor center of the Craig Brook National Fish Hatchery and Fisheries Resource Center. Continue past the hatchery buildings, and then turn right onto the gravel-surfaced Don Fish Road. Follow this road for 0.9 mile to the trailhead parking lot on the right, just before a red-and-white gate and the start of a private road. There is space for six cars; additional parking is along the roadside. *GPS coordinates: 44° 35.752′ N, 68° 40.858′ W.*

TRAIL DESCRIPTION
The 4,500-acre Great Pond Mountain Wildlands was purchased in 2005 by the Great Pond Mountain Conservation Trust. The purchase fulfilled the dream of a local man named Stuart Gross, who founded the land trust in 1993 with a group of local residents. He climbed Great Pond Mountain several times a week to survey the surrounding wildlands and hoped that one day he could buy the land and forever protect it and make it accessible to all. Gross died in 1997 before that dream could be realized. Instead, a logger bought the huge chunk of land, conducted heavy timber harvesting, then put it back on the

market. In 2005, the trust raised nearly $3 million to purchase the 4,300-acre property, a process that took two years to complete.

The property remained separate parcels until 2013, when the trust purchased 200 acres on the summit of Great Pond Mountain, bringing the Wildlands to its current size. The 3,400-acre Hothole Valley parcel includes the extensive valley bounded by Great Pond Mountain to the west; Oak and Flag hills and Flying Moose Mountain to the east; and Hothole Mountain and Condon and Hedgehog hills to the north. The 1,075-acre Dead River parcel includes the summit and the southern and western slopes of Great Pond Mountain west to the Dead River, the northern arm of Alamoosook Lake, and 1.5 miles of waterfront. Four miles of gravel roads and hiking trails provide access to this section of the Wildlands, which includes this described hike.

Across Don Fish Road from the trailhead parking lot, take the blue-blazed Stuart Gross Path into the woods and begin your ascent of the mountain. The often rooty and rocky path heads gently uphill through young hardwoods and hemlocks. In about 0.25 miles, reach a four-way intersection. The wide path straight ahead leads to Gold Brook Trail and on to Dead River Trail. To summit the mountain, turn right at the intersection onto unsigned Mountain Trail. Follow its wide track over bedrock, with moss beds lining the margins of the trail. Beyond a hemlock stand the trail is rocky and eroded. The easy angle lessens and the path breaks out into a semi-open area of mosses, lichens, and bedrock. View windows begin to open up off the right (south) side of the ridge, from the Camden Hills to Blue Hill to Acadia. Alamoosook Lake lies below.

The amazing diversity of terrain in the Wildlands makes it an ecologically rich land, a fact confirmed by a 2006 natural resource inventory, which reported 79 species of birds, including bald eagles, woodcocks, and whip-poor-wills; 400 species of vascular plants; and 14 vegetation communities, such as old growth timber, vernal pools, and beaver flowages.

With the summit of Great Pond Mountain visible ahead and great views of the peaks of Acadia to the right, the trail reenters the woods on the left. The sidewalk-like trail continues through the thick growth of spruce and pines. After a section of gullied trail, the path climbs a series of wide slabs, passing a boulder on the right. Ahead, make a long traverse to the right on sloping slabs. Beyond, the path trends up and left with extraordinary vistas to the south. The very coarse-grained, grayish-white bedrock here is known as Lucerne granite.

Here at the base of the final slope of sweeping granite, an obscure side trail departs ahead (east) and down and to the great cliffs on the south face of the mountain, a very worthwhile short side trip. There, cliff-top views range from Tunk, Caribou, Catherine, Black, and Schoodic mountains well Downeast to

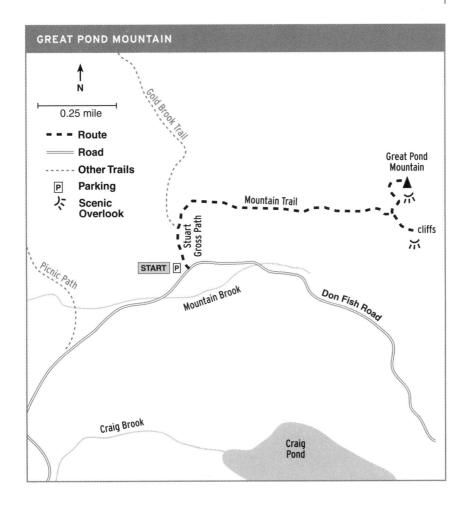

the many peaks of Acadia National Park, and to Blue Hill, Penobscot Bay, and the Camden Hills. Mount Waldo and the Penobscot Narrows Observatory are also visible to the southwest. Craig Pond is just below. A little farther east along the cliffs, views open up over the breadth of the Wildlands to Oak and Flag hills, and to Lead Mountain, as well as Toddy and Patten ponds.

The Wildlands peaks form the southern boundary of the Lucerne Pluton, a huge mass of granite that crystallized from magma that cooled slowly below the surface of the earth. The pluton, which extends northeast for 35 miles and is one of the largest bodies of granite in Maine, has eroded to produce this amazing landscape of lakes and hills and mountains.

Continue on the main trail right and up the wide-open slabs of beautiful granite. Where the slab levels off, continue ahead and slightly right, down over a rock step and into the woods on the right. Wind around to the right, and then bear left (where a muddy track enters from the right). Weave upward through the rocks and ledges amid the fragrant, mossy woods. Out in the open, bear left across a final slab to the true 1,038-foot summit (the sign was missing in 2014, but the post remained), where there are limited views through the trees.

To return, retrace your steps back to Don Fish Road trailhead.

DID YOU KNOW?

The nearby Penobscot Narrows Bridge connecting Verona Island and Prospect is the only bridge observatory in the United States, and one of only four in the world. The observatory is 420 feet above the river and offers 60-degree views over the Penobscot River, including the battlements of historical Fort Knox.

MORE INFORMATION

Great Pond Mountain Conservation Trust (greatpondtrust.org; 207-469-6929). The Wildlands is managed for wildlife habitat, recreation, environmental education, and sustainable timber harvesting. The property is open year-round. Dogs are allowed on-leash. There is no fee, but donations are appreciated. A full-color 18-by-20-inch hard-copy trail map is available from the trust for a small fee; the 8-by-11-inch map may be downloaded online for free.

NEARBY

The Craig Brook National Fish Hatchery in Orland was established in 1889 to raise and stock juvenile Atlantic salmon. In Maine, wild Atlantic salmon are listed as endangered species in eight small and three large rivers. The visitor center is open year-round and features a living stream and watershed, stewardship and historical exhibits, plus a self-guided tour of fry and brooding rearing areas. The adjacent Atlantic Salmon Museum and Display Pool are open seasonally. There are also a picnic area and boat launch and a nice network of nature trails (fws.gov/northeast/craigbrook; 207-469-6701).

MORE HIKING

In addition to the trails described above, the Great Pond Mountain Wildlands is home to eight other foot trails and gravel roads that combine for about 15 miles of walking opportunities.

TRIP 35
WITHERLE WOODS PRESERVE

Location: Castine, ME
Rating: Easy to moderate
Distance: 2.4 miles (loop)
Elevation Gain: 360 feet
Estimated Time: 2 hours
Maps: USGS Castine; *Maine Atlas and Gazetteer,* Map 15 (DeLorme); *Witherle Woods Preserve* (Maine Coast Heritage Trust)

Hike through Revolutionary War and War of 1812 history amid the regenerating hilltop forests at the convergence of the Penobscot and Bagaduce rivers.

DIRECTIONS

From the junction of US 1/ME 3 and ME 175 in Orland, 2.0 miles east of Bucksport, turn right (south) onto ME 175 and drive 8.1 miles to the junction of ME 166 and ME 175. Where ME 175 makes a sharp left, continue straight ahead on ME 166. Follow ME 166 south into the village of Castine and the junction of Main Street and Battle Avenue at 15.5 miles from US 1/ME 3. Here, with the Maine Maritime Academy campus on the left and Fort George on the right, proceed straight ahead on Battle Avenue for an additional 0.5 mile to reach the Witherle Woods Preserve and its trailhead parking lot on the right. The gravel lot has space for four cars. *GPS coordinates: 44° 23.190′ N, 68° 48.684′ W.*

TRAIL DESCRIPTION

Witherle Woods Preserve is a 183-acre parcel on the northwest side of the Castine Peninsula owned and managed by the Maine Coast Heritage Trust (MCHT). The trail network here has been in continuous use for 200 years, first as artillery roads and then as carriage roads.

In the early 1870s, George Witherle bought much of the land here, laid out 4 miles of carriage roads, and opened them for use by residents and summer visitors for walking, carriage rides, and picnics. Witherle, the son of a prominent Castine merchant and ship owner, ran the general store and chandlery. An avid outdoorsman and Appalachian Mountain Club member, Witherle climbed Katahdin nine times. A prominent ravine on the north side of the

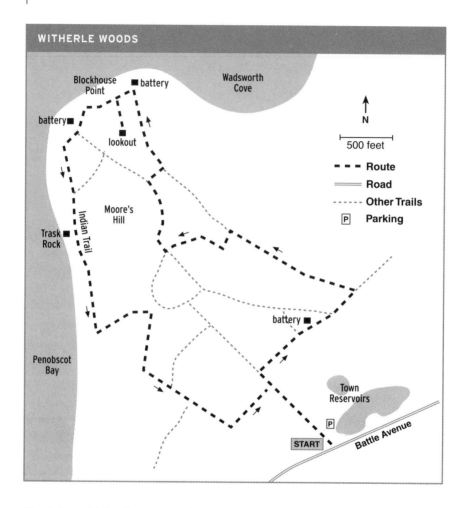

WITHERLE WOODS

Blockhouse Point
■ battery
Wadsworth Cove
battery ■
■ lookout
N
500 feet

- - - Route
═══ Road
- - - - Other Trails
P Parking

Moore's Hill
Trask ■ Rock
Indian Trail

battery ■

Penobscot Bay

Town Reservoirs

P

START

Battle Avenue

Katahdin tablelands is named for him. The preserve as it exists today was pieced together from 1985 to 2006, with most of the land having been donated by the owners.

The high promontory upon which the preserve is situated at the convergence of the Penobscot and Bagaduce rivers is a strategic location that once made it one of the most contested pieces of land in the world. Between 1613 and 1815, control of Castine changed hands eighteen times between the French, Dutch, British, and colonial America, all of whom prized this commanding location for its sheltered harbor and port for the lumber trade and other commerce.

To begin the hike, proceed past the preserve sign and around the gate to follow the gravel road uphill through semi-open fields. Ahead, a foot trail enters the woods on the left. Just beyond, arrive at a junction and an information

From Blockhouse Point, the former site of a British military fortification built during the war of 1812, the vista over Penobscot Bay features the peaks of the Camden Hills and North Haven and Vinalhaven islands.

kiosk. The Castine Town Reservoir—an underground reservoir—is a short distance ahead on the road, but turn right here to follow a grassy trail northeast. Pass a number of stumps that are 8, 10, and even 12 feet high, left behind as wildlife trees after the salvage harvests of years past. Amid the young spruce and fir, birch and alder, a few mature spruce trees remain.

Just into the thicker forest growth ahead, an obscure footpath departs left (easily missed). Continue along on the wide grassy lane to another junction, where a grassy trail on the left departs at a sharp angle. A small white sign on the right points back to Battle Avenue. Continue straight ahead to a small clearing and a trail junction. The trail straight ahead leaves the preserve, but turn left to continue the hike, passing a sign, "Welcome to Witherle Woods," and indicating that this path leads to Blockhouse Point. The forest understory along this next part of the route is primarily oak and birch, spruce and fir, while the scattered canopy trees are of paper birch, spruce, and fir. Cross a dip via a bog bridge, then traverse a wet stretch of trail that reveals a few mature spruce trees.

Much of the land was once cleared for the pasturing of sheep and other livestock but was reclaimed by woods. A major fire in 1903 burned half of the woods, but a century later, a mature forest had returned. By 2000, many of the old conifers were in poor condition from attacks by spruce budworm, spruce bark beetles, and the balsam woolly adelgid, so MCHT began to have some of the dead and dying trees removed. In April 2007, the high winds of the Patriots' Day storm caused extensive blowdowns. Later that September, a microburst leveled 50 acres of trees. After these storms, MCHT had salvage and thinning work done to reopen the trails and remove the downed trees, which posed a significant fire hazard. The results of these weather events and forestry operations are still evident as the young forest of red and white spruce, balsam fir, white pine, and red oak grows back to eventually regain a place in the canopy. It will take time for the forest to mature again, but in the meantime the patchwork of open areas has created significant edge habitat that is beneficial to wildlife.

Ahead, be alert for a junction and a trail leaving to the left. Here, a sign on the right facing the trail uphill indicates that Battle Avenue is to the right while Blockhouse Point is to the left. Turn left onto the grassy, wet, and somewhat obscure trail to make the short, easy climb up the side of Moore's Hill, named for Sir John Moore, an 18-year-old British lieutenant in the Revolutionary War. Ahead, the trail swings right along the ridgetop. Limited views are possible along here north to Wadsworth Cove, Perkins Point, beyond to Penobscot Bay, and along the Penobscot River as far as the Penobscot Narrows Bridge and Observatory. The thick growth to either side of the trail consists of cherry, birch, and red maple. Look for ripe raspberries in season.

Ahead, in a stand of tall spruce, reach a four-way junction and posted map and sign indicating that Battle Avenue is to the left and Blockhouse Point is to the right. Turn right here and walk downhill on a more defined path amid the cool shadows of a spruce grove.

At the base of the hill, reach a junction. Turn right here onto a grassy pathway and quickly reach a signed T junction (sign: "Battle Ave. →, Blockhouse Point ←").

Go left on a wide track through the thick growth of alder, birch, and cherry, then spruce and fir. In a small stand of mature spruce, reach the site of Furieuse Battery No. 1 (1814) on the right. This is the first of two semi-circular artillery batteries, one on each side of Blockhouse Point, and named for the French naval ship *HMS Furieuse*, captured and used by the British during the War of 1812. Any vista that might have been here is now obscured by trees.

Bear left to continue, and in 75 feet, reach the junction with Lookout Trail on the left. Climb the 100 yards up to a bench atop a rocky knob and broad views north and west over Penobscot Bay and the Penobscot River, a vista that includes Islesboro, Sears Island, and Cape Jellison. Scramble a little farther up from the bench for views east to the shapely outline of Blue Hill.

This vantage point makes it easy to see why this location was so important to early settlers. The British regained control of Castine from the French for the last time in 1713, and in 1779 they built Fort George to solidify their position and protect the growing number of British loyalists. Soon after, however, the Americans sent the Penobscot Expedition to seize Castine from the British, but the British held the fort and the Americans retreated, destroying their fleet to avoid having it fall into enemy hands. It is thought to be the worst naval disaster in U.S. history, one that nearly bankrupted Massachusetts, which spent $9 million on the failed campaign. The British finally evacuated Castine in 1874 after peace was declared between Britain and America. The British occupied the site for the final time in late 1814 near the end of the War of 1812.

Return to the main trail and turn left. Enjoy more views over the bay before arriving at the site of Furieuse Battery No. 2 (1814) and a side trail leading 100 feet to a bench and grand views over Penobscot Bay and Islesboro to the Camden Hills.

From the battery side trail, continue south on the main trail to a Y junction. Bear right here and proceed down the short but steep pitch to a shelf some 75 feet above a cobble beach and the waters of the bay. Note the rock along the river here, which is known as Castine formation, a brittle, metamorphosed volcanic rock.

Here at Blockhouse Point, the former site of a British fortification built during the war of 1812, more views of the Camden Hills are possible from this pretty spot, and by looking far to the left down the bay you can see the islands of North Haven and Vinalhaven, the latter adorned with several wind turbines.

From the shelf, continue south on Indian Trail, which is very occasionally marked by splotches of yellow paint. The trailway through this section is somewhat rough in places, uneven with rocks and roots. Enjoy a view window to the west as you pass through areas of severe windthrow that has been cleared by trail crews. Uphill to the left as you go the forest canopy is comprised mostly of oak with some scattered spruce. As you proceed, be on the lookout for Trask Rock, a large glacial erratic deposited along the shore eons ago.

A private property sign and a stone wall mark the preserve boundary. Turn sharply left here away from the bay, and climb the rather rough and rocky trail, marked occasionally by bits of blue flagging tape, to a T junction. Turn right onto the wide grassy lane and proceed into the dense woods ahead. Beyond, into the open again, walk along the margin of a stone wall on the right. Such stone walls at Witherle Woods date back to early agricultural use, even appearing on 1785 property surveys.

Stay straight at the next trail junction to continue along the stone wall to reach a side trail on the right leading to Dyce's Head Light. Ahead, bear left away from the stone wall to join the main gravel road. Turn right here to return to the trailhead parking lot.

DID YOU KNOW?

The area that is now Witherle Woods was first occupied by the Abenaki people, who camped on the hill and dried and ate fish caught in the "Majabigwaduce" or "big tideway river," now known as the Bagaduce River.

MORE INFORMATION

Maine Coast Heritage Trust (mcht.org, 207-729-7366.) Witherle Woods Preserve is open during daylight hours, year-round.

NEARBY

Explore the historic 3-acre grounds of Fort George as well as Dyce's Head Lighthouse at the end of Battle Avenue. Then visit the village of Castine proper, home to numerous eighteenth- and nineteenth-century Georgian and Federal homes, the campus of the Maine Maritime Academy, and a pleasant waterfront area where the state of Maine training ship is docked much of the year (castine.me.us/welcome).

MORE HIKING

Maine Coast Heritage Trust manages more than 100 preserves along the Maine coast, including several other small properties with trails near Castine. The state-owned Holbrook Island Sanctuary on the Cape Rosier peninsula in Brooksville has a nice system of nine hiking trails on its 1,230 acres (maine.gov/dacf/parks, 207-326-4012). The Blue Hill Heritage Trust maintains miles of hiking trails at thirteen preserves in the area between Penobscot and Blue Hill bays (bluehillheritagetrust.org, 207-374-5118).

TRIP 36
BLUE HILL MOUNTAIN LOOP

Location: Blue Hill, ME

Rating: Moderate

Distance: 5.9 miles

Elevation Gain: 1,140 feet

Estimated Time: 3.5 hours

Maps: USGS Blue Hill; *Maine Atlas and Gazetteer*, Map 15 (DeLorme); *Blue Hill Mountain Trail Map* (Blue Hill Heritage Trust)

Make a fine loop over the summit of Blue Hill and around the mountain, with lovely views of Blue Hill Bay and the myriad islands beyond.

DIRECTIONS

From the center of the village of Blue Hill at the intersection of ME 15 and ME 172/ME 176 (Main Street), proceed east on ME 172/ME 176. At 0.2 mile, at the Y junction of ME 172 and ME 176, bear left uphill on ME 172. Pass Mountain Road on the left at 1.4 miles (trailheads and parking for the Osgood and Hayes trails on Blue Hill are a short distance west along this road). Continuing on ME 172, turn left onto Turkey Farm Road at 2.2 miles. Drive west to reach the trailhead parking lot (sign) on the left at 2.9 miles. The gravel lot has space for two cars. *GPS coordinates: 44° 26.934′ N, 68° 34.662′ W.*

TRAIL DESCRIPTION

Blue Hill Mountain, a coastal monadnock that rises to 934 feet, affords outstanding views of the lands and waters of the Blue Hill Peninsula. Since 1975, nearly 500 acres on the mountain have been preserved through a number of generous gifts and conservation purchases. Much of the credit is due to Blue Hill Heritage Trust. Formed in 1985 by local residents, the trust now protects 6,900 acres between Penobscot Bay and Blue Hill Bay in the towns of Blue Hill, Brooklin, Brooksville, Castine, Penobscot, Sedgwick, and Surry.

This loop combines portions of all of the five trails on the mountain, starting and ending with Becton Trail, as well as Tower Service, Hayes, South Face, and Osgood trails.

To begin, descend the steps to the information kiosk (posted trail map) and follow the blue-blazed trail westward over bog bridges into the forest. As

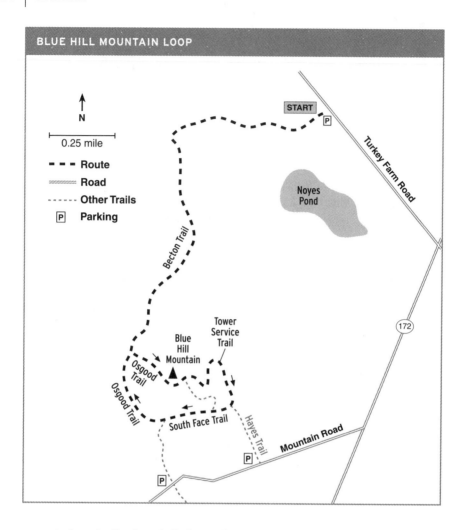

BLUE HILL MOUNTAIN LOOP

N

0.25 mile

- - - Route
≡≡≡ Road
----- Other Trails
P Parking

START

P

Turkey Farm Road

Noyes Pond

172

Becton Trail

Tower Service Trail

Blue Hill Mountain

Osgood Trail

Osgood Trail

South Face Trail

Hayes Trail

Mountain Road

P

P

you wind gradually downhill, the trail passes an orange property stake on the right and a stone wall on the left. Along the base of the slope, pass a large, dead white pine, now an important wildlife tree for birds and small mammals. The trail continues through an understory of mostly spruce trees, with some pines and balsam fir, and lots of mossy green rocks and boulders. The overstory consists primarily of sugar maples, beech, and white birch. Skirt a wetland on the left in a thick growth of young spruce stems. Ahead, there are more mature spruce as well as fragrant balsam fir.

After a quick right around some deadfall, the trail crosses an extensive area of mossy forest floor with impressive spruce trees as large as 24 inches in diameter. Beyond several bog bridges, the trail turns south into a predominantly hardwood forest, with some American elm.

The summit ledges on Blue Hill Mountain reward hikers with fine views over Blue Hill Bay and top the mountain skyline of Mount Desert Island and Acadia National Park.

At about 1.0 mile, a sign on an ash tree on the left indicates it is 1.0 mile to the summit of Blue Hill from this point. The trail continues to wind easily up the slope, which displays some large trunks of white ash. Soon after a 5-foot-high boulder on the left, the path crosses an old woods road.

After passing between a large spruce and a big boulder, the ascent becomes moderate, but soon the angle eases. A long switchback leads to a brief descent; ahead are views north to Toddy Pond. The trail now swings around the west side of the mountain, offering views north to the hills of the Great Pond Mountain Wildlands, including Great Pond Mountain itself.

Continue on through the spruce woods to the junction with Osgood Trail, which enters from the right. A sign here indicates it is 0.75 mile to Mountain Road via Osgood Trail and 1.75 miles to Turkey Farm Road via Becton Trail. Turn left onto Osgood Trail and ascend the wide path over rocks and roots.

Sections of Osgood Trail may have been part of an old mining roadway used in the 1800s, when the top of Blue Hill was mined for rhodonite, a pink or gray silicate of manganese that was used to enhance the durability of iron. The mineral was brought down the mountain, shipped to Bangor, then moved by oxcart north to Katahdin Iron Works in Brownville, where it was used in the smelting of iron ore. The mining roadway was later traveled by horse-drawn carriages, which brought local hotel guests up the mountain to enjoy the view.

Climb over a large slab, and then traverse easily to the east to pass through a small clearing with a clump of red maples on the left. After a walk through a dark grove of spruce, emerge onto the open summit rocks, with the communications tower just ahead over the treetops.

From the summit cairn, bear right and drop down a short distance to the old concrete fire-tower stanchions. A bench is 50 feet or so to the left of this. From here, enjoy the grand view over the south face of the mountain to Blue Hill and its cozy harbor and to Blue Hill Bay and beyond to the mountain skyline of Acadia National Park. Following the devastating fires of 1947, a fire tower was constructed here, and remained in use into the 1990s; it was removed by the Maine Forest Service in 2005. The existing communications tower was built in 1981 and retrofitted in 2005 to accommodate cell phone service.

Beginning in the 1760s, settlers in the area harvested trees for lumber and charcoal and converted the cleared land to agriculture. By 1840, hard as it may be to picture today, Blue Hill was almost entirely deforested. With the eventual decline of farming, much of the forest cover returned, although some open space was used until recently for blueberry cultivation.

To continue, hike east from the summit cairn across the rocks into the woods on Tower Service Trail (no sign). Pass an old mining pit and mossy rock wall, and soon pass behind the communications tower (please keep out!). Just below, reach an unsigned junction. Here, Hayes Trail begins its steep descent of the south side of Blue Hill. Continue straight ahead to remain on Tower Service Trail, a pleasantly winding and gradual descent route that was constructed by Blue Hill Mountain Leasing as access for tower-service vehicles. Near the base of the hill, Tower Service Trail emerges at the top of a large sloping field to join Hayes Trail. From the trail sign and bench, ascend Hayes Trail on a long series of stone steps that lead to a junction with South Face Trail. From here, proceed straight across the south slope of Blue Hill on scenic South Face Trail.

The path is wide open for most of its 0.25-mile length as it contours across old fields and blueberry fields, under a power line and past tangled growth of sumacs and other shrubs. Views of the Blue Hill Fairgrounds, Blue Hill Bay, and Acadia are outstanding at every step.

At a wooden signpost, turn sharply left down and across the slope. Reach the junction with Osgood Trail at a footbridge over a streamlet. Turn right onto Osgood Trail and follow it on a moderate climb up and over the west shoulder of the mountain. A final scramble up rock slabs returns you to the junction of Becton Trail and the close of the loop. Turn left onto Becton Trail and follow it just over 2.0 miles back to the trailhead on Turkey Farm Road.

DID YOU KNOW?

The Abenaki, who lived on the lands in and around Penbobscot Bay, called Blue Hill Mountain *Awanadjo*, meaning "small, misty mountain."

MORE INFORMATION

Blue Hill Heritage Trust (bluehillheritagetrust.org; 207-374-5118). The trails on Blue Hill are open to the public year-round. Dogs are allowed on-leash. A trail map is available online.

NEARBY

Settled in 1762 and incorporated in 1789, the pretty coastal town of Blue Hill is situated on the idyllic bay of the same name. Steeped in shipbuilding and seafaring history, the village is home to a fine library, the Kneisel Hall Chamber Music School, art galleries and craft stores, and a nice selection of other shops, eateries, and lodging (bluehillpeninsula.org). The popular Blue Hill Fair, billed as a "down-to-earth" country fair, is held annually in late August and draws thousands of visitors to its agricultural exhibits, amusement rides, and other fun attractions and entertainment (bluehillfair.com).

MORE HIKING

The Blue Hill Heritage Trust maintains miles of hiking trails at numerous preserves in the area. For even more hiking possibilities, a new 32-page trail guide—a collaborative product of the Blue Hill Heritage Trust , Maine Coast Heritage Trust, and the Conservation Trust of Brooksville, Castine, and Penobscot—is available for $5 and provides directions and maps to 27 public-access recreational sites on the Blue Hill Peninsula (bluehillheritagetrust.org).

TRIP 37
EDGAR M. TENNIS PRESERVE

Location: Deer Isle, ME
Rating: Moderate
Distance: 3.2 miles
Elevation Gain: 295 feet
Estimated Time: 2.0 hours
Maps: USGS Deer Isle; *Maine Atlas and Gazetteer*, Map 15
(DeLorme); *The Edgar M. Tennis Preserve* (Island Heritage Trust)

Explore the interesting human history and understated natural beauty of this rural throwback of an island off the coast.

DIRECTIONS
From the Deer Isle-Stonington Chamber of Commerce Information Center at the junction of ME 15 and Eggemoggin Road on Little Deer Isle, 0.2 mile south of the Deer Isle-Sedgwick Bridge over Eggemoggin Reach, proceed south on ME 15. Pass through the village of Deer Isle proper and soon arrive at the junction of Sunshine Road on the left (there's a gas station on the right). Turn onto Sunshine Road and follow it for 2.5 miles. Turn right onto dirt Tennis Road. In 0.4 mile, enter the Edgar M. Tennis Preserve (sign). The trailhead is just ahead on the left. The first of four small parking areas (two cars each) is located uphill another 100 feet; the others are along the road spaced over the next 0.4 mile. From your parking spot, walk back downhill to the trailhead just above Great Brook on the right. *GPS coordinates: 44° 12.530′ N, 68° 37.787′ W.*

TRAIL DESCRIPTION
The arching span of Deer Isle-Sedgwick Bridge over Eggemoggin Reach is the boundary of a different time zone of sorts, what is often fondly referred to as "island time." The pace of life on Deer Isle seems slower, more relaxed, and perfect for many hours of recreation and leisure activities. And there are plenty of opportunities for both on this 24,000-acre island of bountiful natural beauty, complete with 112 miles of coastline, spruce-scented woods, pink-granite shorelines, deep-green waters, salty ocean air, squawking gulls, and long island views. The Island Heritage Trust has been protecting open space, scenic areas, wildlife habitats, natural resources, and historical and cultural

features here since 1987. The trust owns or manages at least a dozen preserves, four beaches, and eight islands for a total of more than 1,200 acres.

The largest of these protected lands is the 144-acre Edgar M. Tennis Preserve, the former farmstead of the Pickering and Davis families, who resided here in the 1800s. The preserve—owned by the state of Maine and co-managed with the Island Heritage Trust—is bisected by Tennis Road and a chunk of private property. On the east side, a nearly 2-mile loop hike hugs the shore of Pickering Cove and leads to a hidden pocket beach. To the west of the road, the trail snakes through the woods before meandering through the meadows of the Davis farmstead and down to the water's edge at Southeast Harbor.

Archaeological evidence indicates that native people lived on this land for 2,000 years, wintering over and harvesting the abundant fish and shellfish provided by the fertile ocean. Deeds from the late 1700s show that Elijah Toothaker settled the land, which was later farmed by the Pickering and Davis families. The Tennis family purchased the property in 1944.

A blue box at the start of the trail holds trail maps. Beyond, the orange-blazed footpath follows the shore of Pickering Cove. The trail passes through a forest dominated by spruce, some as large as 18 inches in diameter. Farther on, a few cottages appear across the cove, including a lovely red cape. With the small islands of Little Thrumcap and Big Hay directly to the east, the trail turns south along the cove. Lobster boats and sailboats can often be found moored here in these peaceful waters.

Pass through thick undergrowth of balsam fir and cross a stone wall to reach a junction. The trail on the right leads to the old foundation of the Pickering Farm and thence to Tennis Road. Continue straight ahead. Farther on, the trail offers numerous opportunities to scamper out onto the pink-granite shoreline for views across to Freese Island and beyond to Stinson Neck.

Cross a wet area on bog bridges, pass through a grove of aspens and oaks, then cross a shallow gully, the outlet of a small spring. Wind around another point of land to reach a ledge on the left and broad views up and down the cove, where many colorful lobster buoys can be seen bobbing on the surface. After a log bench and a short section of rough, rooty trail, reach a point with far-reaching views south past Stinson Neck and Whitmore Neck to the islands of the Deer Isle Thoroughfare. Here, the trail turns west along Southeast Harbor. A short side trail leads to views across the water to Whitmore Neck.

Just ahead, a blue-blazed trail diverges to the right, a wooded upland route that rejoins the main trail ahead. Continue straight ahead on the orange-blazed trail to follow along the shore. After a short scramble to a rocky viewpoint, the trail winds up and down several times to arrive at a pocket beach of reddish

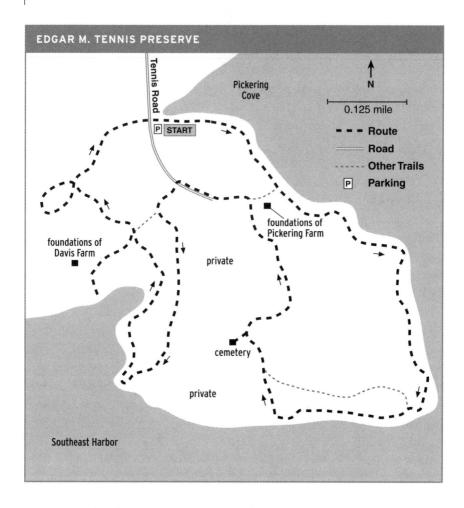

EDGAR M. TENNIS PRESERVE

Tennis Road

Pickering Cove

START

P

N

0.125 mile

- - - Route

——— Road

····· Other Trails

P Parking

foundations of
Pickering Farm

foundations of
Davis Farm

private

cemetery

private

Southeast Harbor

stones. Just ahead is a spur trail on the left that leads around the point to the beach. Use this path to reach the beach and avoid causing further erosion. Beyond, the trail leaves the shore, turning right to switchback up the slope through a stand of big oaks. On the level, the trail makes a sharp right and follows an old moss-covered stone wall, to the junction with the blue-blazed trail. Not far beyond, a side trail leads 250 feet west to the Toothaker Family cemetery, in a small opening in the forest. An interpretive sign describes the colorful history of the Toothakers and the marked and unmarked graves found here.

Returning to the main trail, enjoy pleasant and easy walking through the spruce forest on a soft, needle-carpeted path. In a field beyond is the cellar hole of the old Pickering farmhouse and a trail junction. To the right, a short-cut leads to the shore of Pickering Cove. Turn left to continue the walk, taking

A red squirrel enjoys a snack along the trail amid the mossy green spruce woods at Edward M. Tennis Preserve.

the wide trail out to Tennis Road. Proceed to the right on the dirt road past two parking areas. Ahead, at a sign for "Davis Farm," bear left into the woods on a wide grassy trail. Soon, turn left off the wide trail onto a narrow footpath.

Cross a wet area on bog bridges, then pass through an area of blowdowns. Ascend a short rise, and then descend to the water's edge, crossing two stone walls en route. On the level, a side trail leads to views over Southeast Harbor to cottages and docks on the opposite shore.

Turn north along a shallow cove, with numerous viewpoints. After a few sections of rocky trail, several short ups and downs, and a wet area, turn inland at the head of the cove to reach a four-way intersection. The trail to the right leads out to Tennis Road. Head left and soon arrive at the foundation of the old root cellar of the Roswell Davis Farm in a large meadow. The family eked out a living on the 21-acre farm here from 1873 through the 1930s, as explained by an interpretive sign. Continue through the field between the apple trees down to the shore of Davis Cove and the remains of an old granite pier.

Returning to the four-way junction, turn left, climb a knoll, and saunter through the spruce woods that were once farmland. Pass a short, blue-blazed loop trail on the left. Bear right here, cross a low spot, then navigate a narrow corridor of field before ending on Tennis Road.

DID YOU KNOW?

Prior to completion of the Deer Isle-Sedgwick Bridge in 1939, residents and visitors to the island traveled between Sargentville on the mainland and Scott's Landing on the island by various private ferry services, from open rowboats to scows pulled by a towing boat to steamboat. The last ferry operator, Charles Scott, died twelve days after the bridge was opened.

MORE INFORMATION

Island Heritage Trust (islandheritagetrust.org; 207-348-2455). The preserve is open daily year-round and for day use only. Dogs are allowed on-leash. A portion of the preserve trails and the old cemetery are on private property. Please treat both with respect. A trail map and the island's *Hiking Trails & Public Access* brochure are available online and on-site.

NEARBY

Several small communities make up Deer Isle's year-round population of 2,400 residents. Lobstering and its ancillary businesses are the mainstay of the island's economy, although granite is still quarried here and tourism brings people and revenue to the island. Explore the country roads off the beaten path of ME 15 to get a real feel for this quaint island. And be sure to visit the picturesque town of Stonington at the southern tip of the island for its colorful mix of lifestyles: part fishing village, part artist and artisan enclave, and part summer tourist destination.

MORE HIKING

Six other preserves on Deer Isle—three owned by the Island Heritage Trust, two by The Nature Conservancy, and one by the state of Maine—offer 10 miles of wonderful island hiking. These include Pine Hill, Scott's Landing, Shore Acres, and Barred Island preserves in Deer Isle, and Crockett Cove Woods and Settlement Quarry Preserve in Stonington. There are hiking trails on a handful of offshore islands owned by the Island Heritage Trust. They are in and around the Deer Isle Archipelago and accessible by boat or kayak.

MAINE'S SUSTAINABLE LOBSTER FISHERY

The American lobster *(Homarus americanus)* thrives in the cold, clean waters and rocky bottom habitat found along the coast of Maine. These true lobsters are easily distinguishable from their warm-water cousins by the presence of two large, flesh-filled claws, one known as a pincer and the other as a crusher. Independent fishers harvest Maine lobsters, generally making daily boat trips within 10 to 12 miles of shore to tend their traps, each marked by a colorful floating buoy.

While lobsters are harvested year-round in Maine, the majority of the catch occurs between late June and late December, when the crustaceans are most active. These delicious new or soft-shell lobsters yield a succulent, flavorful meat from a shell that can usually be cracked by hand. Just stop at any Maine coast lobster pound or restaurant and find out for yourself how delicious this fresh ocean delicacy can be, especially when enjoyed with clam chowder and corn-on-the-cob.

The Maine lobster industry, with an annual catch of over 126 million pounds valued at more than $338 million (2012 data), plays a vital role in the state's economy, supporting not only some 5,900 licensed lobster harvesters and their crews, processors, dealers, marine outfitters, boat makers, retailers, and restaurants, but hundreds of communities up and down the Maine coast, all part of a rich lobster-fishing heritage dating to 1840.

Unlike many other sectors of the fishing industry, the Maine lobster fishery—one of the most successful in the world—is thriving, owing to years of sustainable management practices and a high level of cooperation between government regulators and lobster harvesters. Elected councils of harvesters in each of seven lobster management zones determine the maximum number of traps allowed for each license holder, the maximum number of traps that may fished on each line, and the maximum number of harvesters allowed in each zone.

Other rules and regulations ensure the continued health of the lobster fishery. Tail notching of female lobsters is used to identify breeding stock and protect them from future harvest. Minimum size limits allow young lobsters to mature and reproduce before they can be harvested, while maximum size limits protect the healthy breeding adults. Harvesting is allowed by trap only, and each trap must have escape vents for undersize lobsters, along with biodegradable escape hatches for lobsters stranded in lost traps.

TRIP 38
BRANCH LAKE PUBLIC FOREST

Location: Ellsworth, ME
Rating: Easy
Distance: 2.7 miles
Elevation Gain: 160 feet
Estimated Time: 1.5 hours
Maps: USGS Branch Lake; *Maine Atlas and Gazetteer*, Map 23 (DeLorme); *Branch Lake Public Forest Trails Map* (city of Ellsworth)

Enjoy quiet walking through mature spruce and pines and along the undeveloped lower shores of Branch Lake, an important local source of high-quality drinking water.

DIRECTIONS

From the junction of US 1, US 1A, and ME 3 in downtown Ellsworth, travel north toward Bangor on US 1A for 6.6 miles. The entrance to Branch Lake Public Forest is marked by a brown-and-white sign on the left (west) side of US 1A. Turn onto the gravel road and drive through the open metal gate along the blueberry field (Phillips Farm) for 1.0 mile. Park in the small trailhead lot to the left of a locked gate. There is parking here for three to four cars, as well as a portable toilet. The road is generally plowed in winter. *GPS coordinates: 44° 35.472′ N, 68° 31.392′ W.*

TRAIL DESCRIPTION

Acquired by the city of Ellsworth from the Mary C. Fenn Trust in 2010, Branch Lake Public Forest is a 240-acre property on the lake's southeast shore. A 4-mile trail network provides access to a wooded interior and the scenic shoreline of big, beautiful Branch Lake, which is Ellsworth's sole drinking water supply and drains into the Union River and Blue Hill Bay, a nationally significant estuary. This hike combines portions of the main forested gravel tote road and Pine and Lake Loop trails for a walk along the shore of the lake.

The Branch Lake Conservation Initiative—a partnership between the city of Ellsworth, Mary C. Fenn Trust, Forest Society of Maine, The Trust for Public Land, Frenchman Bay Conservancy, and the Maine Department of Conservation—protects nearly 1,200 acres, including this forest and some 3.5 miles of shorefront on Branch Lake. The partners also protect the lake's water quality

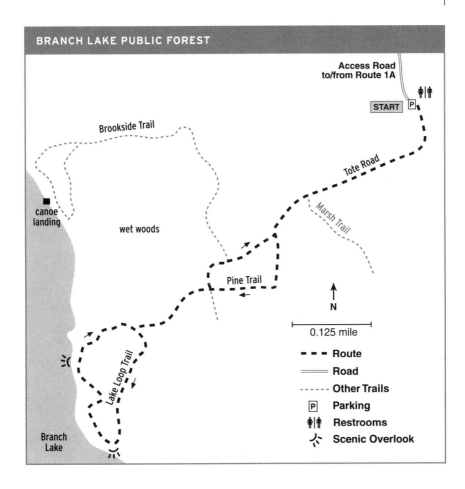

BRANCH LAKE PUBLIC FOREST

Access Road to/from Route 1A

START

Brookside Trail

Tote Road

Marsh Trail

canoe landing

wet woods

Pine Trail

N

0.125 mile

- - - Route
=== Road
----- Other Trails
P Parking
Restrooms
Scenic Overlook

Lake Loop Trail

Branch Lake

through conservation purchases and easements, and develops opportunities for low-impact, nonmotorized recreation and sustainable timber harvesting.

A trail map of the forest is posted on the left side of the gate at the trail-head. Proceed south then west on the gravel tote road, passing through heavily cutover woods and by several old wood yards growing up to grasses and shrubs. About 0.5 mile in, Marsh Trail (sign) departs the road to the left. Not far ahead, in a corridor of young balsams, pines, and firs, turn left onto Pine Trail (sign). Follow the blue-blazed footpath into the forest of spruce, hemlock, and red maples. Cross several bog bridges. Stumps and slash are here and there, evidence of past timber harvesting.

Ahead, Pine Trail intersects the main tote road; proceed straight across past the trail sign. Beyond this junction, the route passes through a more mature forest of white birch, cedars, spruce, and red maples. A few stately white pines easily measure 3 feet or more in diameter, and some of the spruces measure 1.5 feet in diameter. After a wet area, the treadway is soft underfoot as the trail travels through the young softwood growth.

At the junction of Lake Loop Trail, bear left. Observe the mature forest overstory and the next generation of forest growing up underneath; on a warm day the aroma of balsam can be quite heady. The path slopes toward the lake, which soon comes into view. You might hear loons calling from the water. At a junction and sign, a spur trail to the left leads 200 feet to the rocky lakeshore and nice views over the clear waters of Branch Lake, including a view of The Narrows, the passage that leads to the northern half of the lake. Back at the junction, bear left to continue north along the lake. Several short, unmarked spur trails lead to the lake and views west to the bumps of Oak Hill and Flag Hill.

The trail trends away from the water then turns sharply right to close the loop. Bear left at Lake Loop Trail junction to return to the main tote road intersection on Pine Trail. Turn left (north) onto the tote road and follow it for a short distance to a clearing, where the road bears sharply right. Not far beyond is the signed but somewhat obscure start of Brookside Trail on the left.

Continue on the main tote road 0.5 mile back to the trailhead, passing Pine and Marsh trails on the way.

MORE INFORMATION

City of Ellsworth Planning Department (ellsworthmaine.gov, 207-669-2563). Frenchman Bay Conservancy (frenchmanbay.org, 207-422-2328). Branch Lake Public Forest is open from dawn to dusk year-round. Dogs are allowed. Visit Frenchman Bay Conservancy online to download a trail map.

NEARBY

Ellsworth is often referred to as the gateway to Downeast Maine and Acadia National Park. This lively city of nearly 8,000 residents offers an abundance of shopping, dining, lodging, and sightseeing opportunities. Of particular interest are the Woodlawn Museum, the 180-acre estate of Colonel John Black dating to the early 1800s (woodlawnmuseum.com), and the 200-acre Stanwood Wildlife Sanctuary, also known as Birdsacre (birdsacre.com).

MORE HIKING

The Brookside Trail is another short loop hike in the Branch Lake Public Forest that leads to a pocket beach on Branch Lake. Hit the trails at the Frenchman Bay Conservancy's dozen preserves nearby in the US 1 coastal corridor from Ellsworth to Steuben in Hancock County. Their *Short Hikes* pocket brochure describes these walks and is available online.

TRIP 39
AMHERST MOUNTAINS
COMMUNITY FOREST

Location: Amherst, ME
Rating: Moderate
Distance: 3.2 miles
Elevation Gain: 430 feet
Estimated Time: 2.0 hours
Maps: USGS Hopkins Pond; *Maine Atlas and Gazetteer,* Map 24
(DeLorme)

**Fragrant forests of spruce and fir, lush green mosses, and granite
ledges characterize this loop hike to the remote environs of Ducktail and Partridge ponds.**

DIRECTIONS

From the junction of ME 9 and ME 181 in Amherst, travel west toward Bangor for 1.5 miles, where a blue sign on the right that reads, "Amherst" marks
the somewhat obscure entrance road to the Amherst Mountains Community
Forest. Turn just before the guardrail onto the old road, formerly a section of
ME 9, and proceed into the forest. The narrow road of broken blacktop curves
sharply to the right and turns to gravel. In 0.2 mile, reach a large brown entrance sign on the right. Ducktail Pond trailhead and the start of the hike is
2.3 miles past this point on the left; pass the Partridge Pond trailhead en route.
Parking for ten cars is just beyond the trailhead on the right in a lot for the
Indian Stream Day Use Area. *GPS coordinates: 44° 51.424′ N, 68° 23.05082′ W.*

TRAIL DESCRIPTION

The Amherst Mountains Community Forest is a 4,974-acre tract of rugged
forestland encompassing six remote ponds, miles of streams, significant wetlands, and a jumble of granite ledges, hills, and mountains. This route through
the best of the forest's backcountry visits two remote ponds on a scenic loop
that combines Ducktail Pond and Partridge Pond trails. After more than a century of stable ownership by paper companies, this large block of land was sold
three times in six years in the late 1990s and early 2000s. Concerned about the
threat of development and the potential loss of traditional recreational access,
local citizens enlisted the support of the state and the Forest Society of Maine

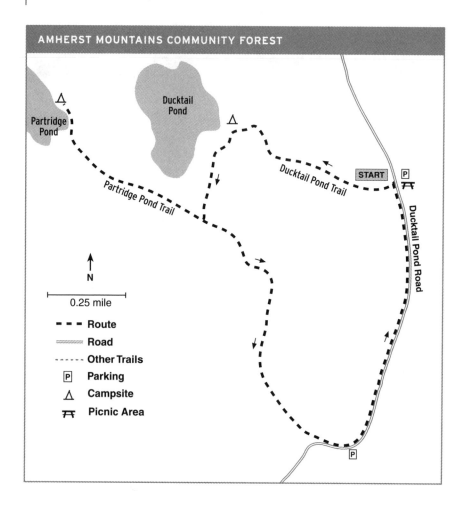

AMHERST MOUNTAINS COMMUNITY FOREST

Ducktail Pond

Partridge Pond

Ducktail Pond Trail

START

Partridge Pond Trail

Ducktail Pond Road

N

0.25 mile

- - - Route
═══ Road
----- Other Trails
P Parking
△ Campsite
🛋 Picnic Area

to help conserve the land. The land was finally protected in 2009 under an uncommon community forest agreement: the town of Amherst and the Maine Department of Agriculture, Conservation, and Forestry, Bureau of Parks and Lands, jointly manage the state-owned property. Together, they promote recreational activities and habitat preservation. The Forest Society of Maine led the conservation effort and now assists the town and the state with forest inventory and management-plan responsibilities on the land.

From the parking lot, walk the driveway back to the main road and angle left across it to the start, marked by a sign and short footbridge. Blue-blazed Ducktail Pond Trail heads uphill into the woods, paralleling Ducktail Brook at varying distances. Beyond a split-log bench on the right, the path levels off, and it is generally easy going the remaining distance to the outlet of Ducktail Pond, reached in just over 0.5 mile. Before you cross, walk ahead on the unmarked

Partridge Pond is one of six pristine ponds found deep in the wilds of the Amherst Mountains Community Forest. A nearby campsite allows hikers to spend the night if desired.

path to the pond. Ignore the dilapidated canoe and kayak in the bushes and enjoy the nice view over the water and good swimming when the weather is right.

To continue the loop hike, return to the outlet. There is no marked route across the outlet (and no blue blazes from here to Partridge Pond Trail), so pick your own route and go. Hop down over the ledge and make your way across, following the edge of the pond as best you can. On the other side, navigate to the large granite boulders just above the pond shore and the obvious campsite and fire pit. Pass a second fire pit just beyond, then bear left easily up the slope through a semi-open grove of red and white pines. Pass an unmarked trail on the right leading to a privy. Beyond, at two large boulders, swing to the right to follow a moss-fringed Jeep track over bare ledges. Soon, bear away from the pond, passing a huge white pine on the right. Continue through mixed woods with a thick understory of spruce and fir.

A little less than a mile into the hike, reach the T junction with blue-blazed Partridge Pond Trail. Left leads to the main road and is your return route. Turn right to head for Partridge Pond. Just ahead, cross a series of bog bridges. The path follows an old Jeep track, crossing more bog bridges as it winds through the rich-green forest of spruce, fir, and pines. At a Y junction, a small sign marked "campsite" points to the right. Bear right at this fork, trending easily uphill. With the pond in sight ahead through the trees, follow along the top of long, sidewalk-like ledge to the wide outlet of Partridge Pond, which drops off to the right in an 8-foot waterfall.

Cross the outlet to reach a primitive campsite and fire pit in a small clearing. A sign for "toilet" just beyond marks the side trail to a box privy. Turn left at the sign and follow the unmarked path through the woods to a large granite "beach" sloping down to the water's edge. The spot is a fine one for picnicking and swimming, and for sunsets if you are camping overnight.

To continue from Partridge Pond, retrace your steps southeast to the previous T junction. Continue straight through the junction, following the blue blazes of Partridge Pond Trail toward the main road. Trend downhill on rocky trail, passing through an area that was commercially harvested for timber in the mid-2000s. The now-level trail follows the edge of the cut on bog bridges, then widens as it merges into an old woods road and becomes a wooded corridor with cut areas on both sides. After a section of thick young hardwoods, cross a cedar-slab footbridge. The trail descends and crosses a brook, then follows a long series of connected bog bridges before emerging at the gravel parking area of the Partridge Pond trailhead (sign).

Turn left onto the main road and follow it for just under a mile back to your car.

MORE INFORMATION

Amherst Mountains Community Forest (parksandlands.com; 207-941-4122). Forest Society of Maine (fsmaine.org, 207-945-9200). The forest is open year-round, but the road into the Ducktail Pond and other trailheads is not plowed in winter. Dogs are allowed. Primitive camping is permitted at Ducktail and Partridge ponds. No trail map is currently available.

NEARBY

Bangor is a major gateway to eastern and northern Maine. Located on the Penobscot River, this thriving city of 33,000 residents is Maine's third largest urban center and the commercial and cultural hub for the region. Once known as the "Lumber Capital of the World," as many as 400 sawmills operated in Bangor and surrounding communities during the nineteenth century. The city features a wide variety of things to see and do, including museums, theaters, shops, restaurants, and a network of urban walking trails (visitbangormaine.com).

MORE HIKING

Within Amherst Mountains Community Forest, hikers can climb to the summit ledges of Bald Bluff Mountain, a 1,011-foot peak reached by a 1.2-mile trail, where fine views may be had of the Lower Penobscot River watershed. The Bald Bluff trailhead is located 6.1 miles from ME 9 and 3.6 miles beyond the Ducktail Pond trailhead.

TRIP 40
TUNK MOUNTAIN AND HIDDEN PONDS

Location: T10 SD, ME
Rating: Moderate
Distance: 4.9 miles
Elevation Gain: 1,060 feet
Estimated Time: 3.0 hours
Maps: USGS Tunk Mountain; *Maine Atlas and Gazetteer*, Map 24 (DeLorme); *Tunk Mountain and Hidden Ponds Hike* (posted at trailhead kiosk)

Extensive areas of open mountaintop ledges provide far-reaching views of the Downeast landscape, while below, a series of pristine ponds dot the spruce woods.

DIRECTIONS

From the junction of US 1 and ME 3 in Ellsworth, 1.0 mile south of downtown, turn left (east) onto US 1. Follow the highway for 4.6 miles to its junction with ME 182 (Tideway Market/Irving Station) in Hancock. Turn left (north) onto ME 182 (Blackwoods Scenic Byway) and follow it for 14.5 miles, passing through the village of Franklin and by ME 200 en route. At the intersection with Dynamite Brook Road, continue ahead on ME 182 for 100 yards to the trailhead parking lot for Tunk Mountain and Hidden Ponds on the left, marked by a blue-and-white state sign. The gravel lot has parking for ten cars, a vault toilet, and an information kiosk. *GPS coordinates: 44° 37.518′ N, 68° 5.346′ W.*

TRAIL DESCRIPTION

The Donnell Pond Public Reserved Land encompasses 15,479 acres in the towns of Franklin and Sullivan and the unorganized townships of T9 SD and T10 SD. Central to the preserve and popular with canoeists, boaters, and campers is the namesake Donnell Pond, hemmed in by the walls of Schoodic and Black mountains. North of ME 182, the preserve includes much of the north and east shores of pristine Tunk Lake, the entirety of Spring River Lake, and a number of small remote ponds, some 6,915 acres in all. Rising high over this northern section is Tunk Mountain, a spectacular 1,157-foot peak offering extensive alpine areas, wide-open granite ledges, and far-reaching views. Five

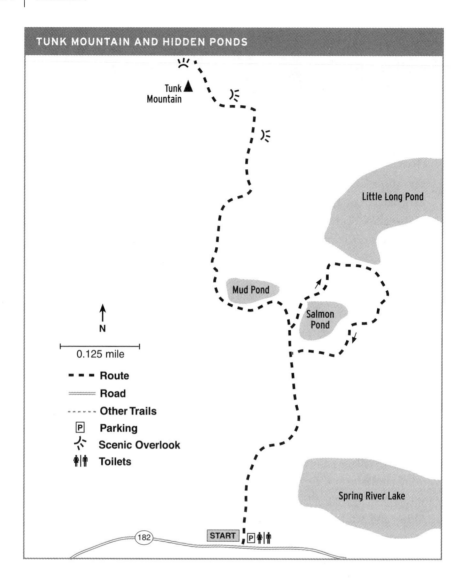

TUNK MOUNTAIN AND HIDDEN PONDS

Tunk Mountain

Little Long Pond

Mud Pond

N

0.125 mile

- - - Route
Road
----- Other Trails
P Parking
Scenic Overlook
Toilets

Salmon Pond

Spring River Lake

182 START P

miles of trails reach to scenic highpoints on Tunk Mountain and to Salmon, Mud, and Little River ponds. This hike visits the entire trail system and all of its attendant natural features.

Tunk Mountain and its environs have undergone a renaissance of sorts thanks to the Maine Bureau of Parks and Lands. In 2011, a new gravel parking lot and vault toilet were constructed at the trailhead on ME 182. This was followed by extensive trail work by the Maine Conservation Corps, which included significant rerouting, rehabilitation of existing trail, and new signage, all to improve public access and visibility.

The extensive open granite ledges high on Tunk Mountain offer far-reaching views over the wild and scenic country threaded by the Blackwoods Scenic Byway.

Tunk Mountain Trail begins to the right of the information kiosk and descends a set of wooden steps to a wide old road that quickly enters the woods. Where an unmaintained trail departs to the left, continue straight ahead on the blue-blazed trail. A sign at this junction indicates that the Hidden Ponds Trail junction is 0.5 mile ahead, while the summit ridge is 1.5 miles ahead.

Soon, bear right off the woods road onto a footpath. Cross a wet area and small stream on bog bridges, then climb over a hump. Pass a series of large boulders to arrive at a streamlet, which can be crossed by rock hopping. The unmarked junction (as of 2013) of the southern end of Hidden Ponds Loop is just ahead on the right. This loop leads 0.9 mile around Salmon Pond, touching the southwestern shore of Little Long Pond halfway along. Just ahead on the main trail, reach the west shore of Salmon Pond. Here, Tunk Mountain Trail continues around the pond to the left to arrive at the north junction of Hidden Ponds Loop on the right.

Continuing straight ahead, Tunk Mountain Trail climbs easily over a rise, then descends to Mud Pond. As you hike along its south shore through the thick growth of spruce, the cliffs of the upper portion of Tunk Mountain come into view. At pond level, a rope swing is tied to a hefty branch of a big white pine at the left end of the pond-side cliffs. Cross the pond's inlet, make your way through mature spruce and pines, then negotiate a gully of boulders.

Here, the trail leaves Mud Pond and climbs steeply over a winding staircase of rock steps. After a level stretch, cross a streamlet, then several bog bridges, before beginning to switchback up the slope. After a final crossing, the winding path ascends at a moderate grade and soon crosses some rock slabs in a semi-open area. Views to the south begin to open up before the trail enters the thick woods at a cairn and makes a traverse west across the face of the mountain.

Ahead, with the upper ridgeline of Tunk in view, the path climbs easily to a side trail on the right leading 100 yards to a series of huge, sloping ledges and far-reaching views south to the Atlantic Ocean, Catherine Mountain, Caribou Mountain, Spring River Lake, and the "hidden ponds" of Mud and Salmon.

At a cairn, enter the woods again and traverse on a very long switchback. After a stretch of moderate to steep climbing, ascend three iron rungs in the rock to a semi-open forest of scrub oaks on rock slabs. Climbing higher, the views get more expansive: Mud Pond, Salmon Pond, Little Long Pond, Tilden Pond; then Tunk Lake and Spring River Lake; Catherine Mountain, Caribou Mountain, Black and Schoodic mountains; then the grand mountain skyline of Acadia and the Atlantic Ocean. Just shy of 2.0 miles into the hike, reach a sign for Monument Vista, a few hundred feet down to the right on a spur trail. A cast plaque here honors the family of Harold Pierce, who generously donated this amazing parcel of land to the state in 1994. From the vista junction, it is 0.2 mile to the Northern Overlook. The trail slabs westerly along the upper face of Tunk before emerging onto the granite summit ledges. Black and Schoodic mountains are clearly visible now to the south.

Follow blazes on rocks and cairns over this mostly open section of alpine terrain. At the crest of ridge high on the northeast shoulder of Tunk the trail bears right, avoiding the true summit. No matter: you have already passed the best views on this side of Tunk Mountain. From this point north you are on The Nature Conservancy's 9,000-acre Spring River Preserve. Continue across the ridge, then drop into a gully and bear sharply left. Make your way north along the gully at the base of a big slab of rock to the end of the trail at a sweeping slab of steep granite that yields a 180-degree view to the north. Forestlands ranging from Calais to Bangor can be seen, including the prominent peaks of Lead Mountain, the hills of Amherst, and Big Chick and Little Chick hills in Clifton. The blueberry barrens in and around Deblois are also visible, as are the obvious nineteen wind towers of the Bull Hill wind power project in T16 MD.

To return, retrace your steps to the north junction of Hidden Ponds Loop at Salmon Pond. Turn left (east) onto the loop trail to follow along the north shore of the pond. In a park-like forest grove, a 75-foot spur leads right to the edge of the pond. Back on the main loop, the trail bears away from Salmon Pond and soon joins the course of a stream to Little Long Pond.

An unmaintained trail continues along the south shore of Little Long Pond, but the main loop bears sharply uphill to the right. After a huge, almost square erratic, the trail traverses mossy ledges above the pond to a viewpoint over a narrow cove hemmed in by cliffs. Finally bearing away from Little Long Pond, the loop swings south and contours across the hillside to Salmon Pond, with good views of the cliffs high on Tunk Mountain. Ahead, atop a low rise, an unmaintained trail heads left. Bear right to remain on the main loop trail, which continues west through the woods above Salmon Pond and reaches the unmarked junction with Tunk Mountain Trail. Turn left (south) to return to the trailhead parking lot.

DID YOU KNOW?

The Tunk Lake Ecological Reserve protects a total of 6,215 acres in and round the Tunk Mountain Pluton, a broad intrusion of igneous rock and one of the most distinctive geological landmarks and natural areas in Downeast Maine. The reserve includes three rare and exemplary natural communities: the raised-level bog ecosystem, low-elevation bald, and lower-elevation spruce-fir forest.

MORE INFORMATION

Donnell Pond Public Reserved Lands (parksandlands.com; 207-941-4412). Trails at Tunk Mountain are open year-round.

NEARBY

The Black Woods Scenic Byway connects the towns of Franklin and Cherryfield via a relatively quiet 11-mile stretch of ME 182 (blackwoodsbyway.org). Both historical small towns offer fine examples of eighteenth- and nineteenth-century architecture, while Cherryfield bills itself as the "blueberry capital of the world" (downeastacadia.com).

MORE HIKING

A 15-mile trail network crisscrosses the southern and larger section of the Donnell Pond Public Reserved Land, reaching the open summits of Schoodic and Black mountains and penetrating the backcountry around Rainbow Pond and Caribou Mountain. Primary access to these trails is from the Schoodic Beach trailhead, located at the end of Schoodic Beach Road.

TRIP 41
LITTLE MAYBERRY COVE TRAIL

Location: Grand Lake Stream, ME
Rating: Moderate
Distance: 5.6 miles (round-trip)
Elevation Gain: 220 feet
Estimated Time: 3.5 hours
Maps: USGS Grand Lake Stream; *Maine Atlas and Gazetteer*, Maps 35 and 36 (DeLorme); *Hiking Trails on the Farm Cove Community Forest* (Downeast Lakes Land Trust)

Meander along the wooded shoreline of expansive and pristine West Grand Lake, part of the 33,708-acre Farm Cove Community Forest conservation lands.

DIRECTIONS
From the post office on US 1 in Princeton, proceed north on US 1 for 2.4 miles. Turn left (west) onto Millford Road (Grand Lake Stream Road). In 10.3 miles (0.1 mile past the Pine Tree Store) cross the bridge over Grand Lake Stream, and 100 feet beyond, turn right (north) onto Shaw Street. In 0.3 mile, turn right into the boat launch parking lot, which also serves as trailhead parking for Little Mayberry Cove Trail. There is parking for up to twenty cars and a pit toilet. *GPS coordinates: 45° 10.854′ N, 67° 46.704′ W.*

TRAIL DESCRIPTION
The 33,708-acre Farm Cove Community Forest, owned and managed by the Downeast Lakes Land Trust, protects 71 miles of undeveloped shorefront and the associated watershed on West Grand Lake, Pocumcus Lake, Third and Fourth Machias lakes, Wabassus Lake, and Sysladobsis Lake. The trust encourages traditional recreational uses and participates in sustainable timber management and harvesting for wildlife habitat enhancement. Little Mayberry Cove Trail meanders nearly 3 miles along the western shore of West Grand Lake from the dam in the village of Grand Lake Stream to Mayberry Cove, threading a route between Daugherty Ridge and the lake itself.

To start the hike, walk north through the parking lot to the boat launch on the south end of the lake, just left of the dam. The bucolic scene here includes a number of camps and cottages hugging the shoreline and a nice view up the lake. The outlet pool below the dam is a popular spot for anglers fly-casting for salmon and trout. Bear left at the boat launch and then quickly right onto Shaw Street, passing a small sign on a tree for Little Mayberry Cove Trail. The pavement soon ends at the town beach, a short stretch of sand on the right and a place to keep in mind for a swim when the hike is done.

Beyond the beach, follow the dirt road out of the village past more camps and cottages. At a fork, bear left uphill. A green-and-black sign reads, "Private Road. Hikers Welcome. Dead End." At the top of a hill near a large boulder, leave the road to the left and follow a wide footpath marked with yellow blazes. A short distance beyond, at a woodpile barrier blocking an old logging trail, bear right off the wide track onto a narrow footpath.

The trail slabs the hillside through mixed woods, then a forest of young beech stems. A camp road is visible through the trees downhill to the right. Follow the gently rolling course of the path, passing a feint side trail on the right. In a grove of good-size spruce and hemlock, meander down to the lake shore amid the mossy boulders scattered across the forest floor. Hike along the lake to reach a spur leading 100 yards to Harriman Overlook, the first of four official viewpoints along the trail route. Extensive views look east across the water, with some camps and lodges visible on the far shore of this deceptively narrow south end of West Grand Lake. The 14,340-acre lake is famous for its salmon fishery, but also holds populations of lake trout, lake whitefish, and smallmouth bass; its maximum depth is 128 feet.

Continuing on, the trail bears away from the lake to avoid a parcel of private property. The impressive trunks of bigtooth aspen through this section are as much as 22 to 24 inches in diameter. Cross an ATV track, then negotiate a wet area of cedars and maple. Beyond, weave through the forest between the mossy rocks. The footing is uneven for a stretch, with lots of roots, as the trail wends through the forest dominated by spruce, pines, and hemlocks.

At about the 2.0-mile mark, a large rock on the lakeshore right next to the trail marks the second viewpoint. Step out onto the rocks for a wonderful view up and down the lake, a big vista over the clear, clean water fringed with low hills. Look across the lake to the east shore, which forms the western boundary of the West Grand Lake Community Forest, a 22,000-acre conservation easement managed by Downeast Lakes Land Trust. The easement also protects the woods and hills ranging east to the Passamaquoddy lands in Indian Township and north to the Sunrise Easement, a 370,000-acre amalgamation of conservation lands managed for sustainable timber harvesting and wildlife habitat, and open to public use for recreation.

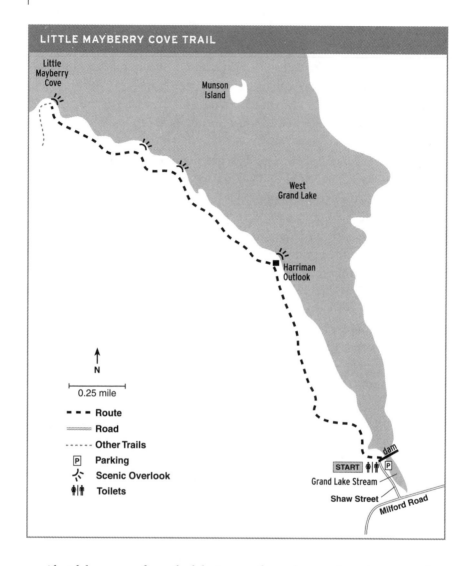

Ahead, bear away from the lake to pass through several semi-open patches of forest where blueberries may be found in high summer. Soon, swing back to the lake to reach the third outlook, marked by a small sign. If you can't wait to return to the town beach, this is a great spot for a refreshing swim.

Farther north, past a large boulder, the trail leads through an understory thick with spruce, cedar, hemlock, and fir. Cross a camp road, and not far ahead, reach an ATV track. Turn left onto the ATV track and in 25 feet turn right off it into the woods. The trail returns to the lake before bearing sharply left to begin a wide arc around a cove.

At a point of land, reach a junction. To the right a spur trail leads a short distance to Little Mayberry Cove, the fourth and final viewpoint on the hike. (To the left, the trail leads a little more than 0.25 mile to the official end of Little Mayberry Cove Trail at a camp/logging road. It is an unmarked and rather uninteresting walk back to Grand Lake Stream this way and not recommended. Unless this is your plan, there is no need to hike this last short stretch.) Take the spur to the right and hike out to the lovely viewpoint, where a bench awaits, as well as a terrific vista north and east over the expansive lake, which at this point is nearly 3 miles wide. State-owned Hardwood Island is due north, while Marks Island can be seen farther out to its left.

Retrace your steps back along Little Mayberry Cove Trail to return to the trailhead at the boat launch parking lot in Grand Lake Stream.

DID YOU KNOW?

The first dam across Grand Lake Stream was built in 1865, 165 feet downstream from the existing dam. Initially built to assist with log drives, the dam later powered the largest tannery operation in the world, which used the natural tannins in the bark of the abundant hemlock nearby.

MORE INFORMATION

Downeast Lakes Land Trust (downeastlakes.org; 207-796-2100).

NEARBY

The Pine Tree Store, an old-fashioned general store in Grand Lake Stream, is worth a visit for a cold drink and a snack, as well as nostalgia's sake. The village of Grand Lake Stream is home to numerous sporting camps and lodges, and the state's highest concentration of registered Maine guides (experienced outdoorspeople who can take you on a memorable boat tour or fishing excursion on the lakes).

MORE HIKING

Downeast Lakes Land Trust maintains several other hiking trails nearby. Pocumcus Lake Trail is a nearly 4.0-mile loop along the undeveloped shoreline of Pocumcus Lake, while Wabassus Mountain Trail climbs 1.0 mile to the hardwoods forest atop the 844-foot peak. Dawn Marie Beach Path leads to an undeveloped beach on Wabassus Lake. Contact the trust for the brochure *Hiking Trails on the Farm Cove Community Forest*.

TRIP 42
LONG LEDGES PRESERVE
AND BAKER HILL EASEMENT

Location: Sullivan, ME
Rating: Moderate
Distance: 4.2 miles
Elevation Gain: 480 feet
Estimated Time: 3.0 hours
Maps: USGS Sullivan; *Maine Atlas and Gazetteer*, Map 24 (DeLorme); *Long Ledges Preserve and Baker Hill Easement* (Frenchman Bay Conservancy)

Meander through the upland forests of two adjoining conservation lands to enjoy ocean and mountains vistas from granite ledges and outcrops.

DIRECTIONS
From the junction of US 1 and ME 3 at the south end of Ellsworth (directly across from McDonald's), bear left (east) onto US 1. In 12.3 miles, turn left (north) onto Punkinville Road in Sullivan. Pass Baker Hill Preserve (sign) on the left at 12.5 miles. Ahead in 0.4 mile, reach Long Ledges Preserve on the left. There is parking for four to six cars. *GPS coordinates: 44° 31.182′ N, 68° 9.888′ W.*

TRAIL DESCRIPTION
Long Ledges Preserve and Baker Hill Easement are adjoining conservation properties just north of Sullivan Harbor at the head of Frenchman Bay. The 318-acre Long Ledges Preserve is owned by the Frenchman Bay Conservancy, a nonprofit land trust that has worked since 1987 to protect 6,300 acres in the Union River and Frenchman Bay watersheds and Eastern Hancock County. Long Ledges features a series of semi-open ridge tops forested mostly with pines and oaks, as well as two ponds, wetlands, granite outcroppings, glacial erratic boulders, and an old quarry. Frenchman Bay Conservancy also holds the conservation easement on the adjacent 58-acre Baker Hill. The extensive granite ledges on the south slope of the hill provide wonderful views extending south to Mount Desert Island and north to the mountains of Donnell Pond Public Reserved Land. Nine trails plus several short connectors combine to

offer more than 5 miles of hiking exploration though both properties. This hike utilizes all or part of each of these trails.

Eastside Trail enters the woods to the right of the register box at the north end of the parking lot. The Frenchman Bay Conservancy's blue diamond markers blaze the trail at first through young aspens and pines, then gently uphill in a spruce grove.

At a trail junction, bear right onto Quarry Trail and contour across a hillside through the spruce, birch, and red maple trees. Slip through a passage in a boulder to enter a mature stand of large spruce and pines towering over the mossy carpet of the forest floor. Soon after a thick stand of young balsam fir, climb three narrow rock steps to reach an area of quarried rock marked by large blocks of granite and drill core marks. After a quarried out amphitheater, climb easily up a shallow ravine to an area of jumbled rocks on the right and a trail junction.

Bear right here onto Upper Ledges Loop and climb a short moderate-to-steep pitch into a semi-open area of ledges. Small cairns mark the way through the oaks, pines, and spruce. From just ahead, limited views peer over the treetops south to the ocean at Frenchman Bay and north to Schoodic and Black mountains. Hike the mildly undulating ridge on a moss-lined path over the pink-granite bedrock, and then finally wind down the slope into a dark forest of spruce. Pass a huge lichen-covered boulder to rejoin Eastside Trail in a ravine.

Turn left onto Eastside Trail and climb along the left side of a rocky ravine. In 100 feet, reach a swampy junction and turn right onto Red Pine Ridge Trail. Beyond a bog bridge, climb easily to a ridge top and a forest of red pines, where there are limited views through the semi-open woods. Meander along the west side of the slope. In a ravine, a connector trail on the left leads back to Eastside Trail. Continue ahead on Red Pine Ridge Trail and quickly regain the ridge.

At 1.0 mile, in a mixed wood of red and white pines, Red Pine Ridge Trail goes left; instead, take the connector trail on the right downslope 100 yards to the West Loop junction. Turn right (north) onto West Loop. Head across and then down a shallow valley. Cross a brook to contour along the west side of the valley. After a thick stand of fir, climb over a low ridge, then descend to Long Pond. After a dip, a short spur on the right leads to the pond. Just ahead, another spur trail leads 100 feet up and over a small hill to a ledge overlooking 59-acre Long Pond, home to native brook trout. The ledge is a beautiful spot to relax, have lunch, and enjoy the view. It's also a good launch spot for a refreshing swim in the crystal-clear water.

Continuing on, Westside Trail leaves the pond and swings west and then south to climb the next ridgeline. Proceed easily across the semi-open hilltop covered with reindeer and sphagnum mosses. A bit higher, the trail enters a

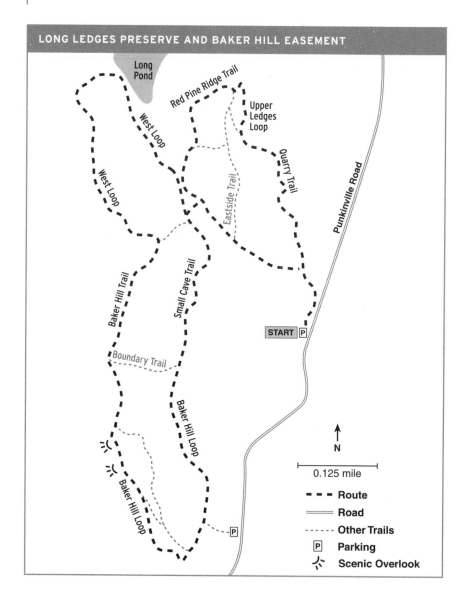

LONG LEDGES PRESERVE AND BAKER HILL EASEMENT

Long Pond

Red Pine Ridge Trail

Upper Ledges Loop

West Loop

Eastside Trail

Quarry Trail

Punkinville Road

West Loop

Baker Hill Trail

Small Cave Trail

START P

Boundary Trail

Baker Hill Loop

N

0.125 mile

- - - Route
Road
----- Other Trails
P Parking
Scenic Overlook

Baker Hill Loop

P

grove of gnarly pitch pines. A number of the pines have been girdled by porcupines. Follow a series of small cairns as you drop easily off the ridge to a wide swath of trail. Cross three bog bridges to reach a junction.

Huckleberry Trail departs to the right but you'll continue straight on Westside Trail, which soon leads into another stretch of semi-open forest and then rises to the top of a yet another ridge a little over 2.0 miles into the hike. This is the boundary line of the Baker Hill Easement. Where Boundary Trail departs to the left, continue straight ahead on Baker Hill Loop.

The lovely 59-acre Long Pond in Long Ledges Preserve is home to native trout and makes a nice summertime swimming spot.

Ahead, the ridge narrows. Beyond the forested high point on Baker Hill, an inner loop trail departs to the left. Continue to the right on the main Baker Loop, which soon swings out onto the semi-open ledges on the southwest side of Baker Hill. From this airy vantage point, lovely views extend to Blue Hill and Acadia National Park, where the profiles of Champlain, Dorr, Cadillac, Pemetic, and Sargent on the east side of Mount Desert Island are visible, as well as Mansell and Bernard mountains on the west side of the island. The village of Sullivan on US 1 is directly below.

Continue right along the edge of the cliff for 100 yards to another large open ledge. From here, the path trends gradually downward along the narrowing ridge through a forest of white pines, with frequent view windows to the west. Avoid an old trail on the right, where old blue paint blazes are still visible. Bear left at this fork and descend a short, steep pitch over the mossy forest floor. Where the trail levels out, an old trail leaves to the right. Ignore it and bear left, and in 25 feet, one of the short Baker Hill loops enters from the left.

Amble easily along the base of the hill to a junction (sign), where a short trail leads right to the trailhead parking lot for Baker Hill Easement. Continuing ahead on the main Baker Hill Loop trail, pass by a wet area, then bear left uphill, climbing steeply through a spruce stand in a ravine. At its head, cross a wet area on logs to reach the property boundary delineating the two preserves and quickly arrive at the junction of Small Cave Trail and Boundary Trail.

Turn right onto Small Cave Trail and trend down through thick woods of spruce and fir. After a short, rough traverse through boulders, cross a creeklet and follow along to the right of a wall of rock ledges. At a sharp right turn you'll find the "small cave," a fissure in a lichen-covered boulder, 1 foot wide and 20 feet long. Pass several unmarked side trails to reach Huckleberry Hill Trail, which enters from the left. Just 30 feet ahead on Small Cave Trail, take the connector trail on the right a short distance to Red Pine Ridge Trail. Turn right onto Red Pine Ridge Trail and follow it to Eastside Trail.

After this junction, hike out on Eastside Trail, crossing a wet area and then climbing easily over a ridge to the trailhead parking lot, passing Quarry Trail en route.

DID YOU KNOW?

Frenchman Bay (often misspelled as Frenchmen's Bay) spans the 7-mile distance between Mount Desert Island and the Schoodic Peninsula, and is named for Samuel de Champlain, the French explorer who visited the area in 1604.

MORE INFORMATION

Frenchman Bay Conservancy (frenchmanbay.org; 207-422-2328). The conservancy's color pocket map and guide, *Preserves—Short Hikes,* is available online.

NEARBY

Tidal Falls, also known as Sullivan Falls, is the most dramatic reversing falls in the region. Located just off US 1 in Sullivan, where the short Taunton River divides Taunton Bay from Frenchman Bay, the falls is a wonderful spot to watch the ebb and flow of the rushing tidewaters as well as eagles, ospreys, herons, and seals. Next to the lobster pound onsite (proceeds benefit the Frenchman Bay Conservancy) is a 4-acre waterfront park and a put-in for canoes and kayaks.

The Schoodic National Scenic Byway (exploremaine.org) extends from Hancock to Prospect Harbor along US 1, ME 186, and the park road through the Schoodic Peninsula section of Acadia National Park. Some 39 points of interest are found en route, most notably the park itself (nps.gov/acad; 207-288-3338).

MORE HIKING

In addition to hikes at thirteen preserves described in the FBC trails guide, four trails in the Schoodic Peninsula section of Acadia National Park climb to Schoodic Head for magnificent coastal vistas (nps.gov/acad; 207-288-3338).

TRIP 43
MAINE COASTAL ISLANDS
NATIONAL WILDLIFE REFUGE

Location: Steuben, ME
Rating: Easy
Distance: 1.8 miles
Elevation Gain: Minimal
Estimated Time: 1.25 hours
Maps: USGS Petit Manan Point; *Maine Atlas and Gazetteer*, Map 17 (DeLorme)

Hike through jack-pine forests and a variety of other habitats to reach the cobble beaches of Pigeon Hill Bay and views of Petit Manan Light, the second-tallest lighthouse along the Maine coast.

DIRECTIONS

From the junction of US 1 and Pigeon Hill Road—3.0 miles east of Steuben and 2.7 miles west of Milbridge—turn south onto Pigeon Hill Road. In 4.5 miles, pass the trailhead for Pigeon Hill Preserve. A short distance ahead, Pigeon Hill Road becomes Petit Manan Point Road and there are signs for the refuge. At 5.7 miles, enter the refuge proper. Just beyond on the right are a parking area, large information kiosk, and trailhead for Birch Point Trail. Continuing on, at 6.1 miles, reach the trailhead for Hollingsworth Trail. Parking is on the right. *GPS coordinates: 44° 25.864′ N, 67° 53.936′ W.*

TRAIL DESCRIPTION

The 8,200-acre Maine Coastal Islands National Wildlife Refuge (MCINWR), managed by the U.S. Fish and Wildlife Service, is composed of three mainland parcels and 55 offshore islands along a 250-mile stretch of the Maine coast ranging from the Isle of Shoals to Cutler. The refuge combines five formerly separate refuges to better reflect the broad scope of its conservation efforts up and down the Maine coast. The island units of MCINWR help protect habitat for nesting seabirds, wading birds, and bald eagles, while the mainland units support habitat for migratory songbirds, shorebirds, and waterfowl.

The 2,160-acre Petit Manan Point Division in Steuben is a diverse landscape of jack-pine forests, raised heath peatlands, blueberry barrens, old hayfields, fresh and saltwater marshes, cedar swamps, granite coastline, and

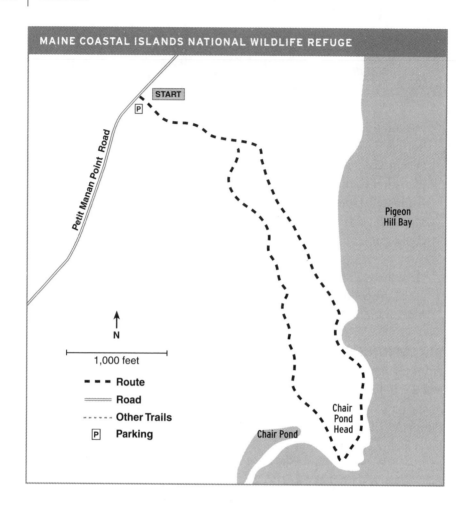

MAINE COASTAL ISLANDS NATIONAL WILDLIFE REFUGE

START

Petit Manan Point Road

Pigeon
Hill Bay

N

1,000 feet

– – – Route
═══ Road
------ Other Trails
P Parking

Chair
Pond
Head

Chair Pond

cobble beaches. The refuge at Petit Manan is one of the featured sites on the Maine Birding Trail, the official state trail and guide to more than 260 of the best birding sites in Maine (mainebirdingtrail.com).

Scenic, 1.8-mile John Hollingsworth Memorial Trail leads to the ocean at Pigeon Hill Bay. The loop's namesake, along with his wife, Karen, devoted many years to photography at this and other national wildlife refuges across the country, generating significant support for wildlife conservation. John Hollingsworth died in 1995. Six interpretive signs along the route describe the various habitats and the wildlife that depends of them, the importance of lighthouses and lobster fishing in Maine's history, significant American conservationists, and the challenges of life in this harsh coastal climate.

From the parking area, cross the road and follow the gravel path through a blueberry field. After a short stretch of boardwalk, enter a forest of scraggly

From Chair Pond Head on hikers can just glimpse the 123-foot tall Petit Manan Light a few miles offshore to the southeast from Chair Pond Head.

jack pine, and then trend gently downslope. Cross a low, wet area of maples, alders, and birch to arrive at a cedar swamp. Ahead, pass through an old field. The fine gravel underfoot changes to larger gravel stones and soon, to a narrow earthen footpath. After stepping-stones beneath a thin canopy of cedar and spruce you'll come to a fork in the loop trail, marked by a signpost but no sign (2013). Proceed to the right on bedrock trail and enter thick woods. Notice the porcupine damage on some of the jack pines along the trail.

Cross another boardwalk, then break out into the open at Chair Pond Cove with a long, sandy beach. Continue along the north shore of the cove to a grassy point and a fine view of Petit Manan Island Light offshore in the distance to the south. At 123 feet, this light is the second tallest on the Maine coast and is listed on the National Register of Historic Places. Here on the mainland, you're likely to see common yellowthroats, American redstarts, and chestnut-sided and yellow-rumped warblers. Ten-acre Petit Manan Island is a critical nesting site for the colorful Atlantic puffins, common eiders, black guillemots, razorbills, Leach's storm petrels, and common arctic and roseate terns. The island is closed to the public, but many tour operators offer birding cruises to its perimeter. Beyond the point, turn east along the ocean and enjoy walking among the rocks and cobbles, seaweed and tide pools on Chair Pond

Head. Enjoy lovely views of Bois Bubert Island's pink-granite shores and dark maritime spruce forests directly across the waters of Pigeon Hill Bay. Leave the shore at an interpretive sign and hike for a time in the trees along the water's edge. At a bench and another sign, take in the view northward to the bump of Pigeon Hill. All too soon, turn inland for the final time and climb moderately to a high point with views back east to the ocean. At the original trail junction, close the loop and turn right to return to the trailhead parking area.

DID YOU KNOW?

Petit Manan, which translates to "little island" from French, was so named by the explorer Samuel de Champlain to distinguish it from the larger Grand Manan island farther north in the Bay of Fundy in Canada. *Manan* is the Micmac word for "island out to sea."

MORE INFORMATION

The Petit Manan Point Division (fws.gov/northeast/petitmanan; 207-546-2124). Petit Manan is open year-round during daylight hours only. Dogs are allowed, but must be kept on hand-held leashes no longer than 10 feet. Blueberry picking is allowed, but only by hand; no rakes. Parts of the refuge are open to hunting; please check in advance for a list of open areas.

NEARBY

The Schoodic Point section of Acadia National Park (nps.gov/acad; 207-288-3338) is located a few miles to the west of Petit Manan, at the southern tip of the Schoodic Peninsula in Winter Harbor. A 6.0-mile, one-way road winds through the park and its pink-granite headlands, rocky beaches, and spruce-fir forests. The park road is part of the Schoodic Scenic Byway, which extends from Hancock to Prospect Harbor.

MORE HIKING

Birch Point Trail is a 4.0-mile round-trip hike that starts near the refuge entrance and leads through a blueberry field and then a forest of mixed woods to the salt marshes of Birch Point on Dyer Bay on the west side of the peninsula. A side trail en route leads to Lobster Point on Carrying Place Cove. At Pigeon Hill Preserve just to the north of Petit Manan, four trails form a 1.7-mile loop through the 170-acre parcel, owned and managed by the Downeast Coastal Conservancy (downeastcoastalconservancy.org). Catch views of the coastal islands from the open ledges of the 317-foot summit, the highest point along the coast in Washington County.

TRIP 44
GREAT WASS ISLAND PRESERVE

Location: Beals, ME
Rating: Strenuous
Distance: 5.0 miles
Elevation Gain: 120 feet
Estimated Time: 4.0 hours
Maps: USGS Great Wass Island; *Maine Atlas and Gazetteer,* Maps
17 and 26 (DeLorme); *Great Wass Island Map and Trail Guide* (The
Nature Conservancy)

**Amble through jack-pine forests and rich peatlands, then hike
along the spectacular ocean shoreline around Little Cape Point on
the east side of Great Wass Island.**

DIRECTIONS
From the junction of US 1 and ME 187 in Jonesboro, 1.1 miles west of the
Jonesboro Post Office, turn south onto ME 187. Follow this scenic road 11.9
miles. In the center of Jonesport, leave ME 187 by turning left onto Bridge
Street to cross the Beals Island Bridge over Moosabec Reach. On the south side
of the bridge at a T intersection, turn left onto Bay View Drive. In 1.2 miles,
just beyond the causeway onto Great Wass Island at another T intersection,
bear right onto Black Duck Cove Road, which is paved at first and then turns
to dirt. At 4.2 miles from Jonesport, reach the trailhead parking lot on the left,
just beyond the Downeast Institute for Applied Marine Research and Education. *GPS coordinates: 44° 28.741′ N, 67° 35.769′ W.*

TRAIL DESCRIPTION
The 1,576-acre Great Wass Island Preserve comprises most of the island of the
same name and almost the entire southern portion of the little town of Beals.
The Nature Conservancy acquired the preserve 1978. Bounded by Eastern
Bay and Western Bay, the island projects farther out to sea than any other land
mass in Downeast Maine. Here, the waters of the Gulf of Maine mix with the
Bay of Fundy, creating a cool, moist climate that supports several rare plant
species and natural communities, well adapted to the often extreme wind, salt
spray, and abbreviated summer growing season.

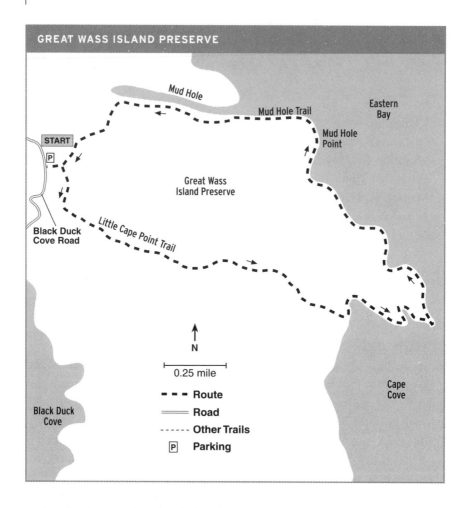

GREAT WASS ISLAND PRESERVE

Mud Hole

Mud Hole Trail

Eastern Bay

START

P

Mud Hole Point

Great Wass
Island Preserve

Black Duck
Cove Road

Little Cape Point Trail

N

0.25 mile

- - Route
Road
Other Trails
P Parking

Black Duck
Cove

Cape
Cove

Hardy plants such as beach-head iris, marsh felwort, blinks, and bird's-eye primrose grow on the exposed headlands. Inland, the island supports one of the largest stands of the twisted and stunted jack pine. The boggy peatlands breed carnivorous pitcher plants and sundews, baked-apple berries, and dragon's mouth orchids. Bird life is plentiful; bald eagles, ospreys, palm warblers, Lincoln sparrows, boreal chickadees, and spruce grouse are all common. Common eiders and great blue herons can be seen offshore. Harbor seals may be seen basking on the rocks in the sun.

Little Cape Trail and Mud Hole Trail penetrate the preserve; this route combines them for a 5.0-mile loop along rugged ocean shoreline.

Start the hike at the information kiosk at the east end of the parking lot. About 100 yards into the woods, reach a junction where Mud Hole Trail diverges left and Little Cape Trail proceeds straight ahead. This is one of four

Little Cape Point Trail cuts through the ecologically-rich wilds of Great Wass Island Preserve to reach the ocean at Cape Cove just south of the rugged headlands on Little Cape Point.

points along the hike where a color photo image of the preserve with GPS points is posted for reference.

Continue on Little Cape Point Trail. Cross a creek on a footbridge deep in a forest of spruce and fir. Follow a boardwalk to the right of a ledge, then hop up onto the ledge and walk the bedrock trail. Cross a gully on a bog bridge and enter a vast forest of jack pines, a species at its southern limit here in eastern Maine. A denizen of these poor, thin soils, jack pine is dependent on fire to release the seeds of its cones, but here on Great Wass Island, these trees appear to be reproducing successfully in the absence of fire.

Atop a rocky knob enjoy views of a large heath or boggy peatland to the west. These ancient bogs originated when sphagnum moss began accumulating in the basins left by retreating glaciers more than 10,000 years ago. Blue paint blazes mark the trail through this area. A low granite ledge about 1.5 feet high makes a perfect seat for a rest stop.

As you pass through an alder swamp on bog bridging, look for the carnivorous pitcher plant and its classic 6-inch, green-and-red, pitcher-shaped cavity filled with liquid, known as a pitfall trap. Unsuspecting insects are lured by nectar to the slippery slope of the rim of pitcher. Waxy scales and downward pointing hairs ensure that the insects can't climb out, eventually drowning and gradually dissolving them in the liquid-filled pitcher, providing nutrients to the plant. Often nearby are the tiny, red, carnivorous sundews, which lure, capture, and digest insects using stalked mucilaginous glands covering their leaf surfaces.

Soon, pass to the left of a large white pine and then a huge spruce. Beyond the spruce grove, climb up around a ledge in the forest on bedrock trail. Ahead, the trail begins to slope toward the water, with limited ocean views through the trees. Emerge from the woods at the base of the slope and scamper out into the open on the rocks of the shoreline at Cape Cove. A sign indicates Little Cape Point Trail here. The promontory of Little Cape Point is in view to the northeast. At low tide, explore among the rocks and driftwood, the seaweed and tide pools, and the usual array of detritus that washes ashore.

To continue the loop, turn left along the shoreline, which forms the route for the next 1.5 miles, marked sporadically with blue blazes. Without a trail to follow and with variable footing—never mind the spectacular coastal scenery—the going can be slow, so plan accordingly.

Meander northward amid the sandy stretches of beach, boulders, cobbles, and ledges. Swing around a cove to the south side of Little Cape Point, passing a square-ended cove with large cobbles. Nearing Little Cape Point, climb to the top of a headland, then scamper along the top of the cliffs some 75 feet above the water. Swing north around the point through the spruce trees. If time and tides allow, explore the spruce-and-fir-studded island just east of Little Cape Point. Beyond the point, Moose Peak Light on Mistake Island comes into focus across Mud Hole Channel to the east. The smaller islands of Water, Knight, and Green lie in front of larger Steels Harbor Island. Farther to the northeast are Head Harbor Island and myriad other islands and ledges.

Ahead, climb up onto a broad granite shelf and follow this around a corner to the north. At the end of the shelf, duck into the woods on the left for a short distance, then return to the beach. Walk the lovely sands of the half-moon cove. The weathered stumps of the trees sticking out of the beachhead are the result of severe erosion and the influence of salt water.

Leave the beach and climb once again onto a rock shelf. Dip into the woods briefly, then return to the rocks and scramble up the shore. Make your way around shallow Sand Cove, marked with occasional rock cairns. Cross another long slab, meander among the cobbles around a bend in the cove, then reach Mud Hole Trail, marked by a sign. Bald eagles are frequently spotted here, as are seals lounging on the rocks of Mint Island and the nearby rocks exposed by the tide.

Proceed on Mud Hole Trail above the shore through the thick woods, including some old growth spruce, mature fir, and old birch, following Mud

Hole inland to the west. Cross a small brook, then ascend an easy slope as you continue along the long, narrow cove, a mudflat at low tide.

At a junction, a spur descends steeply about 100 yards to the edge of Mud Hole. The main trail continues to the left, turning inland away from the water. Roots and mud lead to the higher ground of solid bedrock and more jack-pine forest. A brief descent brings you to the original trail junction and the close of the loop. Turn right and quickly reach the parking lot.

DID YOU KNOW?

Great Wass Island is the largest island in the Great Wass Archipelago, a group of 43 coastal islands south of Jonesport and Beals. On its southern shore, exposed granite bedrock drops precipitously into the ocean, evidence of the Fundian Fault, a long crack in the earth's surface extending from the Bay of Fundy to the coast of New Hampshire.

MORE INFORMATION

The Nature Conservancy (nature.org/maine; 207-729-5181). Great Wass Island Preserve is open daily year-round for day use only; camping is prohibited. Dogs and other pets are not allowed. No fires and no smoking on the trail. If the parking lot is full, visitors are asked to return another time. A trail map is available online.

NEARBY

Machias is the commercial hub of this part of Washington County and has a full range of visitor services. Built in 1810, the Nathan Gates House is home to the Machiasport Historical Society and features an extensive collection of old photographs, period furniture, and housewares, plus a genealogical library that highlights the region's seafaring and shipbuilding history (machiasport historicalsociety.org, 207-255-8461). In Columbia Falls, the Ruggles House is a classic example of 1800s Federal design and Adams ornament (ruggles house.org, 207-483-4637).

MORE HIKING

A wealth of hiking trails on the mainland are within striking distance of Great Wass Island. The Cobscook Trails system offers many miles of outstanding coastal hiking on more than twenty preserves ranging from Cutler to Calais. For more information and a copy of the 56-page guide *Cobscook Trails*, visit downeastcoastalconservancy.org or call 207-255-4500.

TRIP 45
MACHIAS RIVER HERITAGE TRAIL

Location: Machias and Whitneyville, ME
Rating: Easy to moderate
Distance: 4.5 miles (loop)
Elevation Gain: 145 feet
Estimated Time: 2.5 hours
Maps: USGS Machias, Whitneyville; *Maine Atlas and Gazetteer*, Map 26 (DeLorme); *Machias River Preserve Hiking Trails* (Downeast Coastal Conservancy)

Meander along a wild and free-flowing stretch of the Machias River, then loop back to the start via the Downeast Sunrise Trail, a converted rail-to-trail.

DIRECTIONS

From the junction of US 1 and US 1A in Machias, just west of the causeway over the Middle River and opposite a restaurant and motel, turn north onto US 1A. Immediately pass the Machias Town Office on the right. Ahead, US 1A crosses ME 192 and continues westward, passing Machias High School on the right and soon after, the Downeast Community Hospital. The trailhead is on the left, 1.8 miles from US 1. The lot is gravel-surfaced and has space for six to seven cars. *GPS coordinates: 44° 42.858′ N, 67° 29.064′ W.*

TRAIL DESCRIPTION

The Machias River Preserve is part of the Two Rivers Conservation Area, a community conservation project that protects 1,000 acres and 5.5 miles of river frontage on two properties, the other being Middle River Park on the Middle River just north of where it joins the Machias River on the east side of the town of Machias. The Machias River Preserve is managed by the Downeast Coastal Conservancy, which has 40 preserves between Steuben and Pembroke under its stewardship umbrella (twelve are open for public use), for a total of 6,100 acres of land and 62 miles of shoreline. This hike follows the north bank of the Machias River for nearly 3 miles before looping back to the start via section of Downeast Sunrise Trail.

From the kiosk with a posted map and information, located on the edge of the parking area, proceed down the embankment into the spruce and fir forest mixed with some cedars, pine, and birch. The blue-blazed trail trends gradually downslope, crossing a series of bog bridges using old railroad ties as sleepers. You've been following the remains of an old woods road since the trailhead, and about 0.25 mile into the hike, the trail bears sharply left off the wide corridor onto a narrow footpath.

After a quick up, bear right past a white pine measuring at least 4 feet in diameter. Beyond, it's pleasant sidehill walking over the mossy green forest floor. The trail continues to contour through a large cedar grove with also holds some impressive spruce trees. At a double-blaze just shy of 0.5 mile in, with an old trail to the left, turn sharply right and hike downhill. After a series of bog bridges, listen for the sound of the river, which isn't too far off. Turn right to cross a creek on a footbridge to reach a big spruce on the right with some old barbed wire still attached to its trunk. Go left after the bridge along an alder-choked stream. Just ahead, one spur and then another leads about 75 feet left to a viewpoint overlooking the Machias River, a beautiful spot to watch for wildlife, like moose and deer, eagles and ospreys.

From the second spur trail, bear right to continue. For the next 2.7 miles the trail remains relatively close to the river, providing wonderfully easy walking and frequent views out over the scenic river corridor. Good-sized spruce trees line the river here. Pass the foundation of an old cabin on the right. Just beyond, bear right to climb a slope above the river, passing by more large spruce and pine and a five-stemmed clump of maple.

At about the 1.0-mile mark reach a wide bend in the river and a semi-open, park-like grove of fir and spruce, which affords a nice look at the water, which is flowing lazily south to north at this point. Across the river, amid its grassy banks are a couple of rock piles, remnants of the logging days of old when river drives were common and logs were held back by dams until the spring floods.

The Machias River is one of Maine's wildest and most beloved rivers. Flowing 76 miles from its source at Fifth Machias Lake, the Machias River is one of eight wild Atlantic salmon rivers in the state, and contains the greatest amount of juvenile-rearing habitat and the highest estimated smolt (young fish) production. Amid the sounds of riffles on the river, cross a number of gullies by way of bog bridges and foot bridges. As of summer 2014, trail maintainers from the Downeast Coastal Conservancy were systematically working to bridge many of the gully crossings ahead. As time and funds allow, more spans will be built.

Pass a large spruce on the river bank with a long scar on its trunk, indicating it was once hit by lightning. Ahead, pass a sprawling six-trunked cedar on the right and then an old sugar maple copse overhanging the river. The river, about 200 feet wide here, flows calmly by. After a stretch through some tall

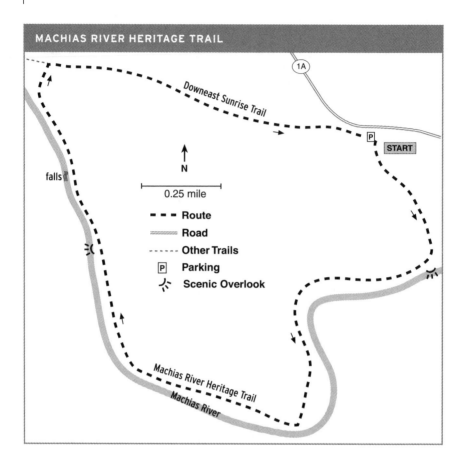

MACHIAS RIVER HERITAGE TRAIL

Downeast Sunrise Trail

1A

START

P

falls

N

0.25 mile

— — — Route
═══ Road
----- Other Trails
P Parking
Scenic Overlook

Machias River Heritage Trail

Machias River

grass, make your way through a pocket of dense young fir. Cross a swampy area, then pass around an old 10-foot high spruce snag. Continue through alders, ferns, and grasses, crossing several low, muddy spots on logs. Listen for the bounty of beautiful birdsongs as you hike through more large spruce.

Halfway along, arrive at a park bench on the right, situated nicely between two large pine trees in a cleared area overlooking the river, a perfect lunch or rest stop. Consider the amazing landscape-scale efforts by the state of Maine and conservation groups like the Downeast Coastal Conservancy that have protected 60,000 acres and 252 miles of river frontage in the Machias River watershed. These actions guarantee recreational access in perpetuity and protect the economically vital commercial forests while eliminating development threats.

Beyond the bench the trail traces a route along the berm of the river, passing a cedar tree with an old 4-foot bolt of pulpwood wedged into its crook. Not far ahead, on the trunk of a huge pasture pine, look close to see if you can make out the "smiley face."

The Machias River Heritage Trail follows a pristine section of one of Maine's wildest rivers, which flows 76 miles from its source at Fifth Machias Lake to Machias Bay.

After the outstretched branches of a huge spruce you'll begin to hear the roar of the river ahead. After a patch of gnarly red maples, reach a viewpoint on the left and an open ledge 15 feet above the river. Here, the rock and ledges of the Machias River form a single ledge drop rapid, and the resulting wave train below flows directly to the viewpoint and beyond. While the view is quite lovely, be sure to check around your feet for blueberries, which are abundant on this spot.

The Machias River has served as an important transportation route dating to the Passamaquoddy, who used the river to migrate between the north woods in winter and the coast in summer. After the arrival of European settlers in the late 1700s, the river was used to transport timber from the woods in the north to the saw mills on the coast at Machias. At the height of the lumbering period there were twenty sawmills operating in Machias. Commercial log drives on the Machias River ended in 1970, and in 1974 the last of the logging dams was removed, thereby restoring the river to its natural free-flowing condition, a boon to canoeists and to wild Atlantic salmon.

Just ahead, the trail reaches a second viewpoint, this one overlooking the top of the ledge drop rapids. Stand and stare long enough at this fine spot and you may well start thinking about a future canoe trip on the Machias River! A short distance beyond is another lookout, a rock ledge with a view upriver.

Cross a series of wet spots (unbridged but with milled lumber piled up and waiting to be installed). Ahead, where the river makes a big bend to the west, find a map posted to a tree and your last river view.

Hike along the margin of an alder swamp, cross a creek on a footbridge, then climb a short slope to merge with Downeast Sunrise Trail, an old railway bed that was converted into a 85-mile-long multiuse recreational trail between Ellsworth and Calais in 2008. Turn right (east) to follow wide, gravel-surfaced Downeast Sunrise Trail. It's straightforward striding along the former railway grade. Pass the old "Mile 56" post, then the town line from Whitneyville into Machias. In another half-mile, pass by blueberry barrens up and to the left.

At the junction of US 1A, turn right. Immediately cross Munsun Pitch Road and pass a white house with black shutters on the right. Walk the shoulder of US 1A for 100 yards to reach the trailhead parking lot and the end of the hike.

DID YOU KNOW?

The Machias River's name is derived from a Passamaquoddy word meaning "bad little falls," which refers to the gnarly stretch of steep falls through downtown Machias just before the river reaches tidewater.

MORE INFORMATION

Downeast Coastal Conservancy (downeastcoastalconservancy.org, 207-255-4500). Machias River Heritage Trail is open every day from dawn to dusk. Dogs are allowed on leash or under voice command and in sight at all times. Note: The trail is closed during periods of high water, such as spring runoff or after heavy rains. High water effectively blocks portions of the trail along the river.

NEARBY

In the tap room of Job Burnham's tavern in Machias, local patriots hatched a plan to capture the commander of the armed British sloop *Margaretta*, which sat anchored in the harbor with its guns trained on the village. Led by Jeremiah O'Brien, the abduction of Lieutenant Moore on June 12, 1775 failed, but it quickly led to a skirmish on the Machias River, where the British ship was captured by two American merchant vessels. This was the first naval battle of the American Revolution. The Burnham Tavern Museum (burnhamtavern.com) is largely the original architecture and houses period furnishings and artifacts of this historic encounter.

MORE HIKING

The cooperative Cobscook Trails (cobscooktrails.org) project is expanding opportunities for nature-based recreation and tourism, particularly hiking in Downeast Maine. Download their free trail map and guide, *Cobscook Trails: Explore Maine's Cobscook Bay & Bold Coast Region* from their website.

TRIP 46
ROQUE BLUFFS STATE PARK

Location: Roque Bluffs, ME

Rating: Easy

Distance: 2.5 miles

Elevation Gain: 120 feet

Estimated Time: 1.5 hours

Maps: USGS Roque Bluffs; *Maine Atlas and Gazetteer*, Map 26
(DeLorme); *Roque Bluffs State Park Brochure and Map* (Maine
Department of Agriculture, Conservation, and Forestry, Bureau
of Parks and Lands)

**The dramatic landscape of Roque Bluffs features maritime forests,
cliffs, cobbles, and more than a mile of oceanfront with a long,
sandy beach.**

DIRECTIONS

From US 1 in Jonesboro, turn right (south) onto Roque Bluffs Road. Follow
this road (which becomes Great Cove Road near its east end) southeast for 5.6
miles to a T intersection. Turn right here onto Roque Bluffs Road and continue
1.4 miles south to the village of Roque Bluffs and a large dirt trailhead parking lot on the right. From US 1 west of Machias, turn left (south) onto Roque
Bluffs Road and follow this for 7.5 miles to the above mentioned trailhead
parking lot. The lot accommodates at least 50 cars. The park entrance, beach
area, picnic area, toilets, and additional parking are located 0.2 mile farther
south on Schoppee Point Road. *GPS coordinates: 44° 36.652′ N, 67° 29.217′ W.*

TRAIL DESCRIPTION

Roque Bluffs State Park features 274 acres of dramatic coastal landscape on
Schoppee Point, including a 0.5-mile long, sand-and-pebble crescent of beach
on Englishman Bay. The Maine State Park Commission established the park in
1969 with proceeds from a public bond to acquire and protect the park land.

The beach at Roque Bluffs is unusual on this stretch of the Maine coast,
which is most often characterized by craggy cliffs and cobble shores. The erosion of the glacial moraine, just to the east, transported sediments here. The
bedrock outcrop at the east end of the beach displays glacial striations, visible
evidence of the powerful glacier's movement through this area.

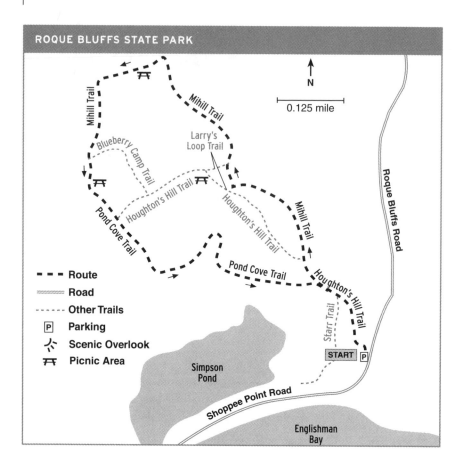

ROQUE BLUFFS STATE PARK

Mihill Trail

Mihill Trail

N

0.125 mile

Larry's
Loop Trail

Blueberry Camp Trail

Houghton's Hill Trail

Houghton's Hill Trail

Mihill Trail

Pond Cove Trail

Pond Cove Trail

Houghton's Hill Trail

Roque Bluffs Road

Starr Trail

START P

- - - Route

▭▭▭ Road

----- Other Trails

P Parking

⋏ Scenic Overlook

☰ Picnic Area

Simpson
Pond

Shoppee Point Road

Englishman
Bay

Just behind the beach is the 60-acre freshwater Simpson Pond. Bordered by wetlands, the pond's south shore sports its own warm-water beach. Directly offshore, south of the beach, are Schoppee Island and, behind it, the bulk of Roque Island. The woodlands to the north of the beach area hold a pleasant 3-mile network of hiking trails. For a good tour of the park, this hike combines portions of the three main trails: Houghton's Hill, Mihill, and Pond Cove.

Houghton's Hill Trail, marked with red blazes, starts at an information kiosk with maps and an iron ranger in the northwest corner of the trailhead parking lot. Starr Trail, which connects to Simpson Pond and the beach at Englishman Bay, joins the route on the left. Continue on Houghton's Hill Trail on a grassy track through an old apple orchard. Stop for a moment to listen to the sound of the ocean surf at the beach a short distance away. Pond Cove Trail soon enters from the left (the loop returns on this trail). Carry on through the field to a junction and a trail sign. Go straight ahead on yellow-blazed Mihill Trail, following along the base of a hill on a wide trail through the spruce-and-birch forest.

On Pond Cove Trail at Rose Ledge, so named for its reddish-colored rocks, hikers can look far out across Englishman Bay.

At another junction (trail sign), Larry's Loop Trail connects left to Houghton's Hill Trail. Stay to the right on Mihill Trail and pass through a thick growth of alders and birch to reach the upper junction with Larry's Loop Trail on the left. Remain on Mihill Trail and enter a dense stand of spruce, then climb moderately through a thicket of young spruce with a vivid, green, mossy forest floor. The short climb soon levels out in a beautiful forest of big spruce, some 14 to 16 inches in diameter, the forest floor pleasantly chaotic with decaying logs, moss, and lichens.

Pass over the hill's highpoint and trend downward to arrive at a picnic table in a park-like wood of spruce trees at the edge of a steep slope. Beyond, descend abruptly then more gradually on a soft carpet of needles, which characterizes much of the path's surface on this hike. After a short section of roots, the water is visible through the trees. Soon enough, the trail flattens and turns left to a lookout over Great Cove, with Pond Cove Island directly in view, and to its left, a floating lobster pound where harvesters temporarily store their catch.

Views are frequent as the path hugs the shore. At a junction, blue-blazed Blueberry Camp Trail departs on the left, Mihill Trail ends, and green-blazed Pond Cove Trail begins. Ahead, Pond Cove Trail follows the top of the steep oceanfront bluffs to Rose Ledge. A picnic table sits in the trees to the left of the trail. On the right, a small point of land juts out into the bay, ending at a ledge of reddish rock. A pocket beach lies to shoreside.

Ahead, continue along the east shore of Pond Cove on the grassy trail, passing a junction with Houghton's Hill Trail. The hull of an old ferry can be seen along the far shore. Leave the cove and soon take a sharp left with a stream on the right (trail sign). It's an easy walk through mixed woods with some wet areas spanned by bog bridges. The trail passes an orchard off to the left, a large tree, and a moss-covered glacial erratic, then emerges from the woods to arrive at a junction. Turn right here onto Houghton's Hill Trail and follow this back to the trailhead.

DID YOU KNOW?

Visible offshore to the southeast of Roque Bluffs State Park is the historical Libby Lighthouse, which marks the entrance to Machias Bay. Built in 1817, it is still an active beacon. Machias Bay was the scene of the first naval battle of the American Revolution, a skirmish between local merchant ships and the British sloop *Margaretta* in 1775.

MORE INFORMATION

Roque Bluffs State Park (parksandlands.com; 207-255-3475). The park is open and staffed from May 15 through October 1, 9 A.M. to sunset. There is a daily entrance fee. Dogs are allowed on-leash. In the off-season, park gates are closed but visitors are welcome. A trail map is available online and on-site.

NEARBY

The four-gun battery at Fort O'Brien in Machiasport actively guarded at the mouth of the Machias River for a 90-year period, during which it was destroyed and rebuilt three times. The fort was one of the few in Maine to be active in three wars: the American Revolution, the War of 1812, and the Civil War. Between Memorial Day and Labor Day, visitors can tour the historic grounds and see the remains of "Napoleon," the bronze cannon used to fire 12-pound cannonballs.

MORE HIKING

There are at least two dozen parks and preserves with hiking trails in the Cobscook Trails in system. Cobscook Trails is a cooperative project of conservation organizations, landowners, and community partners in the region with the goal of expanding opportunities for nature-based recreation and tourism, particularly hiking in Downeast Maine. The partnership produces the excellent trail map and guide *Cobscook Trails: Explore Maine's Cobscook Bay & Bold Coast Region*. Download it for free at cobscooktrails.org.

MAINE'S ICE AGE TRAIL

Maine's landscape has been shaped by the expansion and contraction of vast ice sheets over the surface of the land through the eons. The last of these powerful glaciers, the Laurentide Ice Sheet, flowed southeast over Maine 20,000 years ago, terminating at Georges Bank in the Gulf of Maine. Two miles thick at the coast, the great ice sheet compressed the earth's crust by 3,000 feet. About 18,000 years ago, rising global temperatures caused the ice sheet margin to retreat northward, and as it did, the ocean flowed inland along coastal Maine. Around 13,000 years ago, relieved of the great weight, the earth's crust rebounded, forcing the ocean to recede. Over the next 10,000 years, the land continued to rise along with global sea levels, eventually bringing the land and ocean into their current relative positions.

The prominent glacial landforms left after the retreat are a record of a major global climate change known as the Bolling Warming, which brought summer temperatures to the present levels about 15,000 years ago.

Maine's Ice Age Trail is a self-guided geo-tourism route through Downeast Maine from Blue Hill Bay (Trip 36) east to West Quoddy Head (Trip 49) and north to ME 9, the old Airline Road, which showcases and describes the best and most accessible features of glacial geology formed along the margins of the retreating ice sheet. The trail consists of 46 numbered and signed points along the roads and highways of Hancock and Washington counties where interested visitors can get a fascinating up-close look at moraines, eskers, fans, deltas, raised beaches, marine muds, and fossil shells, as well as historical sites and museums.

The trail's map and guide evolved from extensive glacial geological research conducted by University of Maine Professor Harold W. Borns and others, with financial support from the National Science Foundation. Pamela Pearson, a friend of Dr. Borns, suggested that the research results be presented to the public in a map format similar to Wisconsin's Ice Age Trail. The colorful map and guide, a veritable treasure trove of information for exploring this beautiful region of the Maine coast, was completed in 2007. Detailed driving directions, photos, and GPS coordinates are provided for each site along the Ice Age Trail. The maps are available in a variety of locations around Maine, and online at iceagetrail.umaine.edu.

TRIP 47
CUTLER COAST PUBLIC RESERVED LAND

Location: Cutler, ME
Rating: Strenuous
Distance: 9.9 miles (loop)
Elevation Gain: 1,080 feet
Estimated Time: 6 hours
Maps: USGS Cutler; *Maine Atlas and Gazetteer*, Map 27 (DeLorme); *Cutler Coast Public Lands: Guide & Map* (Maine Department of Agriculture, Conservation, and Forestry, Bureau of Parks and Lands)

A vigorous loop hike along the Bold Coast yields grand views of rugged oceanfront headlands, pocket coves, cobble beaches, peat bogs and grassy meadows.

DIRECTIONS

From the junction of US 1 and ME 191 in East Machias (about 4 miles east of Machias), turn south onto ME 191. Follow ME 191 for 12.6 miles over a very scenic route past Holmes Bay and then Little Machias Bay to the tiny fishing hamlet of Cutler. Just past the town wharf at the harbor on the Little River is a flag pole and bell. Follow ME 191 another 3.8 miles, as it bears sharply left out of town, to the Cutler Coast trailhead parking lot on the right. The two-tiered lot has parking for at least 30 cars, plus a pit toilet. *GPS coordinates: 44° 41.910′ N, 67° 9.475′ W.*

TRAIL DESCRIPTION

The 12,234-acre Cutler Coast Public Reserved Land features 4.5 miles of oceanfront headlands interspersed with pocket coves and cobble beaches, a cool, damp, and windy environment overlooking the Bay of Fundy that also includes maritime spruce and fir forests, grassy meadows, and upland peat bogs. A walk along this rugged and rather lonely stretch of the Maine coast makes it clear why it is nicknamed the Bold Coast.

The state of Maine first acquired land along the coast here in 1989. Nearly 9,500 acres were added in 1997 when The Conservation Fund/Richard King Mellon Foundation and the Maine Coast Heritage Trust donated much of the land north of ME 191. The Maine Bureau of Parks and Lands purchased 570 acres to bring the property to its current size.

This hike combines Coastal Trail and Inland Trail for a grand loop along the ocean before returning through the interior of this ecologically diverse land. The hike mileage can be halved, should conditions warrant, by utilizing Black Point Brook Cut-Off.

Coastal Trail starts from the information kiosk at the left (east) edge of the upper lot. Go down the steps and quickly cross a cedar swamp on bog bridges and then a footbridge. Beyond, climb easily through the mixed forest canopy of big cedars and spruce, balsam fir, paper birch, and red maple. Vivid green moss lines the trail, and more moss hangs from the trees to either side. Descend slightly to reach a junction (sign). Here Inland Trail departs to the right to Black Point Brook Cut-Off and ultimately to Fairy Head 4 miles out.

Continue straight ahead on Coastal Trail and soon cross Schooner Brook on stepping-stones, then navigate more wet terrain. The undulating route, with occasional stretches of rock and roots underfoot, eventually angles gradually down to a patch of semi-open woods high above the ocean waters of the Bay of Fundy. The main Coastal Trail continues to the right, but before you carry on, bear left and down the granite steps and make your way out right on a long, sharp, and rocky promontory. The magnificent viewpoint looks southwest along the rugged coastline to Long Point, previewing some of what you will soon be traversing: the sheer headlands, pocket beaches, and upland peat bogs. Directly north is private property, but there is much more conservation land beyond it. South across the Grand Manan Channel is the long, dark profile of the Canadian island of Grand Manan. The lighthouse at Southwest Head is visible at the far right end of the island. Grand Manan Island is 4 miles long and a mile wide, and its precipitous north side that faces you features cliffs as high as 400 feet. The Fundian Fault separates the island from the mainland, a geologic borderline between the Triassic rocks of the Bay of Fundy and the Silurian-aged rocks of the Cutler coastline.

Climb back up to Coastal Trail to resume your hike west in and out of the dense forest along the cliff tops, which range from 75 to 150 feet above the sea. The undulating path offers frequent viewpoints en route. Use caution near the cliffs, as they are often undercut and the ground above can be unstable. Over the course of the next 4 oceanfront miles you'll find yourself making countless little ascents and descents. The going can be slow and slippery but the reward is the ever-spectacular scenery.

Ahead, pass high above a pocket beach and soon a short spur leads left to a lookout that ranges back to the spine of rock where you first emerged from the

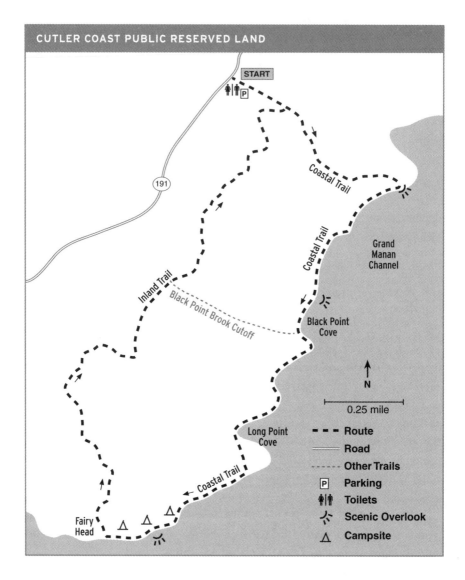

START

191

Coastal Trail

Coastal Trail

Grand
Manan
Channel

Inland Trail

Black Point Brook Cutoff

Black Point
Cove

N

0.25 mile

Long Point
Cove

- - - Route

——— Road

- - - - Other Trails

P Parking

Toilets

Scenic Overlook

△ Campsite

Coastal Trail

Fairy
Head

woods. Below, the colorful cobbles of jasper contrast with the emerald green of the deep ocean waters.

From the airy cliff tops ahead, enjoy the view to the dark, pointed tips of spruce and fir trees on Black Point, as well as the golden grasses of the meadows and the multicolored cobble beaches. Maine's first geologist, Charles T. Jackson, noted "enormous cliffs of greenstone trap" in his 1837 survey of the Cutler area. Such "trap rocks" were also reported by geologist Charles Hitchcock in 1861. These dark-colored rocks were late identified and named Cutler diabase; the vertical fractures in the rock outcrops are called joints.

Coastal Trail leads to a knife-edged rock promontory and bold ocean views southwest along the rugged Cutler Coast as far as Long Point.

Trundle over a large expanse of meadow dotted with alder, spruce, and scraggly birch. In the woods beyond, look for a short side trail on the left leading to the cliff edge and a spruce tree, its trunk distorted with galls. This unusual swelling is caused by an insect known as the spruce gall adelgid. Pass a smaller spruce next to the trail and notice that it too has galls. Beyond the obvious sea stack, the trail trends down toward the water via steps, crosses a stream, then proceeds along the shore over the rocks and cobbles. The way is marked by cairns, but the footing is rough.

Into the brush and ferns above, the path climbs to an overlook. Black Point is just ahead; a large cobble beach is just below it, and a log ladder used to climb up from the beach is also in view. Wind down from the high point to a trail junction. Here, Black Point Brook Cut-Off departs to the right; it leads back to the trailhead in a little under 3 miles. If time is short or the weather is less than appetizing, this is a good route to use.

Continue down through the shrubby growth to reach the beach of large green cobbles at Black Point Cove and the outlet of Black Point Brook. The entirety of Grand Manan Island is now in view. To continue, climb the wooden staircase. Pass a sign indicating that the campsites are ahead (nearly 2 miles actually). The trail bears inland and soon rises to a magnificent high point in the wide open salty air.

Ships and lobster boats often ply the waters offshore. As well, from early summer through early fall astute wildlife observers may also see harbor seals, porpoises, and whales, from the humpback and northern right to the finback and minke. Nearly 200 species of land and sea birds have been identified along the Cutler coast, so you're in for a real avian treat if you've packed binoculars.

Pass high above another pocket beach, which often catches its share of fishing detritus. Beyond, make a long climb to a rocky knob, where there are broad views to the west across a valley. Still following cairns, descend through the grass and shrubs to reenter the woods.

After a stream crossing, the trail arrives at beautiful Long Point Cove. Long Point marks the south edge of the deep cove. Take the stairs down to the beach to explore the cobbles, the smooth surfaces and rounded edges of which are the results of eons of wave action grinding the cobbles and pebbles together. An interesting side note: An archaeological survey of Long Point Cove in 1984 revealed stone tools and fire-cracked rocks, evidence of early Native American use of this part of the coast.

Ahead, the trail cuts across the woods behind Long Point, making several short but steep ascents and descents into and out of gullies and ravines. Beyond a footbridge over a deep gully, the trail emerges into the open at a grassy shelf, then follows the exposed shoreline rocks.

Back into the woods ahead, the trail continues its route west along the edge of the steep cliffs, a rugged stretch of ups and downs. Leave the woods through a slot in the rocks and walk around a corner on slabs to reach a side trail leading to Campsite #1, up the steps to the right and about 100 yards into the woods. Each of the three primitive campsites has space for two tents and a box privy.

As you scramble across the rocks ahead, the Little River Lighthouse at the mouth of the Little River comes into view. Turn inland behind the headland and ascend through a gully to reach a side trail on the left leading 100 feet to Campsite #2, a nice cliff-top spot and a worthwhile side trip. From the rocks in front of the campsite you'll have a full-on view of Grand Manan Island to the southeast and the Little River Light and now the many towers of the Cutler Naval Station to the southwest.

The Little River Lighthouse first shone its lamps in 1848 after Congress appropriated $5,000 to construct the 23.5-foot stone tower on the 16-acre island at the entrance to Cutler harbor. The light was automated in 1975, and in 1981 the U.S. Coast Guard made plans to tear the tower down and sell the island. That plan was tabled after local residents intervened. The American

Lighthouse Foundation restored the various lighthouse structures and relit the light in 2001. In 2002, history was made the Little River Lighthouse became the first light in Maine and New England to be transferred from federal to private nonprofit ownership.

The Cutler Naval Station, also known as the Naval Computer and Telecommunications Station, was commissioned in 1961 and used to maintain contact with submarines in the Arctic and North Atlantic oceans and the Mediterranean Sea. The extensive Very Low Frequency (VLF) transmitter antenna system consists of two arrays of thirteen towers each. The towers are as tall as 998 feet and can be seen for many miles, especially at night.

Beyond the second campsite, traverse some wet ground before breaking out onto the open shoreline rocks. Be sure to look back east for a nice view of the second campsite location atop the headland bluff. Soon enough the path reaches the side trail leading right 150 feet right to Campsite #3. Continuing on, cross a series of rocks slabs, and then skirt a pool of brown water colored by the rich tannin of the peat bogs nearby. As you cross the outlet stream, look for pitcher plants and cranberries growing in the boggy soils along the trail.

The rough, concave face of Fairy Head comes into focus. With one more look at Little River Light, turn inland and leave the coast (sign). Climb through the forest, making your way up through a series of moss-covered ledges. After a short ladder, traverse a narrow ridgetop, then move to higher ground to reach a junction. Here, a sign points to an overlook, a 30-foot scramble left to the top of a knob where you can see over the treetops to the ocean and lighthouse.

Descend the ridge on steps, then join an old road and go right (there's a handmade sign and bench at this turn). Cross a wet area, pass between two huge spruce trunks (24 inches in diameter), and then step over a brook. Contour across the slope, and then climb to a second overlook on the left, reached by a 150-foot spur trail. After the side trail to a third overlook with similar views (200 feet left), descend through the dense alders, maple, and birch. Navigate over a large wet area, then veer sharply left over more wet ground to cross a tiny stream. Make your way around the small pond on the right, the source of Black Point Brook. Finally, climb over rocks to gain an open knob and a wonderful view of the freshwater pond below and the valley beyond leading to the ocean. Be alert for beaver activity.

The undulating route ahead travels over extensive wet areas on bog bridges, log steps, and a footbridge. At the top of a knob reach the junction with Black Point Brook Cut-Off on the right, marked by a signpost and cairn. After a short, steep descent, continue through thick woods, then cross an open stretch of peat bogs with a view across it to a house on ME 192.

Negotiate the ups and downs of several more knolls and drainages, including a tamarack and spruce swamp. After a stretch of thick spruce and fir, cross Schooner Brook on stepping stones and soon close the loop at the junction of Inland Trail and Coastal Trail. Turn left to follow Coastal Trail a little less than 0.5 mile to the trailhead parking lot on ME 192 and the end of the hike.

DID YOU KNOW?

Between the state-owned land at Cutler Coast and West Quoddy Head and Maine Coast Heritage Trust preserves at Moose Cove, Bog Brook Cove, Boot Head and Hamilton Cove, there are more than 15,000 acres of conservation land along the Bold Coast between Cutler and Lubec.

MORE INFORMATION

Cutler Coast Public Reserved Land (parksandlands.com; 207-941-4412). The Cutler Coast unit is open year-round. Dogs must be under control at all times. A trail map is available online.

NEARBY

The Friends of Little River Lighthouse has open houses in the summer when the general public can visit via boat ride, view the lighthouse and the restoration work, and enjoy refreshments and maybe purchase a souvenir to help support the mission. The lighthouse is also available for overnight stays (littleriverlight.org, 207-259-3833). A lone charter company offers half-day excursions in summer to Machias Seal Island, home to the Maine's largest nesting colony of colorful Atlantic puffins (boldcoast.com, 207-259-4484).

MORE HIKING

There are at least two dozen parks and preserves with hiking trails in this region of Washington County. Cobscook Trails is a cooperative project of conservation organizations, landowners and community partners with the goal of expand opportunities for nature-based recreation and tourism, particularly hiking in Downeast Maine. The partnership produces the excellent trail map and guide, *Cobscook Trails: Explore Maine's Cobscook Bay & Bold Coast Region*. Download it for free at cobscooktrails.org.

TRIP 48
MOOSEHORN NATIONAL
WILDLIFE REFUGE

Location: Baring Plantation, ME
Rating: Moderate
Distance: 5.4 miles
Elevation Gain: 530 feet
Estimated Time: 3.0 hours
Maps: USGS Meddybemps Lake East; *Maine Atlas and Gazetteer*, Map 36 (DeLorme); *Wilderness Trails at the Moosehorn National Wildlife Refuge, Baring Unit* (USFWS)

Meander old roads and footpaths through a scenic and diverse landscape managed for the well-being of a wide variety of wildlife.

DIRECTIONS
From the north, at the junction of US 1 and Charlotte Road in Calais, turn south onto Charlotte Road. Drive 2.4 miles to Headquarters Road on the right and a sign for the Moosehead National Wildlife Refuge. From the south, at the junction of US 1 and ME 214 in Pembroke, turn north onto ME 214. Drive 6.1 miles on ME 214 to its junction with Charlotte Road In Charlotte. Turn right (north) here and follow Charlotte Road for 8.4 miles to Headquarters Road on the left. From the refuge entrance, follow Headquarters Road for 0.5 mile west to the refuge headquarters complex. Trailhead parking for about five cars is on the left. The main trail (signed) into the refuge (a gravel road at this point) starts to the left of the obvious flagpole. *GPS coordinates: 45° 6.850′ N, 67° 16.867′ W.*

TRAIL DESCRIPTION
Moosehorn National Wildlife Refuge (NWR) is the easternmost such refuge in the United States, part of a vast federal system designed to protect wildlife and its habitat while providing for wildlife-related education and recreation opportunities. Established in 1937, the refuge is an important stop for migratory birds on the Atlantic Flyway. Moosehorn NWR comprises two geographic units: 20,192 acres in Baring Plantation and 8,872 acres in nearby Edmunds. At Baring, the diverse landscape of hills, ledge outcrops, streams, lakes, bogs, marshes, northern hardwood and spruce-fir forests, and old growth white

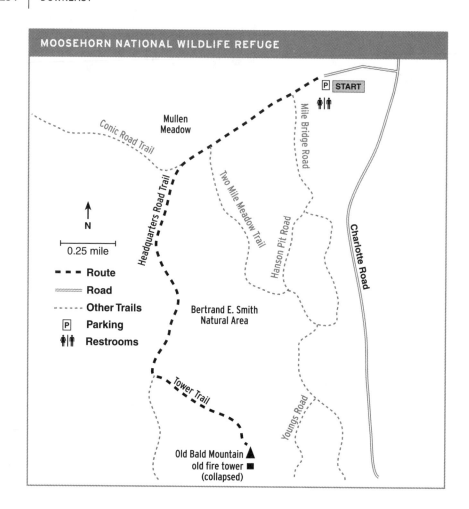

MOOSEHORN NATIONAL WILDLIFE REFUGE

Mullen Meadow

START

Conic Road Trail

Mile Bridge Road

Two Mile Meadow Trail

Headquarters Road Trail

Hanson Pit Road

Charlotte Road

N

0.25 mile

- - - Route
═══ Road
----- Other Trails
P Parking
Restrooms

Bertrand E. Smith Natural Area

Tower Trail

Youngs Road

Old Bald Mountain ▲
old fire tower ■
(collapsed)

pines is home to a wide variety of birdlife, as well as black bears, white-tailed deer, and coyotes. The American woodcock is intensively studied and managed at Moosehorn in an effort to understand and reverse its population decline.

Staff at the refuge office can answer questions and provide maps and brochures. The building directly across from the office houses restrooms. The information kiosk, visitor cabin, and information shelter, all along the entrance road, are worth investigating. This route follows refuge roads—closed to all but official vehicles—and trails to the summit of Bald Mountain.

Start down the gravel road—Headquarters Road Trail—and quickly arrive at a gate. An information shelter is just to the right. Pass around the gate to its right and follow the road as it heads west. A red pine plantation appears on the left, with an interpretive phone box for more information. Mile Bridge Road diverges to the left just ahead, and 200 feet beyond, Barn Meadow Road departs to the right. A shelter with a bench is located at this junction, across from a large field. Markers note that this section of Headquarters Road Trail is also part of the East Coast Greenway, a nearly 3,000-mile multiuse trail route stretching from Key West, Florida, to nearby Calais, Maine.

The road passes several areas that have been clear-cut, a management technique used to provide openings in the forest that spur the young, brushy growth that offers both food and cover to wildlife. Fire is another important tool used at Moosehorn to improve habitat and provide food and cover.

Beyond a lovely forest of tall white pines, Two Mile Meadow Road enters on the left. A kiosk on the right describes the mature forest in this area, which provides important habitat for a variety of plant and animal life. A sign just ahead on the grassy track identifies the area to the right as the Mullen Meadow Wilderness Tract. Continue straight ahead to enter the designated Wilderness proper, which comprises one-third of the refuge and is part of the National Wilderness Preservation System.

Pass a swamp on the left, and then amble up a rise through red pines to reach the wetlands of Mullen Meadow on the right. This wetland and many others like it in the refuge are carefully managed to maintain optimum water levels needed to provide for plant growth as food and cover for waterfowl. In the open area just beyond is a sign: "Wilderness—Foot Travel Only." Here, Conic Trail proceeds straight ahead. Follow Headquarters Road Trail to the left, which soon narrows to a footpath marked with blue blazes.

The trail mildly undulates on the route of an old road through tall red pines and a thick growth of young white pines. Large red pines 2 feet in diameter and larger begin to appear, as do mature white pines. After crossing several wet areas on big culverts, pass a huge white pine on the left that measures at least 4 feet in diameter. Beyond a shallow ravine, the trail enters the Bertrand E. Smith Natural Area, 160 acres set aside in the late 1940s to preserve a representative sample of old growth white pines, which dominate the forest canopy throughout this area of the refuge. Ahead, traverse a cedar swamp, then ascend a rise through more impressive pines, both red and white.

At a junction, take white-blazed Tower Trail left (east) through the beautiful pines, sidestepping around a few blowdowns. The trail rises toward the peak of Bald Mountain, at a moderate grade at first, then more easily. The treadway through the park-like forest becomes somewhat obscure in places, perhaps due to light use, but the path remains blazed and can be followed with a little care.

On the wooded summit of Bald Mountain are the downed remains of the old wooden fire tower, which once towered 100 feet into the sky here. The old concrete stanchions, bolts, cables, a barrel, steps, and a cabin frame are evidence of a bygone era in forest fire protection.

From the top of Bald Mountain, retrace your steps on Tower Trail and Headquarters Road Trail to the trailhead parking lot at the refuge headquarters complex.

DID YOU KNOW?

Moosehorn NWR is named for Moosehorn Stream, which is within its boundaries. Moosehorn is a bit of a misnomer: moose have antlers and not horns.

MORE INFORMATION

Moosehorn NWR (fws.gov/northeast/moosehorn, 207-454-7161). The refuge is open daily year-round, 30 minutes before sunrise to 30 minutes after sunset. Dogs are allowed on-leash. The refuge headquarters office is open Monday through Friday from 8 A.M. to 4 P.M. Trail maps are available at the refuge headquarters.

NEARBY

At the Saint Croix Island International Historic Site (nps.gov/sacr; 207-288-3338) in Calais, learn the story of the first French settlement in the New World, established in 1604 by Pierre Dugua, Sieur de Mons, and mapmaker Samuel de Champlain. The island in the middle of the Saint Croix River is across the modern Canadian border, but the mainland site is in the US and features a ranger station with information, exhibits, and a short interpretive trail leading to a view of the 6.5 acre island (no access).

MORE HIKING

Fifty miles of gravel roads (closed to automobiles) and trails offer plenty of access to the sights and sounds of Moosehorn. Three short trails start near the refuge headquarters. Woodcock Trail is a 0.25-mile, accessible path that introduces visitors to the American woodcock. Raven Trail is a 1.25-mile walk with eleven markers en route that describe the importance of proper habitat for wildlife. Bird Walk is a 0.25-mile trail for bird-watchers interested in some of the 223 avian species that have been identified in the refuge. The miles of gravel roads are ideal for exploring on foot and by bicycle, particularly the Headquarters Loop, a 2.5-mile interpretive walk on Two Mile Meadow and Mile Bridge roads.

TRIP 49
QUODDY HEAD STATE PARK

Location: Lubec, ME
Rating: Moderate
Distance: 3.6 miles
Elevation Gain: 290 feet
Estimated Time: 3.0 hours
Maps: USGS Lubec; *Maine Atlas and Gazetteer*, Map 27 (DeLorme); *Quoddy Head State Park Brochure and Map* (Maine Dept. of Agriculture, Conservation, and Forestry, Bureau of Parks and Lands)

Enjoy rugged oceanfront cliffs, maritime forests, and a unique peatland on a hike through the easternmost point of land in the US.

DIRECTIONS

From the junction of US 1 and ME 189 in Whiting, turn east onto ME 189 and drive 10.0 miles, then turn right (south) onto South Lubec Road. In 4.6 miles, enter Quoddy Head State Park. Just ahead, where the road continues straight ahead to its end at West Quoddy Head Light, bear right and soon enter a large gravel parking lot where there is space for 40 cars. Picnic tables with grills and pit toilets are located here. On the southeast side of the lot are an information kiosk with maps and a green iron ranger (pay fee). Coastal Trail starts from this spot. *GPS coordinates: 44° 48.818′ N, 66° 57.118′ W.*

TRAIL DESCRIPTION

Quoddy Head State Park occupies 541 magnificent acres on West Quoddy Head, the easternmost point of land in the continental United States. The park was established by the state in 1962 on lands acquired from private landowners. It features more than 5 miles of pleasant hiking on six trails. This route wends along four trails on the dramatic coastline, through maritime forests, and into a unique bog on its loop route. The name Quoddy is the Passamaquoddy term meaning "fertile and beautiful."

The park is perhaps best known for its iconic red-and-white striped lighthouse standing tall on the shore of the Bay of Fundy overlooking Canada. The first Quoddy Head Light, commissioned by President Thomas Jefferson, was completed in 1808. The present tower, the third on the site, was built in 1858. The state maintains the light, which was automated by the U.S. Coast Guard

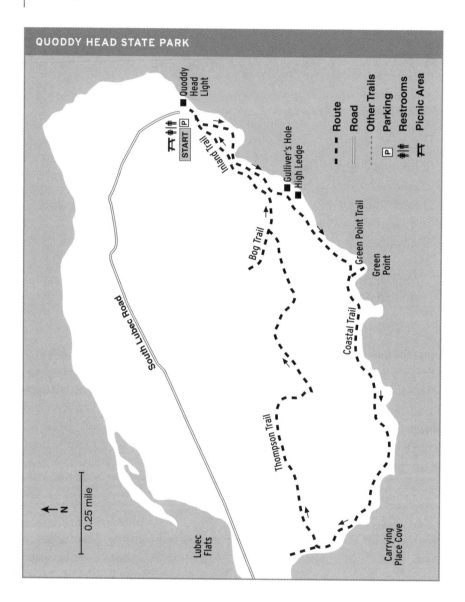

QUODDY HEAD STATE PARK

in 1988, and its powerful 5.5-foot-tall Fresnel lens with the help of the West Quoddy Light Keepers Association. The tower is generally not open to the public, but the former light keeper's quarters are open as a museum preserving the history of the light station and its long list of dedicated keepers.

From the trailhead information kiosk adjacent to the parking lot, turn right and follow wide, graveled Coastal Trail into the woods, where steps on the left lead to the shoreline. The main trail breaks out into the open for a grandstand view over Grand Manan Channel to Canada and the impressive columnar

The steep black cliffs along Coastal Trail at Quoddy Head are composed of gabbro, a dark, course-grained rock of volcanic origin.

basalt cliffs of Grand Manan Island. Beyond, beach peas crowd the trail on the left; ahead are a series of steep black cliffs composed of gabbro, a dark, course-grained rock of volcanic origin. The first 0.25 mile passes at least a dozen benches with ocean views, as well as numerous side trails to scenic outlooks to rugged cliff walls, pocket coves, and cobble beaches. Railings offer protection at the trail's edge in some places.

Ahead, Inland Trail merges with Coastal Trail for a short distance. Cross a footbridge and climb easily, still on a wide trail, to a junction. Here, Inland Trail continues straight ahead. Bear left onto Coastal Trail, pass a bench, and cross a bridge. The path is narrow now, with roots and steps. Pass a section of chain-link fence, then climb a winding staircase to a fenced-in viewpoint at the top of the cliffs overlooking Gulliver's Hole, the narrow chasm in the rocks far below, which booms with a thunderous roar when the tides are just right, much like the famous Thunder Hole in Acadia (Trip 33).

Beyond, pass a connecter trail leading to Inland Trail on the right. Coastal Trail soon reaches a steep staircase leading downward. The undulating, narrow trail soon arrives at wide, grassy High Ledge 150 feet above the ocean. Fine views southwest along the coast may be had from this vantage point, a series of cliffs, cobble beaches, steep headlands, and mountainous little bumps. Soon, the trail turns sharply to a junction. Here, Coastal Trail (sign for Green Point) continues to the left while Inland Trail (sign for parking area) leads right, back to the trailhead.

Continue left on wide Coastal Trail, passing sloping ledges at the water's edge, and then easing through dense thickets of spruce trees. A short spur trail on the left rewards hikers with views to both High Ledge and Green Point. Ahead on the main trail, any of several side paths on the left lead to wide, flat Green Point and its broad vistas of the bold Quoddy coastline. In summer, be on the watch for humpback, minke, and finback whales cavorting offshore.

Beyond Green Point, Coastal Trail journeys westward, at times down close to ocean level, other times high above it. Sections of rough footway with slippery rocks and roots are juxtaposed with delightfully soft carpets of needles edged with green mosses. Lobster boats ply the waters of the channel, and soon a few houses come into view near Carrying Place Cove. Swinging around a cobble cove and a jumble of jagged rocks, the trail ascends wooden stairs and rock steps to emerge into the semi-open with views of the scattered homes on the far shore and boats moored in the mouth of the cove.

Following the west shore of the cove, Coastal Trail soon reaches a junction with Thompson Trail in a grassy clearing with a bench. A spur trail leads straight ahead through the wildflowers of Minzy Field to Carrying Place Cove's long, arching, sandy beach, a great spot for a lunch stop, beachcombing, and perhaps a swim. The cove is so named because it was once a canoe portage site for native people crossing over the narrow peninsula from the ocean to Lubec Flats. The cove is also the former site of the Quoddy Head Life-Saving Station. Completed in 1874, the station housed men and equipment used to search for and aid shipwrecked vessels.

Return to the junction and turn left (northeast) onto Thompson Trail, which rises gently through mixed woods. Soon, the wide track of the old road levels off and proceeds through a corridor of bright-green ferns and wood sorrel. Ahead, the trail gets mucky, but most of the mud can be sidestepped on a faint trail on the right. Enjoy pleasant striding beyond as the trail climbs over a knoll, descends, and bears right through spruce and fir woods.

After a winding section of bog bridges, turn left onto Bog Trail and follow the wide gravel path to West Quoddy Head Bog, the easternmost open peatland in the US. Once a pond formed by glaciers, the bog has evolved over 8,000 years through plant accumulation and decay. A variety of shrubs and plants both familiar and uncommon grow here, including carnivorous pitcher plant and sundew, baked apple berry, black crowberry, cranberry, Labrador tea, laurels, and cotton grass. The dwarf black spruce and tamarack trees may be small in stature, but some are 80 years old. A boardwalk leads from the woods out into the fascinating 7-acre, nearly circular expanse of bog. Small interpretive signs line the final loop. Remain on the boardwalk to protect the fragile surroundings.

To complete your hike, return to the Thompson Trail junction and follow it straight ahead (south) to meet Inland Trail. Turn left (east) onto Inland Trail and stroll easily along, passing two junctions with Coastal Trail on the right en route. Inland Trail ends at the west end of the trailhead parking lot just right of the toilets.

DID YOU KNOW?

West Quoddy Head Light, one of 63 active lighthouses along the Maine coast, has been painted many times in its long history, and the number of red stripes has varied from six to eight.

MORE INFORMATION

Quoddy Head State Park (parksandlands.com; 207-733-9011). The park is open daily from 9 A.M. to sunset from May 15 to October 15, although visitors are welcome during the off-season. There is a daily entrance fee. Dogs are allowed on-leash. A trail map is available online.

NEARBY

Explore the pretty streets of Lubec, which overlooks Lubec Narrows and is the easternmost town in the continental US. The Franklin Delano Roosevelt Bridge connects Lubec with Campobello Island in Canada. The southern end of the island is home to the 2,800-acre Roosevelt Campobello International Park. Established in 1964, the park is a symbol of international cooperation and a memorial to America's 32nd president and the park's namesake, who summered on his "beloved island" most of his life. The park's visitor center houses exhibits on the Roosevelt story and the important ties between the US and Canada. Next door, take a guided tour of FDR's historical 34-room summer home. There is no charge for either.

TRIP 50
SHACKFORD HEAD STATE PARK

Location: Eastport, ME
Rating: Moderate
Distance: 2.3 miles
Elevation Gain: 360 feet
Estimated Time: 2.0 hours
Maps: USGS Eastport; *Maine Atlas and Gazetteer*, Map 27 (DeLorme); *Shackford Head State Park Guide and Map* (Maine Department of Agriculture, Conservation, and Forestry, Bureau of Parks and Lands)

Explore the dramatic oceanfront headlands of Shackford Head, a wild and scenic natural gem located in sight of the easternmost city in the US.

DIRECTIONS

From the junction of US 1 and ME 190 in Perry, turn right (east) onto ME 190 toward Eastport, passing through the Passamaquoddy Indian Reservation en route. In 6.5 miles, turn sharply right onto Deep Cove Road. Follow this for 0.7 mile, and with the boatyard and buildings of the Maine Marine Technical Center just ahead, turn left into Shackford Head State Park on a gravel way that quickly leads to the trailhead parking lot in a cul-de-sac at Cony Beach on Broad Cove. Pay the fee at the green iron ranger on the western edge of the parking lot near the information kiosk and pit toilet and trailhead. *GPS coordinates: 44° 54.332′ N, 67° 0.766′ W.*

TRAIL DESCRIPTION

Shackford Head State Park, a 90-acre gem owned and managed by the Maine Department of Agriculture, Conservation, and Forestry, Bureau of Parks and Lands, comprises most of a rugged peninsula bounded by Cobscook Bay to the west and Broad Cove to the east. The area is named for one of Eastport's earliest settlers, the Revolutionary War soldier Captain John Shackford. He brought his family here in 1783 and lived most of his 87 years on the headland. Shackford died in 1840 and is buried alongside his wife in nearby Hillside East Cemetery. In the 1970s, Shackford Head was the site of a proposed oil refinery, but the project was strongly opposed because of the navigational hazards imposed by Cobscook Bay and the scenic and wildlife values of the land. The

Pittston Company abandoned its refinery plan in 1983, and the state acquired the land in 1989. Seven trails wend through the park, totaling nearly 3 miles of hiking. This loop combines Shackford Head, Schooner, Ship Point, and Overlook trails into an excellent tour of the park's many natural highlights. The park is also a stop on the Downeast Fisheries Trail (downeastfisheriestrail. org), which links 45 active and historical fisheries sites from Penobscot Bay to Cobscook Bay.

Interpretive signs in the grassy circle of the parking area describe the Civil War ships burned at Cony Beach between 1901 and 1920. The *Minnesota, Vermont, Wabash, Franklin,* and *Richmond*, all part of the Union Navy, were brought here to be salvaged for their metal—copper, brass, and iron—and other onboard valuables, and then burned. The extreme tides at this location meant that the ships could be sailed in at high tide and worked on before the tide receded.

A warning sign notes that the park is experiencing an infestation of stinging red fire ants. While this is normally a good hike for kids, and dogs are welcome on-leash, it may not be the best place for either until the situation changes. For all other hikers, the park may indeed be safely enjoyed, but long pants, socks, and closed shoes are recommended. As of summer 2013, the fire ant problem seemed confined to the north and west areas of the park.

Before starting your hike, take the short trail down to Cony Beach for a nice view over Broad Cove (active aquaculture pens are just offshore), and beyond to Estes Head and the entrance to the busy harbor at Eastport, the deepest natural port on the East Coast of the US.

Wide and well-traveled Shackford Head Trail enters the woods at the western edge of the parking lot and reaches a second information kiosk, then a trail junction just a few minutes into the woods. As of 2013, a portion of the trail directly ahead was closed due to the fire ant infestation. Hikers must bear right here and follow a bypass trail through lush spruce woods.

In about 100 feet, turn right onto blue-blazed Schooner Trail. After a sharp left, cross several wet areas on bog bridges to reach a spur trail on the right to an overlook atop a rocky bluff on Deep Cove. In view are a long pier, lobster and sail boats, several small islands, and Seward Neck across the bay in Lubec. After a pocket beach, the trail hugs the shoreline, undulating easily along the slope of the headland and passing numerous spur trails to waterfront views.

Where Deep Cove Trail enters from the left, a side trail on the right leads to a beach and a close-up look at the aquaculture pens. These circular enclosures floating on the surface of the water are used for raising Atlantic salmon. Nets cover the top of the pens to keep out aerial prey. The young salmon are

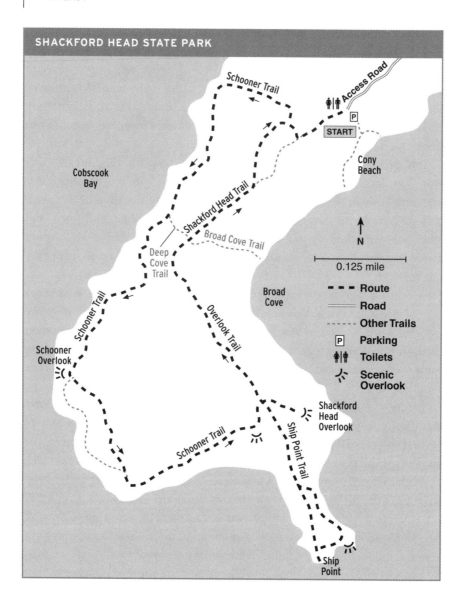

SHACKFORD HEAD STATE PARK

Schooner Trail

Access Road

Cobscook
Bay

Shackford Head Trail

Broad Cove Trail

Deep
Cove
Trail

Schooner Trail

Overlook Trail

Schooner
Overlook

Broad
Cove

Shackford
Head
Overlook

Ship Point Trail

Schooner Trail

START

Cony
Beach

N

0.125 mile

- - - Route
——— Road
- - - - - Other Trails
P Parking
Toilets
Scenic
Overlook

Ship
Point

put into the pens when they are 6 inches long and take about two years to mature to market size. Farms such as this are an important part of Maine's seafood industry.

Continuing southward, the trail climbs through thick balsam woods to a semi-open area in an aspen grove, and then drops down among hardwoods. The path crosses several gullies before arriving at Schooner Overlook above the bay. Just beyond, an obscure alternate trail descends to the right to follow a lower-level route. Ahead, the trail meanders through the woods away from

From Ship Point on Shackford Head, hikers can enjoy views southeast over Broad Cove as far as Campobello Island in Canada.

the water and, after a few ups and downs, reaches the lower junction of the alternate trail, which reenters from the right.

The trail beyond traverses the top of a bluff, with outstanding vistas and several nice picnic spots in the slope-side grass. The long and rocky arm of Ship Point comes into view, as does the long, curving beach at its western base. Spread across the horizon to the southeast is the bulk of Campobello Island in Canada.

Scramble higher on the rocks ahead, then through the woods to reach a four-way junction. Follow yellow-blazed Ship Point Trail down a rocky slope in a beech wood, with rock steps at its base. Then cruise easily along the spine of land to the junction of a short loop trail. Bear right onto the loop, through big white spruce trees and a small meadow, then down the slope through a carpet of juniper and Atlantic white cedar to the rocky end of Ship Point. Here, enjoy more views over Broad Cove and its aquaculture pens to a fish processing plant on Estes Head.

Close the loop through more big spruce, pass along the edge of the cove, then swing up the slope and head back to the four-way junction. Bear right onto Overlook Trail, a 250-foot spur to the top of Shackford Overlook, a spectacular open ledge 173 feet above Broad Cove. Plunk down on the log bench on top and drink in the fine view.

Return to the four-way trail junction and turn right onto your return route: Shackford Head Trail, a wide old woods road that leads easily along, past mossy ledges and through lovely stands of yellow birch and white spruce. At a junction, Deep Cove Trail to the left is a shortcut back to Schooner Head Trail on Cobscook Bay; Broad Cove Trail leads right a short distance to the cove. Not far beyond the junction, bear left onto the bypass trail, which circumvents the closed section of boardwalk trail. Soon, Schooner Trail enters from the left. Ahead, bear left onto Shackford Head Trail to return to the trailhead.

DID YOU KNOW?

Old Sow, the largest tidal whirlpool in the Western Hemisphere, lies on the international boundary between Moose Island in Eastport and Deer Island, New Brunswick. Called "Old Sow" for the piglike sounds made by its churning waters, the whirlpool area can be as large as 250 feet in diameter.

MORE INFORMATION

Shackford Head State Park (parksandlands.com; 207-941-4014). The park is open daily from 9 A.M. to sunset from May 15 to October 15, although visitors are welcome during the off-season. The park is not staffed at any time. There is a daily entrance fee. A trail map is available online.

NEARBY

Eastport is the easternmost city in the US, although nearby Lubec claims to be the easternmost town in the country. Eastport is built on a series of islands that are linked by causeways, connections that were part of a now long-defunct attempt to construct a huge tidal dam project. This busy fishing and shipping port has experienced quite a revival in recent years, and its pretty waterfront downtown now boasts a variety of shops, galleries, museums, and restaurants that are well worth a visit (eastportchamber.net).

MORE HIKING

There are at least two dozen parks and preserves with hiking trails in the Cobscook Trails in system. Cobscook Trails is a cooperative project of conservation organizations, landowners, and community partners in the region, with the goal of expanding opportunities for nature-based recreation and tourism, particularly hiking in Downeast Maine. The partnership produces the excellent trail map and guide *Cobscook Trails: Explore Maine's Cobscook Bay & Bold Coast Region*. Download it for free at cobscooktrails.org.

INDEX

ABOUT THE AUTHOR

CAREY MICHAEL KISH has been exploring the hiking trails along the coast and in the mountains of Maine for more than four decades. Carey is a freelance outdoors and travel writer and photographer, editor of AMC's *Maine Mountain Guide* and the AMC Maine Chapter's *Wilderness Matters*, and writes a regular hiking and camping column for the *Portland Press Herald/Maine Sunday Telegram*. His writing and images have also appeared in a variety of online and print publications, including *AMC Outdoors* magazine. A Registered Maine Guide and Wilderness First Responder, Carey has thru-hiked the Appalachian Trail and completed more than two dozen other long-distance backpacking treks in the US, Canada, and Europe. Carey has a Bachelor of Science in Forestry and a Master of Business Administration from the University of Maine and a Bachelor of Arts in Geography and Anthropology from the University of Southern Maine. Carey lives in Southwest Harbor, Maine, on the edge of Acadia National Park with his wife, Fran Leyman, two cats, and a mountain of well-used outdoor gear.

BE OUTDOORS™

Since 1876, the Appalachian Mountain Club has channeled your enthusiasm for the outdoors into everything we do and everywhere we work to protect. We're inspired by people exploring the natural world and deepening their appreciation of it.

With AMC chapters from Maine to Washington, D.C., including groups in Boston, New York City, and Philadelphia, you can enjoy activities like hiking, paddling, cycling, and skiing, and learn new outdoor skills. We offer advice, guidebooks, maps, and unique eco-lodges and huts to inspire your next outing.

Your visits, purchases, and donations also support conservation advocacy and research, youth programming, and caring for more than 1,800 miles of trails.

Join us!
outdoors.org/join

ABOUT THE AMC IN MAINE

Through the Maine Woods Initiative, AMC has permanently protected 66,500 acres of forestland in the state while creating new opportunities for nature-based tourism through its Maine Wilderness Lodges. The Maine Woods Initiative seeks to address regional and economic needs through outdoor recreation, resource protection, sustainable forestry, and community partnerships. To learn more about AMC's regional conservation efforts, visit outdoors.org/conservation/wherewework.

AMC's Maine chapter offers a wide variety of hiking, backpacking, climbing, paddling, and skiing trips each year, as well as social and young-member programs, instructional workshops, and trail volunteer opportunities. To view a list of AMC activities in Maine and across the Northeast, visit activities.outdoors.org.

AMC BOOKS UPDATES

AMC Books strives to keep our guidebooks as up-to-date as possible to help you plan safe and enjoyable adventures. If we learn after publishing a book that relevant trails have been relocated or route or contact information has changed, we will post the updated information online. Before you hit the trail, visit outdoors.org/books-maps and click the "Book Updates" link.

While hiking, if you notice discrepancies with the trip descriptions or maps, or if you find any other errors in the book, please let us know by submitting them to amcbookupdates@outdoors.org or to Books Editor, c/o AMC, 10 City Square, Boston, MA 02129. We will verify all submissions and post key updates each month. AMC Books is dedicated to being a recognized leader in outdoor publishing. Thank you for your participation.

Maine Mountain Guide, 11th Edition

Compiled and edited by Carey Michael Kish

For more than half a century, the Appalachian Mountain Club's *Maine Mountain Guide* has been hikers' and backpackers' quintessential resource for trails in Maine's spectacular mountains. Thorough trip-planning and safety information—along with full-color, GPS-rendered, pull-out maps featuring trail segment mileage—make this the trusted, comprehensive hiking guide to Maine.

$23.95 • 978-1-62842-097-5

Outdoor Adventures: Acadia National Park

Jerry and Marcy Monkman

Outdoor Adventures: Acadia National Park spotlights 50 hiking, biking, and paddling trips for all ability levels. Covering the popular Mt. Desert Island, as well as the hidden gems of Isle au Haut and Schoodic Peninsula, this is the definitive guide to enjoying the best of New England's only national park.

$19.95 • 978-1-62842-057-9

AMC's Best Sea Kayaking in New England

Michael Daugherty

This concise guide, written by a Registered Maine Guide and inveterate paddler, features 50 of the best sea kayaking adventures in New England, from Maine's Bold Coast to the mouth of the Connecticut River. Many trips can be done in a day or turned into an overnight for all ability levels.

$18.95 • 978-1-62842-006-7 • ebook available

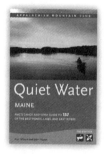

Quiet Water Maine, 3rd Edition

John Hayes and Alex Wilson

With its first revision in more than a decade, the fully updated *Quiet Water Maine* reveals more than 100 spectacular ponds and lakes ideally suited for canoeing and kayaking. Each trip includes a detailed summary of paddling time, distance, and difficulty, with a special focus on flora and fauna.

$19.95 • 978-1-62842-066-1 • ebook available